'OUR SOUTHERN ZION'

By the same author:

Princeton Seminary, Vol. 1: Faith and Learning
Princeton Seminary, Vol. 2: The Majestic Testimony

'OUR SOUTHERN ZION'
OLD COLUMBIA SEMINARY
(1828 – 1927)

'Almighty God had called us . . . to light up another sun which shall throw farther west the light of the Gospel.'
(Address to the Public, 1826)

David B. Calhoun

THE BANNER OF TRUTH TRUST

THE BANNER OF TRUTH TRUST
3 Murrayfield Road, Edinburgh EH12 6EL, UK
P.O. Box 621, Carlisle, PA 17013, USA

*

ISBN: 978 1 84871 172 3

*

Typeset in 11/15 pt Sabon Oldstyle Figures at
The Banner of Truth Trust, Edinburgh
Printed in the USA by
Versa Press, Inc.,
East Peoria, IL

To

William S. Barker, Joseph H. Hall,
Sean M. Lucas, and Michael W. Honeycutt,
valued friends and able colleagues in the
Church History Department of
Covenant Theological Seminary

CONTENTS

ILLUSTRATIONS

PREFACE

I have long admired the historical/theological writings of Dr David Calhoun (of Covenant Seminary) because he has the rare gift of combining historical accuracy, wide and deep cultural perception, theological insight and best of all, the fragrance of Christ and his gospel. His most recent volume on the first century of Columbia Theological Seminary (then in South Carolina), 1828-1927, exhibits all of these qualities in a beautiful combination.

Columbia, along with Union in Virginia, were until the late nineteenth century the major training grounds of the ministry of the Southern Presbyterian Church. The great Calvinist scholar and statesman, Robert L. Dabney, was for much of his lifetime professor in Union, while his South Carolina colleagues at Columbia (also strong Calvinists) were such justly famous preachers, professors and authors as Thornwell, Palmer, Plumer and Girardeau. Their theology, preaching, statesmanship and writing made a profound mark upon the Southern mind and heart in those states that for a few years called themselves 'the Confederacy.' They were leaders not only of the Presbyterians, but also of the Southern *intelligentsia* in general—both for good and for bad.

David Calhoun's scholarly integrity shows itself as he honestly evaluates a tradition he loves (coming from Southern Presbyterian roots himself, as does this reviewer). He does not attempt to hide the ugliness and sin of significant aspects of the Southern experience: particularly slavery and then racial segregation. He grieves that so many evangelical Christian leaders, of whom the world could have expected a higher standard, failed to rise above the self-serving, sinful assumptions of their own time—notably on racial issues.

Without excusing that which should not be excused, realistically one must note that Christians in every culture, to some degree or other (not infrequently, hidden from their own explicit awareness) carry 'this treasure in earthen vessels' (cf. 2 *Cor.* 4:7). Yet somehow, in every age and culture, rays of the transcendent power and glory of God manage to shine through in spite of imperfect witnesses and sub-Christian attitudes. And thus we may gladly learn much truth and come into contact with real beauty in cultures where there is a great deal of which we would not approve.

Dr Calhoun opens the heart of South Carolina history from the 1670s to the 1920s. He manifests the qualities of Calvin's 'clarity and brevity' in so doing. The revival Christianity from the Southern evangelist, Daniel Baker (1790s to 1850s) to the pastor/theologian J. L. Girardeau (1820s to 1890s) is the spiritual context of old Columbia Seminary.

Old Union and Old Columbia Seminary drew much inspiration from Old Princeton Seminary. All enthusiastically shared a high commitment to careful scholarship in the Calvinist stream of the Reformation, especially as it was channelled through the experience of the Scottish Presbyterians and English Puritans. Dr Calhoun accurately points out certain differences of emphasis between Princeton and Union on the one hand, and Columbia on the other. Hodge of Princeton and Dabney of Union did not really accept the teaching of John Calvin on the spiritual presence of Christ in the Lord's Supper, whereas Thornwell, Adger and Girardeau made much of it. It has been my own impression as I have been reading these varying traditions for many decades that Hodge and Dabney laid less emphasis on the doctrine of union with Christ (so strong in Calvin) than did the theologians of Columbia.

Dr Joseph Ruggles Wilson (father of World War I President of the United States, Woodrow Wilson) was connected both with Columbia Seminary and its parent, First Presbyterian Church. Woodrow Wilson was named for his uncle, Dr James Woodrow, who for many years taught at Columbia. His adherence to theistic evolution was to bring controversy, decline, and for some years—closure—of Columbia Seminary. Dr John L. Girardeau (a fellow professor at Columbia) was an ardent opponent of Woodrow's evolutionary compromises with the Genesis text. David Calhoun charts fair-mindedly this painful controversy, which is far from ended in evangelical and Reformed institutions. There is much to be learned from how this controversy unfolded in the late nineteenth century, whatever side one may take today.

Douglas F. Kelly
Charlotte, NC
February 2012

INTRODUCTION
'ANOTHER SUN'

COLUMBIA Theological Seminary began in 1828 in Lexington, Georgia. In 1830 it moved to the city of Columbia, South Carolina, where it remained for almost a hundred years, until relocating in Decatur, Georgia, in 1927. Part collective biography and part narrative history, this book follows the story of the seminary during its Columbia years, hence the subtitle—*Old Columbia Seminary*. The title, *Our Southern Zion,* is an expression used by Presbyterians in the Old South for their church and its institutions, including Columbia Seminary.[1] The word *Zion* is found often in the Bible, mostly in the Psalms and Prophets. It refers to a geographical place in Israel, the 'city of David,' and to its temple; to the 'heavenly Jerusalem'; and most frequently to the Old Testament 'church'—the place where God meets his people. Psalm 74:2, for example, concerns the first and mainly the last of these—'Remember thy congregation, which thou hast purchased of old; the rod of thine inheritance, which thou hast redeemed; this mount Zion, wherein thou hast dwelt.'

Columbia Seminary became a notable place in its day. 'Here gathered a young but brilliant faculty,' writes historian Erskine Clarke, 'that would make Columbia Theological Seminary the most formidable theological school in the Old

[1] Erskine Clarke uses the expression in the title of his book *Our Southern Zion: A History of Calvinism in the South Carolina Low Country, 1690-1990* (Tuscaloosa, Ala.: University of Alabama Press, 1996).

South and one of the most important in the country during the antebellum period.'[2] According to John Leith, 'It is not likely that any abler group of Presbyterian ministers was ever congregated in so small an area [Columbia and its surroundings] in the history of American Presbyterianism.'[3] Leith's statement would be more accurate if we expand the geographical area around Columbia to include the state of South Carolina, especially Charleston and the Low Country.

The founders of Columbia Seminary stated that in beginning the new seminary, Presbyterians in the South would 'light up another sun which shall throw still farther west the light of the gospel.'[4] That vision was realized as the graduates of the seminary took the gospel further west. At the semicentennial of the seminary in 1881, George Howe said that Columbia Seminary had trained about 550 students. 'More than three-fourths of the ministers and licentiates of the Synod of South Carolina, more than half of those of the Synod of Georgia, about one-third of those of the Synods of Alabama and Arkansas, nearly one-half of the Synods of Memphis and Mississippi were students of this Seminary.'[5] Some graduates of Columbia Seminary went out to serve the Choctaw and Chickasaw Indians. Others went to the slaves on the Southern plantations. By 1881 some twenty-one had

[2] T. Erskine Clarke, in J. McDowell Richards, *As I Remember It: Columbia Theological Seminary, 1932-1971* (Decatur, Ga.: CTS Press, 1985), pp. 2-3.

[3] John H. Leith, 'James Henley Thornwell and the Shaping of the Reformed Tradition in the South', in Elsie Anne McKee and Brian G. Armstrong, eds., *Probing the Reformed Tradition: Historical Studies in Honor of Edward A. Dowey, Jr.* (Louisville: Westminster/John Knox, 1989), p. 425.

[4] *Memorial Volume of the Semi-Centennial of the Theological Seminary at Columbia, South Carolina* (Columbia, S.C.: Presbyterian Publishing House, 1884), pp. 139-40.

[5] George A. Blackburn, ed., *The Life Work of John L. Girardeau, D.D., LL.D.* (Columbia, S.C.: The State Company, 1916), p. 165.

gone overseas as missionaries to Syria, Turkey, Persia, India, China, Japan, Africa, and South America.

The 'Old Columbians' purposed to honor Christ in their teaching and living. That they failed to do so perfectly does not detract from their desire and effort. According to Louis LaMotte: 'These men have more or less clearly perceived the truth and more or less fully lived it.'[6] But not completely. They failed in many small ways and in one major way—their support for slavery before the War Between the States and for segregation thereafter. John Leith writes about James Henley Thornwell, the most famous of the 'Old Columbians,' that 'Thornwell's innocence or blindness to the brutality or inhumanity of slavery that historians record and that must have been apparent is difficult to understand and impossible to justify.'[7] Douglas Kelly states that the Southern theologians' reading of Scripture 'was hampered and twisted by the degree of fallenness which remained in their culture. The United States of America and the still largely segregated churches of the land have not yet ceased to pay a price for this woeful failure.'[8] Nothing is more disheartening, writes Eugene Genovese, than to see firmly orthodox Christians in the post-Reconstruction era, who 'turned to the Bible for guidance on every subject, plunge into arguments from sheer prejudice that hardly pretended to be scripturally based.'[9] The Old Columbians to a man supported slavery before the Civil War

[6] Louis C. LaMotte, *Colored Light: The Story of the Influence of Columbia Theological Seminary 1828-1936* (Richmond, Va.: Presbyterian Committee of Publication, 1937), preface.

[7] Leith, *Probing the Reformed Tradition*, p. 437.

[8] Douglas Kelly, *Preachers With Power: Four Stalwarts of the South* (Edinburgh: Banner of Truth, 1992), p. xxiv.

[9] Eugene D. Genovese, *A Consuming Fire: The Fall of the Confederacy in the Mind of the White Christian South* (Athens, Ga.: University of Georgia Press, 1998), p. 95.

and accepted segregation thereafter. They did not so much try to defend it, but neither did they oppose it. 'In the contest between their abhorrence of race mixing and their fidelity to the Bible,' Genovese writes, 'the Bible lost.'[10]

Thankfully, we have moved beyond the racial views of these 'ancestors.' Their attitudes and practice toward black people, however, were more complex and nuanced than generally thought. Among the men who taught at Old Columbia three gladly gave large portions of their lives in ministry to African Americans. It was through their efforts, and others like them, that by the middle of the nineteenth century there were more African Christians in America than in Africa. Professors C. C. Jones, John Adger, and John Lafayette Girardeau loved the slaves and were loved by them. When Girardeau was contemplating leaving his black congregation at Charleston's Zion Presbyterian Church in 1871, he wrote to them:

> I can scarcely bear the thought of parting with you—no more to preach to you the precious gospel of Christ, no more to mingle my prayers and praises with yours on earth, no more to minister to you in times of affliction and distress. There is not one of you whom I am not conscious of tenderly loving in Christ Jesus, and I would fain believe, not one of you who does not feel affectionately towards me.[11]

Despite their failures, there is much we can learn from the lives and thought of the 'Old Columbians.' While rejecting the 'enormity' of slavery and racial prejudice, Genovese laments the current

> neglect of, or contempt for, the history of Southern whites, without which some of the more distinct and noble features

[10] Genovese, *Consuming Fire*, p. 80.
[11] Blackburn, *Girardeau*, p. 151.

> of American national life must remain incomprehensible. The northern victory in 1865 silenced a discretely southern interpretation of American history and national identity, and it promoted a contemptuous dismissal of all things southern as nasty, racist, immoral, and intellectually inferior.[12]

In describing his early alienation from the Dutch Calvinism of his childhood and his later respect for much of it, James Calvin Schaap writes

> But if you, like me, are too much a Calvinist to trust progressivism, to truly believe the world is a better place because we're smarter, more morally sound, or less judgmental than [our] ancestors, then a question we have to ask is 'What might have been lost?'[13]

As we follow the story of Old Columbia Seminary, we will learn from the mistakes and sins of Christian leaders. But if we abandon what Morton Smith calls the 'orthodox, Old School, Presbyterian theology' of the 'Old Columbians,' we must have the wisdom to ask, 'What is lost?' And we must have the humility to ask, 'Where do we fall short in our convictions and practices? What will succeeding generations say about us?'

* * * * *

An important source for the early history of Columbia Seminary is the *Memorial Volume of the Semi-Centennial of the Theological Seminary at Columbia, South Carolina*

[12] Eugene D. Genovese, *The Southern Tradition: The Achievement and Limitations of an American Conservatism* (Cambridge, Mass.: Harvard University Press, 1994), pp. xi-xii.

[13] James Calvin Schaap, 'Emily Dickinson, Peter De Vries, and the Strangely Unshakeable Calvinist Character', *Pro Rege* (June 2010), p. 22.

(1884). This book contains addresses given on the occasion of the semi-centennial, including 'History of Columbia Theological Seminary' by George Howe, and 'History of Foreign Missions, as Related to the Southern Presbyterian Church and Columbia Seminary.' It also includes memorial sketches of deceased professors and students.

William Childs Robinson's Harvard University dissertation was published as *Columbia Theological Seminary and the Southern Presbyterian Church: A Study in Church History, Presbyterian Polity, Missionary Enterprise, and Religious Thought* (1931). In his review of this book Paul Wooley of Westminster Theological Seminary wrote: 'Robinson has given us a concise, clear and scholarly survey of the development and present state of Presbyterian doctrine and life in one of the great areas of our Lord's vineyard.'[14]

Louis C. LaMotte wrote *Colored Light: The Story of the Influence of Columbia Theological Seminary, 1828-1936* (1937). In the preface to his book LaMotte writes:

> To the writer [LaMotte] the history of Columbia Seminary seems a wonderfully interesting story. Perhaps this may be due to his personal association with the venerable school of the prophets. He was born and lived the first thirteen years of his life only a block and a half from the campus in Columbia, South Carolina. He learned to play tennis as a small lad upon that campus. It was while kneeling in prayer in the home of one of the members of the Columbia faculty that he made his first definite conscious acceptance of and commitment to the Christian life. To Columbia Seminary he returned from college and there studied three years until graduation. The old campus still well-nigh arouses slight nostalgia. The transfer to Atlanta was decided upon in the writer's senior year.

[14] Paul Wooley, 'A Study in Church History', *Evangelical Quarterly* (January 1932), p. 89.

J. McDowell Richards' *As I Remember It: Columbia Theological Seminary, 1932-1971* (1985) includes some information on the early twentieth-century history of the seminary, as well as the years 1932 to 1971 when Richards was president.

For most of its first hundred years, Columbia Seminary was located near Columbia's First Presbyterian Church and happily shared a theological and spiritual heritage. See my bicentennial history of the church, *The Glory of the Lord Risen Upon It: First Presbyterian Church, Columbia, South Carolina, 1795-1995* (1994).

Douglas Kelly's *Preachers With Power: Four Stalwarts of the South* (1992) surveys the lives, and studies the preaching, of four men, each of whom served the First Presbyterian Church and three of whom taught at Columbia Seminary. Daniel Baker supplied the pulpit at First Presbyterian Church for a few months during 1832. James Henley Thornwell was pastor twice (1839-41 and 1856-61). Benjamin Morgan Palmer was pastor from 1843-55 and preached again at the church during the Civil War. John Girardeau was a frequent preacher at First Presbyterian during his years at Columbia Seminary. Thornwell taught at Columbia Seminary from 1855 until his death in 1862. Palmer was a teacher there from 1853-56, and Girardeau from 1876-95.

Morton Smith wrote *Studies in Southern Presbyterian Theology* (1962) as his doctoral dissertation under the direction of Professor G. C. Berkouwer of the Free University of Amsterdam. In this book Smith surveys the theology taught at Columbia Seminary from its beginning through the professorship of J. B. Green.

* * * * *

For help in the writing and production of this book, I would like to give special thanks to:—

• Covenant Theological Seminary for my beautiful office on campus and to the seminary library for generous help.

• Wayne Sparkman, director of the Historical Center of the Presbyterian Church in America, for untiring interest in this projcct and skillful assistance.

• Barry Waugh, church historian, for permission to use the outstanding collection of photographs that he has given to the Historical Center.

• Erica Hoyt, South Carolina artist, for permission to use her watercolor painting of the Mills Building in Columbia, South Carolina—the home of Columbia Theological Seminary for almost a hundred years. Erica Hoyt's painting of the First Presbyterian Church of Columbia graces the cover of my bicentennial history of First Presbyterian, *The Glory of the Lord Risen upon It.*

• Douglas Kelly, Richard Jordan Professor of Theology at Reformed Theological Seminary (Charlotte), for reading an early version of this book, for his encouragement, and for writing the preface.

• The Banner of Truth Trust and all their staff for invaluable service to the Lord's church.

• Anne Calhoun for careful proofreading.

• Our loving and sovereign God for sustaining and enabling me to write this book during a time of physical challenges in my life.

I

A NEW TOWN

ON March 24, 1663, King Charles II of England granted a charter for the province of Carolina, which included part of North Carolina and all of South Carolina and Georgia. The first English settlement in South Carolina began in 1670 at Charles Town on the west bank of the Ashley River; it was moved ten years later to the present site of Charleston, on the peninsula between the Ashley and Cooper rivers. From its earliest days, the colony of South Carolina was dominated by this wealthy city of sophisticated social and cultural life. By the 1740s, however, a steady flow of frontier farmers had begun to fill the South Carolina Upcountry. Some settled in the central part of the state in Pine Tree Hill (later Camden), in Winnsboro, and in several places along the Congaree River. By then the native Indians—the Congarees, Waterees, Catawbas, and Saludas—had departed, leaving little behind except the names of the region's rivers.

At the end of the Revolutionary War, South Carolinians of the Upcountry and the Midlands, often alienated from the government of the planters and merchants of the Low Country, were agitating for a more centrally located capital. Several sites were proposed, including Camden and General Thomas Sumter's Stateburg in the High Hills of the Santee. On March 6, 1786, John Lewis Gervais introduced a bill in the House of Representatives to locate the capital in a new town on the Congaree River near the center point of the state. On March 22, the General Assembly approved this plan and named the town Columbia, a feminine adaptation of the name of Christopher Columbus. The next month, five commissioners were authorized to purchase 2,471 acres from ten property owners. In 1787 the town of Columbia was laid out in four hundred square blocks, with lots of half an acre each and a pattern of sixty-foot-wide streets.

Columbia was written into the state constitution of 1790 as the permanent capital of South Carolina. Someone observed that exactly one hundred and twenty years after the first English settlement at Charleston, the capital was moved about one hundred and twenty miles, from Charleston to Columbia. Many people saw opportunity in the new town, and sales of property were brisk. The few native Carolinians were joined by settlers from New England and Virginia. Immigrants came from England, Scotland, and Ireland, as well as from France and Germany.

* * * * *

Presbyterians were among the earliest settlers in South Carolina. One of the first churches in the colony, organized in Charleston between 1680 and 1690, was called the Independent Church, or 'Old White Meeting House' because of its color, and later the 'Circular Church' because of its shape. It comprised Presbyterians chiefly from Scotland and Ireland and Congregationalists from England and New England. In 1731 the Presbyterian members of the Independent Church withdrew and moved down Meeting Street to establish First (Scots) Presbyterian Church.

Out in the countryside there was an important colony of New England Congregationalists. These Puritans had come from Devon, Dorset, and Somerset in England to Massachusetts in 1630. In 1695 some of them and their children came south to Charleston, sailed up the Ashley River, and settled at a place they called Dorchester, near the site of the present town of Summerville. There they celebrated their first Communion under a spreading oak on December 14, 1695. In 1754, seeking more and better land, most of these colonists moved to Liberty County, Georgia, where they began the Midway Church—a people and church that would have great influence in Southern Presbyterian history and in the story of Columbia Seminary.

French-Calvinist Huguenots driven from France by the Revocation of the Edict of Nantes in 1685 found their way to South Carolina. Years earlier, in 1562, two years before John Calvin died, a small colony of Huguenots had lived for a short time on the shores of Port Royal Sound, before being overcome by the Spanish. Later Huguenots who came to South Carolina became Anglicans, joined Presbyterian churches, or formed their own Huguenot church in Charleston.

Low Country Presbyterian congregations, especially strong on the islands south of Charleston, were served by well-educated ministers, mostly from Ireland and Scotland. The earliest presbytery in the South was organized by the Charleston-area churches before 1722; it maintained close ties with the Church of Scotland.[1]

George Whitefield visited the colony several times, beginning in 1738. His preaching produced a 'great awakening' and contributed chiefly to Baptist and Presbyterian growth. By the

[1] The Charleston Union Presbytery, as it was known, affiliated with the Presbyterian Church in the United States of America in 1823.

middle of the eighteenth century, large numbers of Scotch-Irish immigrants, who poured into the Carolina Upcountry by way of Philadelphia and Virginia, founded Presbyterian churches in towns and villages where they settled. 'They knew how to use the axe and the rifle,' wrote Henry Alexander White. 'They carried with them the Bible, the Westminster Confession of Faith and the Catechisms.'[2] These Presbyterians had closer links with Philadelphia than with Charleston. Many of their ministers were educated at the Presbyterian college in Princeton. By the time of the American Revolution, these Scotch-Irish settlers made the Presbyterian Church the largest denomination in South Carolina.

The first American presbytery was organized in 1706 in Philadelphia; it was largely the work of Francis Makemie, who came from Rathmelton in Donegal, Ireland, as a missionary to Virginia in 1684. In 1716 the Synod of Philadelphia was formed. The church divided in 1741 into the Old Side (Synod of Philadelphia) and the New Side (Synod of New York). The Old Side opposed the methods of the Great Awakening; the New Side was made up of enthusiastic supporters of George Whitefield and his preaching. Three years before the schism ended in 1758, the New Side Presbyterian Church organized Hanover Presbytery, which included the area from western Pennsylvania to Georgia. Four ministers and three elders were present for the first meeting; Samuel Davies, later president of Princeton College, was elected moderator. There had been decades of Presbyterian labor in the South before Hanover Presbytery was formed, but it was Hanover that was to become 'the mother of Southern Presbyterianism.' In 1770

[2] Henry Alexander White, *Southern Presbyterian Leaders 1683-1911* (New York: Neale Publishing Company, 1911; reprint, Edinburgh: Banner of Truth, 2000), p. 31.

Orange Presbytery was created from Hanover and included all territory south of Virginia. South Carolina Presbytery was established in 1784.[3] In 1786 the churches in Georgia were set apart as Hopewell Presbytery. The first General Assembly, meeting in Philadelphia in May 1789, divided the one Synod of New York and Philadelphia into four: New York and New Jersey, Philadelphia, Virginia, and the Carolinas.

In 1788 there were only eleven Presbyterian ministers in South Carolina. Three years later the Synod of the Carolinas sent out four missionaries to work within its bounds, directing them 'not to tarry longer than three weeks at the same time in the bounds of twenty miles, except peculiar circumstances may appear to make it necessary.'[4] By 1799 there were fifty-seven Presbyterian congregations in South Carolina Presbytery. In 1813 the Synod of the Carolinas was divided into the Synod of North Carolina and the Synod of South Carolina and Georgia. The latter synod comprised the presbyteries of South Carolina, Hopewell, and Harmony. The Presbytery of Georgia was set off from Hopewell in 1821.

* * * * *

There were other Presbyterians in the state—independent Presbyterian churches in the Low Country and Associate Reformed Presbyterians in the Upcountry. The Associate Reformed Presbytery of the Carolinas and Georgia was organized at Long Cane, South Carolina, on February

[3] In 1800 South Carolina Presbytery was divided into First and Second South Carolina Presbyteries. First South Carolina was succeeded by Harmony Presbytery in 1809.

[4] T. Watson Street, *The Story of Southern Presbyterians* (Richmond, Va.: John Knox Press, 1960), p. 29.

24, 1790, with four ministers and forty-four congregations. This church traced its history back to two Scottish Presbyterian movements: the sturdy Covenanters of the seventeenth century, who took the name 'Reformed Presbyterians,' and the Seceders of the eighteenth century, who called themselves 'Associate Presbyterians.' The Covenanters stood for a Presbyterianism that honored the convictions of the martyrs in the struggle with the Stuart kings. The Seceders opposed interference with Presbyterian polity by prominent nobles or landowners and attempted to call the church back to the pure doctrines of grace against the creeping moralism of the time. The Associate Reformed Presbyterian Church in America's South was composed mainly of Seceders who came from Ireland after the Revolutionary War. They found homes in Chester, Lancaster, Fairfield, and Abbeville counties in South Carolina. On May 9, 1803, at the Old Brick Church in Fairfield County, the Associate Reformed Synod of the Carolinas was organized. In the little town of Due West, the ARPs would establish a college and theological seminary called Erskine—after Ebenezer and Ralph Erskine, brothers who led the 'secession' from the Church of Scotland in the 1730s.

* * * * *

The Presbyterians were 'the first religious society' established in the Richland district.[5] There was a church on the banks of Cedar Creek before the Revolutionary War, but in the district's first years there was no church in Columbia. Presbyterian services were held in the chapel of South Carolina College. Members of the congregation were seated in the

[5] F. D. Jones and W. H. Mills, *History of the Presbyterian Church in South Carolina since 1850* (Columbia. S.C.: R. L. Bryan, 1926), p. 32.

galleries, and the students below. South Carolina College was chartered in 1801; of the thirteen members of the first board, seven were Presbyterians. By 1809 Columbia Presbyterians were 'a numerous and wealthy congregation.'[6] Property on Marion Street was acquired, and in October 1814 the uncompleted new building was dedicated when Harmony Presbytery met in Columbia. Presbyters, church members, and visitors sat on rough seats that were brought in for the occasion and heard the dedication sermon from the text 'Be thou faithful unto death, and I will give thee a crown of life' (*Rev.* 2:10). When the building was finished, regular services were moved there from the college chapel; students walked the several blocks to worship with the congregation in their new church. A few years later a Sunday school building, or Lecture Room, as it was called, was constructed. The ground level provided classrooms for white children, and the basement was used for the 'oral instruction' of black people.

* * * * *

Columbia's central location on a river, its importance as the state's seat of government, and its promising college produced rapid growth in population and influence. In 1820 South Carolina was the leading cotton-producing state in the nation, and much of this business passed through Columbia. By 1826, the Columbia Canal—designed to enable boats to navigate the rocky rapids on the Broad River—was opened, and soon boats transported cotton and other goods to Charleston. Joined by stagecoach lines to Camden, Charleston, Greenville, and Augusta, Columbia welcomed

[6] David Ramsay, *The History of South-Carolina from Its First Settlement in the Year 1670 to the year 1808* (Charleston, 1809), 2:16.

many visitors. Times were good, the price of cotton was high, and the future looked bright indeed. South Carolina emerged from the War of 1812 a patriotic and nationalistic state, but it turned toward an aggressive sectionalism in the face of Northern abolitionism and federal tariffs that penalized the agricultural South. In 1832 the nullifiers, as they were called, won control of the state government. They organized a convention that met in Columbia and passed an ordinance nullifying certain acts of the Congress of the United States. They talked of secession, but the state was not of one mind. A Union party opposed to secession held a convention on September 10, 1832—at First Presbyterian Church. After President Andrew Jackson's threats to invade South Carolina, a compromise of sorts was achieved and the federal tariff was dropped. But hostile feelings and mutual suspicions remained. From the 1830s until the War between the States—a time called by David Duncan Wallace 'the bitter generation . . . a generation of brilliant and swift absorbing drama'—South Carolina was obsessed with debate on nullification, slavery, and secession.[7]

[7] See David Duncan Wallace, *South Carolina: A Short History, 1520-1948* (Columbia: University of South Carolina Press, 1961), pp. 396-408. The doctrine of nullification held that it was legal for a state to refuse to obey an act of Congress.

2

A NEW THEOLOGICAL SEMINARY

PRESBYTERIANS of South Carolina and Georgia contributed generously to the support of the General Assembly's seminary at Princeton, New Jersey. In 1820 Columbia's First Presbyterian Church sent to Princeton two collections received at Communion services. That same year the Synod of South Carolina and Georgia united with the Synod of North Carolina in an effort to endow a chair in the seminary and sent more than $42,000 to Princeton. But distance from Princeton and the growing desire to have a seminary for the 'Southern Church' led, in 1828, to the founding of the Theological Seminary of the Synod of South Carolina and Georgia—ambitiously first known as 'The Classical, Scientific and Theological Institution of the South.' It was decided, however, to make the new school a theological seminary only, so as not to compete with 'literary institutions now existing within the bounds of Synod.'[1]

'The spiritual needs of the entire Southeastern part of our country were resting upon the hearts of the men who founded Columbia Seminary,' wrote Henry Alexander White.[2] In an 'address to the public' the founders stated that

[1] LaMotte, *Colored Light*, p. 34.

[2] White, *Southern Presbyterian Leaders*, p. 256.

> we are conscious 'the ground on which we stand is holy' . . . Andover and Princeton have already told us what part theological seminaries are destined to bear in the illumination and reformation of the present age; and when we find another about to rise... surely 'the ears of the deaf must begin to hear, and the tongue of the dumb to sing, and the lame to leap as a hart.'[3]

Thomas Goulding, pastor of the Presbyterian church in Lexington, Georgia, was chosen as the seminary's first professor, and five students joined him for classes in his study. Goulding was born in Liberty County, Georgia, on March 14, 1786, and grew up in the community surrounding Midway Church—the remarkable settlement with roots in South Carolina and, earlier, in Puritan New England. Although a Congregational church, Midway sent scores of its sons into the Presbyterian ministry as preachers, missionaries, and professors. John Wells was thinking mainly of this church when he wrote that 'one of the strains that has gone into the making of our Southern Presbyterian Church is the English Puritan.'[4]

Goulding went to the North to study at Yale College but was so dismayed by practices at the school that he did not become a student there. He stayed in Connecticut, however, to study privately in the town of Wolcott. There he met Anne Holbrook, whom he married in November 1806. After the birth of a daughter, the Gouldings moved to Georgia, where Thomas studied law while he taught school to provide for his family. Thomas Goulding had no conversion experience to which he could point. He said that 'if ever he was regenerated, it was while he was asleep.' Wearied with his burden of

[3] *Memorial Volume*, p. 140.

[4] John Miller Wells, *Southern Presbyterian Worthies* (Richmond, Va.: Presbyterian Committee of Publication, 1936), p. 78.

sin, 'he had sunk despairingly into a profound slumber, from which he awoke praising God for his great salvation.'[5]

Early in 1811 two close friends, without any plans to do so, came on the same day from some distance to urge Thomas to consider the ministry. He was convinced that they were right. He studied theology privately and was licensed by the Presbytery of Harmony in 1813. He became stated supply at White Bluff, a settlement of Saltzburghers, who were Lutheran and Reformed Germans, near Savannah. On January 1, 1816, Thomas Goulding was ordained and installed as pastor of that church. He liked to say of himself that he was 'the first native of Georgia that became a Presbyterian minister since the foundation of the world'![6]

Goulding began to suffer from severe illness, and, after six years as a pastor in White Bluff, he moved to Oglethorpe County, Georgia, where he had purchased a small farm. In 1824 he became pastor of the Presbyterian church in Lexington, the county seat. He was awarded the doctor of divinity degree by the University of North Carolina in 1829, the same year in which he began to teach in the synod's theological college.

* * * * *

The Synod of South Carolina and Georgia considered various locations for the new seminary, including Athens, Georgia, and Pendleton and Winnsboro, South Carolina. Winnsboro was the home of the famous Mount Zion School, incorporated in 1777, which had produced thirteen of the

[5] *Memorial Volume,* p. 186.
[6] *Memorial Volume,* p. 181.

thirty-four men from the South who became Presbyterian ministers between the Revolutionary War and 1800. The synod finally decided on Columbia. William Childs Robinson wrote: 'Columbia, at that time, was regarded as the center of the Synod; the place in which was concentrated the most wealth, literary advantages, and moral force; and at which the influence of the Seminary could be brought to bear on the largest number of immortal beings.'[7]

In his history of the city of Columbia, John Hammond Moore speculated that the transfer of what he called 'this ultra-conservative school to South Carolina's capital was inspired, no doubt, by grim resolve to counteract the religious views of one Thomas Cooper,' the 'free-thinking' president of South Carolina College.[8] Born in London and educated at Oxford, Cooper had taught at the University of Virginia and was a close friend of Thomas Jefferson. Cooper denied the Mosaic authorship and inspiration of the Pentateuch and described the book of Genesis as a collection of 'absurd and frivolous tales.' It may have occurred to South Carolina Presbyterians that it would not be a bad thing to have an orthodox seminary in the same town with the state college, but their purpose was not merely, or mainly, to counter the influence of the college's president. The seminary's constitution stated that 'the design of this institution is, and ever shall be, to educate young men for the gospel ministry, who shall believe, love, and preach the doctrines of the Bible, as set forth

[7] William Childs Robinson, *Columbia Theological Seminary and the Southern Presbyterian Church: A Study in Church History, Presbyterian Polity, Missionary Enterprise, and Religious Thought* (Decatur, Ga.: Dennis Lindsey Printing Company, 1931), p. 13.

[8] John Hammond Moore, *Columbia and Richland County* (Columbia: University of South Carolina Press, 1993), p. 115.

in the Confession of Faith of the Presbyterian Church in the United States of America.'[9]

Early in 1830 Dr. Goulding, accompanied by his family and slaves, moved from Lexington, Georgia, to Columbia. Goulding was inaugurated on March 17 in the First Presbyterian Church. Dr. William A. McDowell preached the sermon from 2 Corinthians 1:24—'Not that we have dominion over your faith, but are helpers of your joy: for by faith ye stand.' Dr. Benjamin Morgan Palmer Sr. inducted Dr. Goulding into office. Palmer, pastor of the Circular Congregational Church of Charleston, was the first chairman of the seminary's board of directors. Classes were held on Marion Street in the former manse of the First Presbyterian Church, but soon, through the generosity of local supporters of all denominations, and led by First Presbyterian elder Colonel Abraham Blanding, the school acquired a splendid house of its own a few blocks from the church.

Designed by famous South Carolina architect Robert Mills for Ainsley Hall, a prominent Columbia merchant, it was a classical building of red brick with a four-columned portico on a raised brick arcade.[10] The house had three levels—a

[9] *Constitution of the Theological Seminary of the Synod of South Carolina and Georgia* (1826).

[10] A Southerner opposed to slavery, and a Unionist who cherished states and local rights, Robert Mills was the first native-born and American-trained architect. He executed commissions from Newburyport, Massachusetts, to Mobile, Alabama, and worked in Philadelphia, Baltimore, Columbia, South Carolina, and Washington, D.C. Mills published architectural works, as well as proposals for canals, steam locomotion, railroads—including an elevated railway for New York City—and urban water supply. As a young man, Mills was greatly helped by Thomas Jefferson, who made his library available to him and involved him in the process of completing Monticello. From 1801 to 1803 Mills lived at Monticello. Robert Mills is best known today for his Washington National Monument—in the words of the accomplished late-nineteenth-century American architect Ralph Adams Cram, 'the noblest architectural structure in the United States.' Above all, Robert Mills was a devout

principal floor, a 'chamber' or bedroom floor, and a full raised basement. The basement contained a central hall and four rooms, each having a fireplace and windows on two sides. Intended as a service area, the basement was 'plainly and neatly' finished with an unglazed brick floor and rough plastered walls.[11] Two small, unpretentious buildings, intended for the use of servants, stood on each side of the main house. These at first were used for student accommodations. It was said that in their second floor rooms the students were obliged to uncover their heads and bow—not for reverence but so they could stand without hitting the ceiling! Later the top floor and basement of the main building also were used for student rooms. Classes and chapel were held on the middle floor. A gardener's house became a refectory and dining room. On January 25, 1831, the seminary opened in its new location with six students. 'The same rooms that were intended for the home life, merriment and hospitality of Ainsley Hall, who died before the building was finished,' a later historian

Christian who read and studied the Bible from childhood. Raised a Presbyterian in Charleston, South Carolina, he remained a faithful member of that denomination all his life. In 1821, when he lived in Columbia, South Carolina, Robert and his wife, Eliza Barnwell Smith Mills, joined the First Presbyterian Church. In 1824 Robert Mills was elected an elder. Later he regularly attended a Presbyterian Church in Washington, D.C., until his death on March 3, 1855. Among Robert Mills's writings are devotional and theological works. A typical comment in his journal is the prayer 'O Lord, I beseech thee to renew my spirit. Blessed Jesus, let me taste the fullness of thy grace.' In a letter to his wife, Eliza, dated September 15, 1816, Mills wrote: 'O may we, my dearest Eliza, appreciate the blessings we enjoy, and improve the privileges which we are favored with, in striving through faith in the blessed promises of the Gospel to enter in at the strait gate, and realize the bliss in store for all the redeemed of the Lord. Ah! What avails all that this world calls good! Of what advantage is it to us to possess the honors, riches, pomp and power of this life, if we have not an interest in the Redeemer's Kingdom, if we cannot call Jesus our Savior, Brother, Friend.'

[11] See John M. Bryan, *America's First Architect: Robert Mills* (New York: Princeton Architectural Press, 2001), pp. 194-99.

wrote, now 'echoed to the droning or stimulating or inspiring lectures or to class-room discussions.'[12]

When the First Presbyterian Church pastor, John Rennie, visited Europe during the summer of 1830, Thomas Goulding occupied the pulpit. When Rennie resigned in 1831, Goulding and his seminary colleague, George Howe, were joint supply pastors for a year and a half. Throughout its Columbia history, seminary professors often preached at the church or served as interim pastors. Many of the church's pastors gave lectures at the seminary. The seminary students attended the church, in which two pews were set aside for their use. They heard good sermons, learned the Bible, and observed first-hand the life and mission of the church.

* * * * *

Columbia's sesqui-centennial history states that 'the Seminary faculty from the first included vigorous characters, fluent in spoken and written argument, who rapidly became leaders of the large Scotch-Irish element of up-country South Carolina.' They were the beginning of 'the long line of Presbyterian presidents and professors of the University, the outstanding Presbyterian publishers and publications, that were to give a decided tone of Edinburgh to this town set among Episcopal planters and German Lutheran farmers.'[13]

Although the seminary was located in the new town of Columbia, Presbyterians and Congregationalists of Low Country South Carolina and Georgia played a major role in founding

[12] Jones and Mills, *The Presbyterian Church in South Carolina*, p. 420.

[13] Helen Kohn Hennig, ed., *Columbia: Capital City of South Carolina, 1786-1936* (Columbia: The State Printing Co., 1966), p. 196.

and supporting the new school. Columbia's board of directors was dominated by men from the Low Country. Most of the early financial support for the seminary came from the Low Country. William Seabrook of Edisto Island made the largest contribution in the seminary's early history. Many of the seminary's teachers had Low Country roots. Thomas Goulding and C. C. Jones came from the Midway Congregationalist Church in Liberty County, Georgia. New Englander Aaron Leland served for years as a pastor in the Charleston area before going to Columbia Seminary. Benjamin Morgan Palmer, Bazile Lanneau, and John Adger all came to the seminary faculty from the Low Country, as did John Lafayette Girardeau.

* * * * *

George Howe came to Columbia Seminary in 1830 to teach Greek and Hebrew and the next year was elected professor of biblical literature. A native of Massachusetts, Howe was the son of William, who traced his line back to one of the pilgrims of Plymouth Rock, and Mary, who was related to Timothy Dwight, the president of Yale College. A studious boy, George began his study of Latin by reading Cotton Mather's *Magnalia*. He graduated from Middlebury College, with first honors, in 1822. George Howe studied for the ministry at Andover Seminary and taught at Dartmouth College as professor of theology before coming to South Carolina for the benefit of his health. Turning down an invitation to become pastor of Charleston's First Presbyterian Church, he chose instead to accept the appointment at the new seminary in Columbia. On August 25, 1831, Howe married Mary Bushnell. She died on September 18, 1832, and was buried in the cemetery of the First Presbyterian Church.

In his sermon before the Synod of South Carolina and Georgia, young George Howe likened the fluctuation of faith to 'the magnetic needle that comes to rest at north just as the soul comes to rest in Christ.' Dr. Moses Waddel, former president of the University of Georgia who had himself declined a faculty position at the seminary, was heard to whisper, 'Sublime.'[14]

[14] LaMotte, *Colored Light*, p. 42. Moses Waddel was born in 1770 on a farm in Rowan County, North Carolina, to a Scotch-Irish family. The sickly Waddel baby was expected to die. When he lived after all, he was named 'Moses' for the biblical patriarch who was providentially preserved to become a leader of his people. Moses studied first at school in North Carolina but, at the age of fourteen, began to teach himself with wonderful success. At eighteen, he opened his own school at Bethany, Georgia (near the Ogeechee River). The Reverend Daniel Thatcher had organized a Presbyterian church there, and it was under his ministry that young Moses Waddel was led to 'embrace, receive, and rest upon the Saviour for the whole of his salvation.' Waddel decided to study for the ministry. He graduated from Hampden-Sydney College in 1791. He was licensed to preach by the Presbytery of Hanover on May 12, 1792—a day he recorded in his diary and remembered for the rest of his life. Waddel went to Charleston, South Carolina, where he preached at several churches until 1794, when he returned to Georgia. He was elected clerk at the first meeting of Hopewell Presbytery in 1796. Moses Waddel married Catherine Calhoun, older sister of John C. Calhoun. Catherine died in childbirth in 1796; Moses married again in 1800. In 1801 he moved to Vienna, South Carolina, and then to Willington, where he set up an academy in which he prepared students for their junior year in college. Waddel's school at Willington has been called 'the best academy in the South, maybe in the nation.' In fifteen years the Willington Academy educated more than one thousand boarding students, many of whom became leaders in the South. At the first commencement of South Carolina College, in 1807, Moses Waddel was awarded the honorary title of doctor of divinity. On March 1, 1819, Dr. Waddel was elected president of the University of Georgia. He passed through a period of agonizing prayer, trying, as he did 'in all the business of life,' to discover God's will. He longed to preach, but he felt constrained to accept the call to the university. According to historian Thomas Walter Reed, the eighteen-year-old college was reborn when Waddel came, 'for on that day about all that remained to be done was to lay it in its shroud and usher it into the land of memories.' Reed states that Waddel 'put upon the University of Georgia the stamp of religion. There wasn't a moment in his ten years as president of the University when he was not the preacher as well as the teacher.' On December 25, 1820, Moses Waddel organized the Presbyterian Church in Athens, Georgia, and served as the church's minister. From time to time this famous educator preached at Augusta's First Presbyterian Church. After retiring from the presidency of the University of Georgia, Waddel led his school in Willington. He died in 1840. See William B. Sprague, ed., *Annals of the American Pulpit*, vol. 4.

Fifty years later, at the celebration of his long service to the seminary, Dr. Howe reflected on how all this came to be. He said:

> I believe in a Providence, a Providence which rules over all things. I believe in a special providence. And I have reason to 'know that the way of man is not in himself: it is not in man that walketh to direct his steps.' There is a power above us that stirs up our nests, and thwarts our purposes, forecast them as we will, and this, too, for our own best good. In my early manhood a malady which is most often fatal had overtaken me, and, after a partial recovery, the frosts of the succeeding winter had brought on a relapse, and my medical friends thought it necessary that I should avoid the severities of another. I came, a stranger, not without solicitude, to the port of Charleston, but only to receive the kind hospitalities of those who seemed to know how to dispel the forebodings of a stranger's heart. The Synod of South Carolina and Georgia met in the city of Augusta on the 2nd of December, 1830. Dr. Goulding had asked for an assistant who should teach the original languages of the Scriptures. My name was brought before the Synod by the Board of Directors. I was unanimously elected to this office for the year; accepted the office, first for three months, but was prevailed upon to stay till July... On the 3rd of December, 1831, the Synod of South Carolina and Georgia, meeting in [Columbia], elected me as Professor of Sacred Literature and Biblical Criticism.[15]

Howe organized the curriculum and set the tone for Columbia Seminary, following the models of Princeton and his own alma mater, Andover. He was an exceptional teacher. It was said that he so skillfully taught the Bible in the original languages that 'sound methods of Hebrew and Greek exegesis

[15] *Memorial Volume*, pp. 11-12.

were disseminated by him throughout our Southern country.'[16] When George Howe declined a call in 1836 from the new Union Theological Seminary in New York City, he wrote:

> I must now say, that it appears still my duty to cast in my lot and earthly destiny with the people of the South, among whom I have made my home. When I accepted the professorship which I hold, it was with the hope that I might be the means of building up the wastes, and extending the borders, of our Southern Zion. This motive still holds me here.

Howe wanted to do his part, he said, to 'transmit to the men of the next generation an institution which will bless them and the world.'[17]

* * * * *

'The world' was on the mind of the seminary faculty and students from the very beginning. On the evening of February 7, 1831, several weeks after the seminary had moved to its new home, two students, John Leighton Wilson, a South Carolinian, and James L. Merrick, a native of New England, began the Society of Inquiry on Missions. Wilson read a paper to a small gathering of students, faculty, and visitors: 'What Has Been and What Ought to be Done by the Southern Presbyterian Church in behalf of Foreign Missions.'

There was a serious desire for deeper commitment to God among the students. James Merrick wrote in his diary for May 25, 1831:

> This evening several of the brethren met in my room for prayer. We confessed our faults one to another, and prayed

[16] Wells, *Southern Presbyterian Worthies*, p. 258.
[17] *Memorial Volume*, p. 410.

> one for another. Our hearts flowed together; the Holy Spirit seemed present to bless; it appeared to be a little reviving in our midst. I think that we are all desirous of living more to the glory of God than we have done . . . Lord Jesus, aid us.[18]

* * * * *

For a few months during 1832, well-known Presbyterian preacher Daniel Baker supplied the First Presbyterian Church pulpit. Descended from Puritans, Baker was born on August 17, 1791, in Midway, Liberty County, Georgia, the birthplace of Dr. Goulding. Baker was educated at Hampden-Sydney and Princeton colleges. At Princeton he led the few Christian students in praying for 'a revival of religion in college.' Revival did come, with numerous conversions, and about twenty or thirty of the young men went on to become ministers of the gospel. Baker attempted theological studies with the Reverend William Hill, pastor of the Presbyterian church in Winchester, Virginia, but as soon as Baker settled in, William Hill went off on a visit and stayed four months, leaving him in charge of two congregations! In 1816, Baker married Elizabeth McRoberts of Prince Edward County, a 'lady of piety and kindness.'[19] In the fall of 1816 he was licensed to preach, although presbytery was concerned about his scanty theological training. Baker's sermon before presbytery, however, was impressive. One man who heard it attributed his own conversion to that sermon.

For three years Daniel Baker was pastor of two churches in Rockingham, Virginia. During a missionary tour in western

[18] LaMotte, *Colored Light*, p. 53.
[19] Kelly, *Preachers With Power*, p. 15.

Virginia he began to have, he wrote, 'a hankering after a missionary life.'[20] That 'hankering' never left him, although he served short pastorates. The first was at Second Presbyterian Church in Washington, D.C., where John Quincy Adams and Andrew Jackson, later United States presidents, were among his parishioners. Baker then accepted a call to the large and important Independent Presbyterian Church in Savannah, Georgia.[21] When Baker became discouraged with himself and the state of things in the church, he took Payson's *Memoirs* early one morning and spent nearly the whole day in a distant graveyard, reading, fasting, and praying.[22] 'That day,' writes John Wells, 'marked an epoch in his life. The channels that had been clogged by self and sin, restraining the work of the Spirit in the life, were opened by grace.'[23] After revival came to the Savannah church in 1830 and 1831, Daniel Baker felt constrained to return once more to his first love—itinerant preaching. He was appointed evangelist by the Synod of South Carolina and Georgia, and preached widely and constantly throughout the Southern states.

During Daniel Baker's short stay in Columbia, the city

[20] William M. Baker, *The Life and Labors of the Rev. Daniel Baker, D.D.* (Philadelphia: William S. & Alfred Martien, 1854), p. 134. See also Kelly, *Preachers with Power,* part one, 'Daniel Baker: Evangelism with Power,' pp. 3-57.

[21] See David B. Calhoun, *Splendor of Grace: Independent Presbyterian Church 1755-2005* (Greenville, S.C.: A Press, 2005), chapter 11, 'Preacher with Power,' pp. 139-51.

[22] Edward Payson was an American Congregational pastor (1783-1827) in Portland, Maine. A collection of his sermons, with a memoir by Asa Cummings, was published in 1828. The memoir was published separately in 1830 by the American Tract Society. According to Iain Murray, Payson's memoir 'was probably the most influential ministerial biography to appear in the United States in the first half of the 19th century.' Iain H. Murray, *Revival and Revivalism* (Edinburgh: Banner of Truth, 1994), p. 194. The life of one of the daughters of Ann and Edward Payson is given in *Elizabeth Prentiss, 'More Love to Thee'* by Sharon James (Edinburgh: Banner of Truth, 2006).

[23] Wells, *Southern Presbyterian Worthies,* p. 84.

was refreshed by a 'gracious outpouring of God's Spirit; and a large addition was made to the communion of the church.' The town's Methodists and Baptists joined with the Presbyterians in a series of meetings. John Leighton Wilson, a student at Columbia Seminary, wrote to his sister in Sumter:

> We have an interesting season in Columbia. Mr. Baker has been here nearly three weeks and has preached almost every night during the time... Deep feelings have attended Mr. Baker's preaching from the outset—upwards of twenty persons have been converted and [are] now rejoicing in Christ. About fifty are enquiring 'What shall we do?' Mr. Baker has been indefatigable in his labours and I have seldom heard any minister preach the gospel in so much simplicity and power. His whole soul seems to be entirely absorbed in the work of his master... O how exceedingly desirable is it that we shall have a glorious revival of religion in this town. It is the central town of the state—the center of political influence—a wealthy community—the college here—the seminary here. O pray earnestly for this community![24]

The session of First Presbyterian Church met on July 31, 1832, at 'the lodgings of Rev. Mr. Baker' and approved visitation to every family in the town by Baker and one of the elders. During his ministry in Columbia, Baker traveled to Nazareth Church in Spartanburg District and to Winnsboro for preaching missions. Many other places were urging him to help them, including the churches at Pendleton, Newberry, and Walterboro. On September 7, Mr. Baker requested release from his engagement as supply at First Presbyterian to attend 'various protracted meetings.'

After leaving Columbia until the end of his life in 1857, Daniel Baker worked in fairly short pastorates (by far the

[24] Calhoun, *The Glory of the Lord Risen Upon It*, p. 38.

longest in Holly Springs, Mississippi, where he stayed for nine years) and much longer fruitful evangelistic tours. After a meeting during which Baker preached a number of times, he received a letter closing with the words 'In the hour of death I think I shall see you, sir, as your finger ran over the precious promises in the third chapter of John.'[25] In 1838 Baker was challenged by the words of a friend, 'Brother Baker, you are the man for Texas.' The rest of his life was spent in three long missionary tours of Texas, interspersed with brief pastorates and preaching missions back in the states east of the Mississippi River. On December 10, 1857, during the last hours of his life, Baker said to his son William that he wanted the words carved on his tomb: 'Here lies Daniel Baker, Preacher of the Gospel. A sinner saved by grace.' 'Remember,' he added, 'a sinner saved by grace.'[26]

John Miller Wells sums up Baker's preaching with six points.

First, no other minister of the Presbyterian Church in the South preached so widely. His journal lists 165 places where he held preaching missions, from Ohio to Texas. He returned often to South Carolina and Georgia. In 1852 he was in Sumter, South Carolina, where Donald McQueen, 1836 graduate of Columbia Seminary, was pastor. Baker wrote: 'Last night, amid circumstances of very special interest and solemnity, our meeting in this place came to an end, and truly, a most delightful, blessed meeting it has proved, a soul refreshing season indeed.'[27]

Second, no one has excelled him in the fitness of his preaching to lead souls to Jesus Christ. As a student, he wrote

[25] Wells, *Southern Presbyterian Worthies*, p. 88.

[26] White, *Southern Presbyterian Leaders*, p. 279.

[27] Jones and Mills, *History of the Presbyterian Church*, p. 832.

in his diary: 'O may I never become a cold, lifeless, sentimental preacher, but may I imitate the zeal of a Whitefield, the tenderness of a Hervey, the affection of a Baxter, and blend all with the pure, sound, evangelical principles of a Doddridge.' After a series of meetings in South Carolina in 1854, Baker wrote: 'If my preaching was crowned with a remarkable blessing, I believe that one reason was this: bearing in mind that the Word of God, and not the word of man, is quick and powerful, I was a man of one book, and that book the Bible; and taking the hint from an inspired Apostle, I made Jesus Christ and him crucified my constant theme.'[28] Writing to one of his sons, a young minister, Baker exhorted him: 'Remember, my son, this saying of your father, that the sermon that does not distinctly present Christ in the beauty and glory of his mediatorial character is no better than a cloud without water, a casket without a jewel, a shadow without the substance or the body without the soul.' Baker preached the great doctrines of the Bible. He wrote: 'I am free to say that I think the religious movement among us is due mainly to plain, frank, undisguised presentation of these great doctrines in their own solemn Scripture attire.' A pastor said that Baker preached divine sovereignty, election, total depravity, vicarious atonement, and efficacious grace with such love and tact that 'a beautiful and cordial union prevails; Presbyterians, Methodists and Baptists commingled their tears under the droppings of a sublime Calvinist theology.'

Third, the methods that he employed were sane and scriptural. The shouting and crying that marked many evangelistic meetings during this time were largely missing from

[28] Ernest Trice Thompson, *Presbyterians in the South* (Richmond, Va.: John Knox Press, 1973) 1:429. See Kelly, *Preachers With Power,* part one, 'Daniel Baker: Evangelism with Power,' pp. 3-57.

his services. He remembered only 'eight or ten cases of outcries,' and in nearly all of them, he wrote, order and stillness were immediately restored when he simply repeated this beautiful passage of Scripture, 'The Lord is in his holy temple, let all the earth keep silence before him.'

Fourth, he believed in personal evangelism. Ashbel Green, the president of Princeton College during Baker's time there, wrote that Baker went through the college speaking to each person 'privately and tenderly on the subject of religion.'

Fifth, he believed in and used prayer as a powerful factor in evangelistic work. In his life of sixty years, wrote John Miller Wells, 'between the child praying in the cornfield and the saint praying on his deathbed, lay a life of continued prayer.'

Last, he was used of God in most wonderful revivals, in which God's people were richly blessed and very many souls were saved. How many? Too often, in Baker's reports and in writings about him, there are specific numbers of 'hopeful conversions' reported. It is better to sum up his life work as Wells does: 'From one end of our church to the other, this flaming evangelist passed, holding up the blood-stained cross. Only eternity will measure his work.'[29]

[29] Wells, *Southern Presbyterian Worthies*, pp. 97-104.

3

JOHN LEIGHTON WILSON

OF the seminary's first graduating class of six, three chose to go as foreign missionaries. One of them, James M. Adams, was accepted by the American Board but was prevented from going overseas by family considerations. He became a pastor, serving churches in the Carolinas until his death in 1862. Two men from that first class, James Merrick and John Leighton Wilson, did become missionaries overseas.

James Merrick was born in Monson, Massachusetts. He graduated from Amherst College in 1830 and Columbia Seminary in 1833. In Columbia Merrick worshipped at First Presbyterian Church and sometimes preached there. On a return visit to Columbia he wrote in his diary for May 25, 1834: 'Preached in the Presbyterian Church morning and afternoon. Probably for the last time I have entered those courts where for years I have listened to the glad news of salvation, and where in months not long since gone by, I have again and again proclaimed the messages of Christ.'[1] James Merrick, greatly influenced by the example of Henry Martyn, wanted to work with the Muslims of Persia. He reached Istanbul in November 1834, studied Turkish, the

[1] LaMotte, *Colored Light*, p. 75.

language of northern Persia, then traveled to Tabriz in the fall of 1835. He was tutor to the prince of Persia. Merrick married Englishwoman Emma Taylor in 1839. They served in Persia and in the mission to the Nestorians before coming back to the United States in 1845. Merrick became pastor of the Congregational church in South Amherst, Massachusetts, and professor of the Persian language at Amherst College. There were no conversions, as far as is known, through his missionary work in Persia, but 'no doubt his prayers, as well as those of Henry Martyn, whom he so much admired, in behalf of that people, will yet be answered in a way that was entirely unknown to them as well as ourselves.'[2]

* * * * *

John Leighton Wilson was a descendant of the Scots-Irish colony of Presbyterians who settled along South Carolina's Black River in 1734.[3] 'Godly folk they were,' writes John Wells, 'worshipping God, reading His Word, keeping His day, and bringing up their children in the nurture and admonition of the Lord.'[4] William Wilson married Jane James and they became the parents of John Leighton Wilson, born on March

[2] *Memorial Volume,* p. 168. The quotation is from John Leighton Wilson.

[3] For John Leighton Wilson, see the biography by Hampden C. DuBose, *Memoirs of Rev. John Leighton Wilson. D.D., Missionary to Africa and Secretary of Foreign Missions* (Richmond, Va.: Presbyterian Committee of Publication, 1895); and the chapter in John Miller Wells, *Southern Presbyterian Worthies,* pp. 50-76. Wilson's middle name, 'Leighton,' was probably in honor of the Scottish minister Robert Leighton, who was principal of the University of Edinburgh from 1653 to 1662. Despite his Presbyterian connections and views, Leighton agreed with hesitation to accept appointment as Archbishop of Glasgow in 1670, hoping to bring about some degree of conciliation between the Episcopalians and the Presbyterians. His commentary on 1 Peter was published a few years after his death in 1684 and has rarely been out of print since.

[4] Wells, *Southern Presbyterian Worthies,* p. 50.

25, 1809. Their son, according to Hampden DuBose, 'was a Wilson in humility of soul, simplicity of life, loveliness of character, and consecration to the Church; but it was the James' blood coursing through his veins that made him a Joshua to the Southern Church in her days of poverty and desolation.'[5] Wilson grew up in the flat country of South Carolina, which is interlaced with swamps through which flow sluggish creeks and rivers turned brown by juniper and cypress trees. The higher ground was covered with forests of long leaf pine and beautiful oaks. As a child John listened in the slaves' cabins to stories about Africa. He finished his preparatory studies at the well-respected Mount Zion College, a secondary school in Winnsboro, South Carolina. Rejecting South Carolina College because of its 'atheistic' influences, John Leighton Wilson went to Union College in Schenectady, New York, where fellow South Carolinian John Adger was his best friend. Adger was a major influence on Wilson's decision to enter the ministry and become a missionary. John Adger went to Princeton Seminary, and Wilson, after graduating from Union College in 1829, came home to South Carolina. Another important influence in Wilson's early life was his uncle, Robert Wilson James, who was pastor of the Salem, Black River Presbyterian Church, and one of the founders of Columbia Seminary. James preached not only to his white congregation but also to the slaves who came in large numbers from nearby plantations to hear his sermons. This, no doubt, contributed to Wilson's desire to be a missionary to Africa.

In January 1831, John Wilson entered Columbia Seminary as part of the first graduating class of six. One of his classmates was the genial Francis R. Goulding, son of Dr.

[5] Wells, *Southern Presbyterian Worthies*, pp. 50-51.

Goulding. After graduating, Francis Goulding served churches in South Carolina and Georgia. One of his books, *The Young Marooners,* was widely read and translated into several European languages. Joel Chandler Harris, author of the Uncle Remus stories, called it a classic. Another classmate of Wilson's was William Moultrie Reid. Wilson recommended Reid to Mount Zion, Wilson's home church, where William Reid served for forty years—honored as 'Father Reid.'

Wilson's early reading at the seminary included the works of Richard Baxter and John Newton and Edwards' *Life of Brainerd*. He sought to know 'the blessing and presence of God' above all else, he wrote to his sister.[6] Wilson often remembered the southwest corner room of the ground floor of the seminary building as 'a place of peculiar sanctity,' because it was there that he learned 'what consecration to God meant' as he knelt in prayer with Dr. Howe.[7] When John Wilson returned home after making his decision to become a foreign missionary, his father refused to give his consent. 'Father,' said John, 'would you be willing to pray with me?' The father agreed and so they began, 'Our Father which art in heaven, hallowed be Thy name, Thy kingdom come, Thy will be done on earth as it is in heaven.' Brought face to face with the world-embracing love and purpose of God as expressed in the Lord's Prayer, the father could no longer resist. Slipping his arm around his son's shoulders, he told him he could go.[8]

On September 8, 1833, Harmony Presbytery met at Mount Zion to ordain John as a foreign missionary. His uncle Robert Wilson James preached the ordination sermon and Dr. Howe gave the charge. That afternoon Wilson preached to the slaves

[6] DuBose, *Wilson,* p. 34.
[7] *Memorial Volume,* p. 166.
[8] Robinson, *Columbia Theological Seminary,* p. 110.

on the subject of missions. Afterwards an old man came up to the young preacher and said that he believed it was in answer to his prayers that Wilson was going as a missionary to Africa and that he would 'add to his prayers one dollar for the spread of the gospel' there.[9]

While he was a student at the seminary, John heard about two sisters in Savannah, Jane and Margaret Bayard. Descendents of General McIntosh of Revolutionary War fame, the sisters were born on Cumberland Island, off the coast of Georgia, on their mother's plantation. Both their parents died when they were little girls. They were popular, talented, and wealthy young women; they were also dedicated members of Savannah's Independent Presbyterian Church. Both sisters wanted to go to the Sandwich Islands as missionaries, but the American Board of Commissioners for Foreign Missions would not accept them because the board did not send unmarried women to foreign mission fields. John decided that it was worth going to Savannah to see the sisters. Since he was set on a missionary career himself, he was interested in these young women who had 'made up their mind to the work of missions with no parents to say they shall not go.'[10]

John's first sight of Jane came when she was teaching her class at the African Sunday School sponsored by the Independent Church. She was tall, slender, and graceful, with light hair, blue eyes, and a winsome smile. Two weeks later he was writing to her that she was 'now the nearest and dearest object to my heart on the face of the earth.' 'I cannot be induced to turn away my eyes from Africa,' he wrote. 'My heart is fixed upon that injured, neglected people, and

[9] DuBose, *Wilson*, p. 56.

[10] DuBose, *Wilson*, p. 42.

I rejoice that yours is also. We must be subject to many trials and deprivations, but, Jane, this is food for the children of God. Englishmen can penetrate the heart of the country for wealth, and shall we not go for the love of Christ?'[11] According to his friend John Adger, Wilson wanted to serve in Africa because it had been neglected by Christian nations and because America owed the gospel to Africa, 'inasmuch as so many of her children were held in bondage' in America.[12] Not everyone understood or sympathized with Wilson's plan. He went away as a missionary to Africa, according to George Howe, 'amid misconceptions, sneers, and bitter words on the part of many.'[13]

In 1833 Wilson studied Arabic at Andover Seminary and made an exploratory trip to western Africa. Aboard his ship he taught Bible to children and adults, and studied Greek, Hebrew, and medicine. He had been offered the position of governor of Liberia but wrote to Jane that he loved 'the privilege of preaching the gospel too much to give it a serious consideration.'[14]

On May 21, 1834, John Wilson and Jane Bayard were married. A few weeks later they departed for Cape Palmas, Liberia, as missionaries with the American Board of Commissioners for Foreign Missions. After arriving in Africa, Wilson wrote to a friend:

> We anchored at Goree after a voyage of thirty days. The sight of land, and especially of the continent of Africa, was refreshing to us, yet not without melancholy reflections. Goree, like many other spots on the coast of Africa, has been the scene

[11] DuBose, *Wilson*, p. 47.
[12] DuBose, *Wilson*, p. 40.
[13] *Memorial Volume*, p. 405.
[14] DuBose, *Wilson*, p. 54.

of much inhumanity and cruelty. It was once a most extensive slave-market, and although the trade has been suppressed at this place for many years, I fancied I could almost see traces of human guilt upon her mouldered wall. Indeed, the stone walls which were originally reared to confine the slaves still remain, a monument of the sufferings of the Africans and the reproach of the Christian name.[15]

The Wilsons' mission station was beautifully situated near the ocean. To the north stretched a plain of grass through which wound a stream. They named it 'Fair Hope.' Wilson wrote, 'I do not know that I have ever seen any place where beauty and grandeur of nature are more harmoniously united.'[16] In Liberia they planted a church, started a school, developed a system of writing for the Glebo language, and translated parts of the Scriptures. In 1842, after seven years at Cape Palmas, the Wilsons turned over their work there to the Protestant Episcopal Church and launched a new mission among the Mpongwe in Gabon, within the territory north of the Congo River claimed by France. Wilson learned the Mpongwe language, prepared a grammar and dictionary, and published books in that language.

John Wilson explored western Africa, eventually gathering his findings in the book *Western Africa: Its History, Condition, and Prospects* (1856).[17] David Livingstone pronounced Wilson's book the best that had been written about western Africa.[18] The longer Wilson experienced Africa, the more he

[15] DuBose, *Wilson*, p. 212.

[16] DuBose, *Wilson*, p. 71.

[17] John Leighton Wilson, *Western Africa: Its History, Condition, and Prospects* (London: J. Wilson, 1850). Wilson's book was reprinted by Harper & Brothers (New York) in 1856 and 1969. In 1970 it was published by the Negro University Press in Westport, Connecticut.

[18] DuBose, *Wilson*, p. 190.

became critical of the European role on the continent. It had destroyed, he believed, some positive elements of African culture and had made some unfavorable things, such as slavery, worse. Wilson at first supported the American Colonization Society, and resettled in Liberia the thirty slaves his wife had inherited. Observing colonization's failure in Liberia, however, he came to oppose the plan. Many Americans, though, including Abraham Lincoln, continued to believe that blacks should be deported to Africa or some other place, because they believed that they could not live on equal terms with whites in America.[19] Wilson developed more and more respect for the variety, integrity, and basic coherence of African cultures. He praised the traditional Glebo system, finding it so different from 'the arbitrary despotism which prevails in certain parts of Africa, that it may be regarded as the purist specimen of republicanism to be found in the world.'[20] Wilson became a member of the Royal Oriental Society of Great Britain. On subjects connected with the fauna and flora of Africa he was an established authority.

John Leighton Wilson felt keenly the tragedy of slavery. On a journey to the interior in 1836, he wrote, 'How affecting to trace the footsteps of white men in Africa! I have reference to slave-dealers, who form the great majority of those who have visited her shores! They are to be traced in wars, in bloodshed, in tumults, in distress, in misery, and in everything that can degrade and render savage the heart of man.'[21] He openly attacked the Atlantic slave trade with every weapon at his

[19] See Eric Foner, *The Fiery Trial: Abraham Lincoln and American Slavery* (W. W. Norton & Company, 2010).

[20] Henry H. Bucher, Jr.., 'John Leighton Wilson and the Mpongwe: The "Spirit of 1776" in Mid-Nineteenth Century Western Africa,' *The Journal of Presbyterian History* (Fall 1976), p. 295.

[21] DuBose, *Wilson*, pp. 212-13.

command. 'God reigns, and this vile traffic in human beings must come to an end,' he wrote in 1842.[22] 'Ending the slave trade,' he wrote hopefully in 1852, 'will be regarded as one of the most noble achievements of the nineteenth century.'[23] When there was a move in England to withdraw the British fleet from its patrol of the waters off the African shore, because it was felt by many that it was accomplishing nothing, Wilson objected. He wrote a paper that was printed in England in an edition of 10,000 copies and widely distributed in prominent circles. Wilson's voice, claimed Hampden DuBose, 'was heard by the English nation,' and her people accepted his three conclusions: first, that the blockade had done much for Africa; second, that it must be continued until its work was accomplished; and third, that the fastest ships be placed in this service.[24] By his writings and persistence, the South Carolina missionary became an important agent in the permanent suppression of the African slave trade.

Wilson deplored slavery in America, pointing out that 100,000 slaves in the United States meant the death of 150,000 other human beings in the total slave enterprise. He had freed the slaves that his wife inherited, giving them the choice 'to go to the North, to Africa, or to any other place where they could enjoy their freedom.'[25] He tried to emancipate two slaves, John and Jessie, whom he had inherited when he turned twenty-one, but they refused to leave the Wilson farm in South Carolina. When the mission board put pressure on Wilson after Northern newspapers claimed that he was a common slaveholder, he asked the mission if he should

[22] DuBose, *Wilson,* p. 218.

[23] Bucher, 'John Leighton Wilson,' p. 301.

[24] DuBose, *Wilson,* p. 226.

[25] DuBose, *Wilson,* p. 100.

force his slaves to be free, noting subtly the irony of such a suggestion. Wilson wrote his own emancipatory document for the two slaves and mailed it to his father. John and Jessie decided to remain on the Wilson farm as hired labor.[26] Wilson wrote to Dr. Rufus Anderson, secretary of the American Board of Commissioners for Foreign Missions, that he had 'used every means, short of coercion, to induce them to go where they could safely accept their freedom.'[27] Wilson's approach to this situation caused some extremists in the South to regard him as 'a rampant abolitionist' and some in the North to denounce him as 'a vile slave-holder, or, to use their modest language, manstealer,' Wilson wrote.[28]

In 1848 Wilson contributed an article to the *Southern Presbyterian Review* on 'The Moral Condition of Western Africa.' Nothing, Wilson stated—not 'the suppression of the slave trade, as devoutly as this object is to be desired,' nor 'the development of commercial resources'—would change the moral condition of Africa except the preaching of the gospel. Wilson believed that if the Africans 'shall be among the last to receive the blessings of the Gospel, they will be unsurpassed in their devout and steady adherence to the cause of their Saviour.'

Because of his wife's failing health and his own, John Wilson returned to the United States in 1852, after serving almost twenty years in Africa. The Presbytery of Harmony chose him

[26] In a chapter about B. B. Warfield, Bradley J. Gundlach describes 'the dilemma of the antislavery slaveholder—feeling it wicked to hold people in bondage, but wicked too to release them unprepared into a society unprepared to receive them fairly.' Bradley J. Gundlach, '"Wicked Caste": Warfield, Biblical Authority, and Jim Crow,' in *B. B. Warfield: Essays on His Life and Thought* (Phillipsburg, N.J.: P&R Publishing, 2007), p. 143.

[27] DuBose, *Wilson,* p. 100.

[28] DuBose, *Wilson,* p. 99.

as a commissioner to the General Assembly of 1853, which met in Philadelphia. It was probably the first he had ever attended. The assembly elected him secretary of the Board of Foreign Missions of the Presbyterian Church, whose offices were in New York. Wilson served in that position for the next eight years. When the clouds of war darkened, the Wilsons packed up and returned to the South and to the old Wilson homestead near Mayesville, South Carolina, 'to suffer with [their] people.'[29] A close friend, Charles Hodge of Princeton, who was related to Jane Bayard Wilson, sadly remarked: 'Our wisest man is gone out from us.'[30] In 1861 Wilson became the missionary voice and conscience in the new Southern Presbyterian denomination, serving as secretary of its Board of Foreign Missions for twenty-five years.

William Childs Robinson called John Leighton Wilson 'Columbia's foremost exemplar of the missionary spirit.'[31] Wilson, wrote Henry H. Bucher Jr., was 'one of the most eminent American churchmen of the nineteenth century... There is no question that he was a rare combination of apostle, philosopher, linguist, and explorer.'[32] With his vision, his great heart, and his writings, Dr. Wilson, more than any other man, helped to keep the missionary vision alive in the Southern Presbyterian Church both before and after the War between the States.

[29] DuBose, *Wilson,* p. 247.

[30] DuBose, *Wilson,* p. 243.

[31] Robinson, *Columbia Theological Seminary,* pp. 124.

[32] Bucher, 'John Leighton Wilson,' pp. 291, 309.

4

AN OLD SCHOOL SEMINARY

DR. William A. McDowell, pastor of Third Presbyterian Church in Charleston, was called as professor and 'financial agent' for Columbia Seminary in December 1832. He declined, stating that 'in the present awful crisis everything in our state is at this moment in a state of agitation.' A year later McDowell left his pastorate in Charleston to become secretary of the Home Missions Committee of the Presbyterian Church.[1]

* * * * *

In 1833 the Rev. Aaron W. Leland was chosen for the chair of theology at Columbia Seminary, and Dr. Goulding moved to ecclesiastical history and polity. Aaron Leland, like George Howe, was from Massachusetts. After graduating from Williams College in 1808 (he was there when the famous Haystack Prayer Meeting occurred in 1806), he moved to Mount Pleasant, near Charleston, South Carolina, where he taught school. In 1809 he married the oldest daughter of James Hibben of Christ Church Parish. About this time Leland decided to become a minister. He was licensed in 1811 and supplied vacant churches of Harmony Presbytery for a

[1] Robinson, *Columbia Theological Seminary*, p. 22.

year. On May 2, 1812, he was ordained and was called to the First Presbyterian Church, also known as Scots Kirk, in Charleston. Several years later Leland dedicated the impressive new sanctuary of the church to the worship of God. In 1814 he received an honorary master of arts degree from Brown University, and in 1815, at the age of twenty-eight, he was granted the degree of doctor of divinity by South Carolina College. From 1825 to 1833 Aaron Leland served the Presbyterian church on James Island, where he came to know a remarkable boy who would himself become a revered teacher at Columbia Seminary, John Lafayette Girardeau. In becoming a professor at the seminary, Leland, as had Goulding and Howe before him, and as would the professors who followed, subscribed to the Westminster Confession with these words:

> In the presence of God and these witnesses I do solemnly subscribe the Confession of Faith, catechisms and other standards of government, discipline, and worship of the Presbyterian Church in the United States as a just summary of the doctrine contained in the Bible, and promise and engage not to teach, directly or indirectly, any doctrine contrary to the Scriptures as interpreted in those standards while I continue a professor in this seminary.

At first Dr. Leland taught theology and later, at his own request, preaching and pastoral theology. He was a superb preacher, 'magnificently endowed with natural gifts, both of body and mind,' wrote William Childs Robinson. 'His vigorous powers of thought, his vivid imagination, his fervid emotional nature, his splendid voice and majestic form combined to place him in the front rank of pulpit orators.'[2]

[2] Robinson, *Columbia Theological Seminary*, pp. 18-19.

'While the predominant element in the Presbyterian Church in the Southeast has been Scotch-Irish,' Robinson wrote in his history of Columbia Seminary, 'Puritanism has had a commendable part in the planting and nurturing of Presbyterianism in this section.'[3] Robinson asserted that 'one hope in the founding of the seminary was that by fostering education and religion the dangers arising from an ignorant or irreligious sectionalism might be allayed. It is a tribute to the statesman-like vision of these founders that... of the first three professors, two were Massachusetts born [Howe and Leland] and the other of New England Puritan descent [Goulding].'[4]

'The state of the seminary is bad,' Aaron Leland wrote on August 12, 1834, to his Charleston friend Thomas Smyth. 'We talk of peace but there is no kinship or cordiality. The efforts of Dr. G[oulding]... against Br. H[owe] are secret but untiring. The accusation now is heresy.'[5] There were differences that could well have made for tension between the two men: Goulding was from the South, Howe from the North; Goulding was self-taught, Howe had an impressive academic record; Goulding was the seminary's first leader, Howe's presence threatened that position. But the basic difference was theological. When George Howe came to the seminary he used as one of his textbooks the *Theological Lectures* of Leonard Woods, one of Howe's teachers at Andover Seminary. Although basically a conservative Calvinist, Woods was suspect for favoring the governmental theory of the atonement, which views Jesus' sacrifice as upholding the sanctity

[3] Robinson, *Columbia Theological Seminary*, p. 20.

[4] Robinson, *Columbia Theological Seminary*, p. 30.

[5] E. Brooks Holifield, *The Gentlemen Theologians: American Theology in Southern Culture 1795-1860* (Durham, N.C.: Duke University Press, 1978), p. 195.

of the law by exhibiting the consequences of its breach by a sinful humanity. Southern critics of the governmental view of the atonement generally agreed that those advocating this view were correct in what they affirmed but mistaken in what they denied—the doctrine of penal satisfaction.

Dr. Goulding, troubled by the problems he perceived in the seminary, returned to Georgia and to the pastorate in 1834. He served the Presbyterian Church in Columbus, Georgia, until his death on June 21, 1848—'with his harness on,' which had been his oft-repeated wish.[6] On the evening of June 21, with great effort he preached on Psalm 63—'O God, thou art my God; early will I seek thee; my soul thirsteth for thee; my flesh longeth for thee in a dry and thirsty land where no water is... I will bless thee while I live. I will lift up my hands in thy name.' Shortly after his sermon, Goulding was stricken. He suffered greatly in his last moments. His son, who was holding him, heard his father's last words, 'Come, Lord Jesus, come quickly.'[7] Just an hour after he had pronounced the benediction upon his people, Dr. Goulding was called 'to hear the benediction upon himself from the lips of the Savior whom he loved, Well done, good and faithful servant; enter thou into the joy of thy Lord.'[8] At the time of his death he was the oldest of fifteen Presbyterian ministers from the Midway Congregational Church in Liberty County, Georgia.

Dr. Goulding was described by his contemporaries as a 'thorough Calvinist of the Genevan school' whose 'heart was open to embrace all evangelical Christians.'[9] Like his famous successor at Columbia Seminary, James Henley Thornwell,

[6] *Memorial Volume*, p. 183.
[7] White, *Southern Presbyterian Leaders, p.* 257.
[8] *Memorial Volume*, p. 184.
[9] Smith, *Studies in Southern Presbyterian Theology*, p. 108.

Goulding regarded the doctrine of justification by faith as the center of Christian theology.

* * * * *

For a number of years Dr. Ebenezer Porter, president and professor of preaching at Andover Seminary, came south to avoid the bitter New England climate, which he thought was affecting his health. He declined the presidency of South Carolina College, but during the winter of 1833-34 taught homiletics at Columbia Seminary, where he was reunited with his friend George Howe. Porter told the Columbia students:

> Next to a warm and sanctified heart, and a sound understanding, knowledge respecting his own sacred employment is necessary to make the preacher a workman that needeth not to be ashamed. No man can learn to preach by study merely. He must be taught of God, or he will never understand the gospel. He must love Christ, or he will never feel the motives of the gospel, nor exhibit its truths in demonstration of the Spirit and with power. But neither will piety alone render him skillful and powerful in the pulpit. Besides respectable native endowments, he must have others that can result only from study [of the science of preaching].[10]

Dr. Porter died on April 8, 1834, shortly after completing and publishing his *Lectures on Homiletics and Preaching*. His book went through several editions and was widely considered the best treatise on preaching then available.

* * * * *

[10] Ebenezer Porter, *Lectures on Homiletics and Preaching* (Andover, Mass.; Flagg, Gould and Newman, 1834), p. iii.

In 1835, at the age of thirty, Charles Colcock Jones was elected to the board of directors of Columbia Seminary, and the next year he joined the seminary faculty to teach church history and polity. The year before, Andrew Maybank, a wealthy planter in Liberty County, Georgia, had died. Having no wife and family, he left his possessions to various Christian organizations, including Columbia Theological Seminary, and to Charles Jones and his wife, Mary, whom he regarded as his own children. As a result of Andrew Maybank's will, Charles Jones found himself the owner of a second plantation and fifteen more slaves. He was the executor of Andrew Maybank's estate, which included the management of the legacy left to the seminary.

Charles Jones was from Liberty County, Georgia, and the Midway Congregational Church, as were Thomas Goulding and Daniel Baker. He was born on December 20, 1804, to John and Susannah Jones. Susannah was a Girardeau from the South Carolina Huguenot family. Charles Jones studied in the North at Andover and Princeton seminaries.[11] He wrote from Andover to his fiancée Mary Jones (first cousins, they married in 1830), that the more he looked at slavery, 'the more enormous does it appear.' Slavery is a 'violation of all the laws of God and man at once,' he wrote. It is 'a complete annihilation of justice. An inhuman abuse of power, and an assumption of the responsibility of fixing the life and destiny

[11] For the life of C. C. Jones, see the remarkable family correspondence edited by Robert M. Myers, *The Children of Pride: A True Story of Georgia and the Civil War* (New Haven: Yale University Press, 1972) and *A Georgian at Princeton* (New York: Harcourt Brace Jovanovich, 1976). See also Eduard N. Loring, 'Charles C. Jones: Missionary to Plantation Slaves, 1831-1847,' Ph.D. diss., Vanderbilt University, 1976; Erskine Clarke, *Wrestlin' Jacob: A Portrait of Religion in the Old South* (Atlanta: John Knox Press, 1979), and *Dwelling Place: A Plantation Epic* (New Haven: Yale University Press, 2005). and Iain H. Murray, *Heroes* (Edinburgh: Banner of Truth, 2009), pp. 173-258.

of immortal beings, fearful in extreme.'[12] At Princeton Charles struggled to find his calling, finally responding to Archibald Alexander's advice that he return to Georgia and begin a ministry to the slaves. After serving Savannah's First Presbyterian Church for eighteen months as pastor, he resigned to give himself to the task of missions to the slaves on his own and other plantations. In 1832, Jones organized the 'Liberty County (Georgia) Association for the Religious Instruction of the Negroes' and traveled about the South 'stirring the churches of every name as with the blast of a trumpet.'[13] In 1833 the Synod of South Carolina and Georgia adopted and published an exhortation written by Jones stating that 'religion will tell the master that his servants are fellow-creatures; and he has a Master in heaven to whom he shall account for his treatment of them.'[14]

Charles Jones had little preparation for the subjects he was to teach at Columbia Seminary—church history and polity—other than his studies at Andover and Princeton. What appealed to the seminary directors, however, was not so much his knowledge of these subjects as his calling and ministry to the slaves. They persuaded him that he could 'do more good for the Negroes, by directing the minds of the young men [at the seminary] to them as a field for pastoral and missionary labours,' than he could by his 'own direct labours' in Liberty County.[15]

Mary and Charles Jones missed their family and their 'people'—their slaves—in Georgia, as well as the Low Country

[12] Erskine Clarke, *Dwelling Place: A Plantation Epic,* p.117.

[13] White, *Southern Presbyterian Leaders,* p. 295.

[14] Thompson, *Presbyterians in the South,* 1:440. Thompson states that 'Dr. Jones did as much as any man in the country to arouse the church to its responsibility for the African's religious training.'

[15] Clarke, *Dwelling Place,* p. 173.

culture. They found Columbia to be a somewhat 'lawless and corrupt place,' but in time came to appreciate much about it—its dogwoods, azaleas, and spring flowers, the intellectual stimulation of the seminary, especially that of Dr. and Mrs. Howe, and the presence of Mary's brother John Jones, who was a student at the seminary. John helped with the Sabbath school for slaves that Charles had started down by the river. Charles Jones also preached to the black people of First Presbyterian Church on Friday nights and taught a Sunday afternoon class of over two hundred, leading his students through the study of a catechism he had prepared for their instruction.[16] The 150-page catechism presented God as Creator, Lawgiver, and, through Jesus Christ, Savior to fallen humanity. It does not matter, declared the catechism,

> what country one comes from, whether we are from the East or from the West, the North or the South. It does not matter what color we are, whether of white, or brown, or black. It does not matter of what condition we are, whether rich or poor, old or young, male or female, bond or free, Jesus is able to save all who come unto him.[17]

Jones's catechism set forth a simple but comprehensive Reformed and evangelical presentation of the Christian faith, along with a conservative description of the relationship of parents to children, of husbands to wives, and of masters to servants, with four pages dealing with the 'duties of masters and servants.' The catechism was not only used by many of those who were teaching African American Christians, but

[16] C. C. Jones's *Catechism for the Oral Instruction of Colored Persons* was widely used among the slaves in the South and was translated into several foreign languages by missionaries.

[17] Charles C. Jones, *A Catechism of Scripture, Doctrine and Practice: for Families and Sabbath Schools, Designed for the Oral Instruction of Colored Persons,* 3d. ed. (Savannah, Ga.: T. Purse, and New York: Leavitt, Trow, 1845), p. 69.

was also translated into a number of languages for use on the foreign mission field.

Dr. Jones taught at Columbia Seminary for only three years. He found himself discouraged by the smallness of the school and by the theological wrangling that marked the times. 'His irenic spirit, his experience of working with different denominations, and his piety,' comments Erskine Clarke, 'left him less than enthusiastic about denominational divisions.'[18] He was more and more pulled to the love of his life—preaching to the slaves of the plantations in coastal Georgia. After his departure students at the seminary, one of whom was Benjamin Morgan Palmer, carried on his work among the black people of Columbia. Another student, Charles Allen Stillman, who graduated in 1844, served churches in Alabama. With some ministerial colleagues, he presented an overture to the 1875 General Assembly calling for a theological training school to be established for African Americans. The school began in 1876 with two students. Charles Stillman taught its first classes and served as superintendent of the school, now known as Stillman College, until his death in 1895.

Samuel G. Alexander of the class of 1861 was one of the founders of a school for African Americans in Charlotte, North Carolina. This school, called Biddle University and then Johnson C. Smith University, came under the government of the Northern Presbyterian Church. R. C. Reed, who became professor of church history at Columbia Seminary in 1899, wrote that the Northern Presbyterian 'brethren' at Biddle 'teach Calvinistic doctrine and Presbyterian polity in the use of the very text-books that we ourselves would select if the matter were referred to us.'[19]

[18] Clarke, *Dwelling Place,* p. 178.

[19] R. C. Reed, 'The Southern Presbyterian Church and the Freedmen,' *Southern*

* * * * *

During the early nineteenth century, some Presbyterians in the North were influenced by the views of New England Congregationalists on doctrine, church polity, and slavery. Other Northern Presbyterians vehemently rejected 'the New England theology' and insisted on a strict interpretation of the Westminster Confession of Faith. They favored Presbyterian agencies for missions and church planting over the 'independent' boards and societies that the 'New School' supported. They rejected the innovative revival techniques promoted by Charles Finney and his followers. They were moderate on the slavery issue, whereas the 'New School' openly supported the abolitionists. These issues led to an intense struggle in the churches, publications, and courts of the Presbyterian Church, and in 1837 resulted in a division into separate Old School and New School denominations. More than three-quarters of Southern churches adhered to the Old School Assembly.

The presence of two Columbia Seminary professors from New England—George Howe and Aaron Leland—caused some Presbyterians in the South to question whether or not the seminary was wholeheartedly committed to the Old School position. Howe and Leland defended their Old School 'orthodoxy' but refused to follow a narrow partisan line. 'Some will not be satisfied until we enter deeply into the agitating question of party,' they wrote, 'until we cause the discordant notes of theological warfare to issue from these walls where that quiet should reign in which alone the studies

---

Presbyterian Review (January 1885), p. 108.

of the institution can be successfully pursued. We have thus far felt that we have something more important to do.'[20]

A year after the Old School-New School division, the Synod of South Carolina and Georgia, meeting in Columbia, adopted a 'Testimony' setting forth its Old School position—affirming belief in the imputation of sin and righteousness, the satisfaction view of the atonement, and regeneration as a direct, immediate, and invincible act of the Spirit—and pledging that 'no contrary doctrines shall be taught in [Columbia] Seminary or in our pulpits.' Professors Howe and Leland were both examined as to their teaching and, although explaining their tendency in earlier days to lean toward some New School views, strongly affirmed their present allegiance to the 'Testimony.' Synod then asked James Henley Thornwell and two other ministers to draft a letter to the churches explaining the professors' true views and reporting the synod's unanimous resolution expressing 'unabated confidence in, and affection for, these men of God, who are sedulously engaged in training up our pious young men for the office of the sacred Ministry in our Southern Church, and the world at large.'[21]

In 1839 the Synod of South Carolina and Georgia received a proposal from the Synod of Virginia and the Synod of North Carolina to merge Union and Columbia seminaries. (Union Theological Seminary had been founded in 1812 as the theological department of Hampden-Sydney College.) The Synod of South Carolina and Georgia favored the plan only

[20] Thompson, *Presbyterians in the South* 1:503. William Childs Robinson notes that 'the temperament of these early professors—Goulding, Howe, and Leland—seems to have been irenic rather than polemic.' Robinson, *Columbia Theological Seminary*, p. 36.

[21] Smith, *Studies in Southern Presbyterian Theology*, p. 336.

if the seminary was located in South Carolina or Georgia, and not in a location closer to Princeton Seminary. In 1845 the Georgia presbyteries were set off into a separate Synod of Georgia, while retaining the ownership and direction of Columbia Seminary with the Synod of South Carolina. Dr. Goulding was the first moderator of the new synod.

5

JAMES HENLEY THORNWELL

IN May 1839, twenty-eight-year-old James Henley Thornwell, professor at South Carolina College, was invited to serve as supply at First Presbyterian Church; five months later he was called to be the church's pastor.

Thornwell was born in the Marlborough District in Upcountry South Carolina on December 9, 1812. His father, a plantation overseer, died in 1819. James's father was 'generous, hospitable, and accumulated nothing,' wrote John M. Wells.[1] James's mother, Martha Terrell Thornwell, was a devout Baptist who taught him from the cradle 'those eternal principles of grace which the Westminster Confession contained.'[2]

James showed early promise and was sponsored by wealthy friends to study at a local academy and later at South Carolina College. At first he found himself attracted to the Deism popular in the college at that time and promoted powerfully by the college president, Dr. Thomas Cooper. Before long, however, Thornwell became disillusioned with Cooper's Deism. 'I found it a system that would not hold water,' he

[1] Wells, *Southern Presbyterian Worthies*, p. 12.

[2] James Henley Thornwell, *The Collected Writings of James Henley Thornwell* (Edinburgh: Banner of Truth, 1974), 1:576.

said.[3] Thornwell's way out of the Enlightenment philosophy of Cooper came through careful investigation; this was also his way into biblical faith and Calvinistic theology. By simply reading it through, Thornwell came to the conviction that the Bible was the revelation of God. Then, during an evening walk, he found in a Columbia bookstore a copy of the *Westminster Confession of Faith*. He had never heard of it, but he bought the little book for twenty-five cents and read it through that night. 'He studied carefully its text and proofs and accepted its premises,' wrote John M. Wells. 'The conclusions confirmed him as a Calvinist, and made of him a Presbyterian.'[4]

Thornwell graduated from South Carolina College at the age of nineteen with the highest distinction the college could confer. He 'rose up early and sat up late to store [his] mind with that knowledge which [he] then designed to make only an instrument of ambition.'[5] He remained at the college for another term as a tutor and then took a teaching position in Sumter. 'God never had a more rebellious subject,' he wrote. 'Feeling guilty, condemned, and miserable, I was determined to fight it out to the last, that it was not my fault . . . God made me as I am, and I can't help my wickedness.' But at last, 'light began gradually to break in upon me, and by degrees I came out, as I believe, a Christian.'[6] Henry Alexander White wrote:

> Prior to this confession, a fierce conflict took place in his mind with reference to the Bible doctrines of sin and

[3] Benjamin Morgan Palmer, *The Life and Letters of James Henley Thornwell* (Richmond, Va.: Whittet & Shepperson, 1875), p. 79.

[4] Wells, *Southern Presbyterian Worthies*, p. 16.

[5] Thornwell, *Collected Writings*, 1:574.

[6] Palmer, *Thornwell*, pp. 26, 27.

> salvation. With this issue adjusted, and the principles of the gospel firmly established in his understanding, the Spirit entered and assumed control, but in a manner so quiet that Thornwell was unable to point out the exact time he became a Christian.[7]

Thornwell joined the Concord Presbyterian Church near Sumter on May 6, 1832, and was baptized a week later. In time he came to see that undergirding his own search for the truth were the prayers and testimony of his mother.

Thornwell taught at his old school in Cheraw for a year and a half. In the spring of 1834 he met Dr. Ebenezer Porter, who was returning to Andover Seminary after his winter of teaching homiletics at Columbia Seminary. Porter invited young Thornwell to study at Andover without cost. Thornwell went north, and for a few months in the summer of 1834 he studied at Andover Seminary and Harvard College. He disliked the New School teaching at Andover and the liberal theology he encountered at Harvard and, fearing the northern winter, Thornwell returned to South Carolina in October. He planned to prepare himself for the senior class at Columbia Seminary, 'being deficient only in Hebrew,' he wrote.[8] However, before the seminary term began in January, he was licensed to preach by Harmony Presbytery—at Tolerant Presbyterian Church.[9] During Thornwell's examination, seminary professor Dr. Goulding is reported to have said, 'Brethren, I feel like sitting at this young man's feet as a learner.'[10] Early in 1835 Thornwell was ordained and installed as pastor of the newly

[7] White, *Southern Presbyterian Leaders,* p. 311.

[8] Palmer, *Thornwell,* p. 116.

[9] Tolerant Church was a chapel of Beaver Creek Presbyterian Church in Kershaw, South Carolina. It was founded in 1771. It is not clear whether the church is named for an attitude or for a geographical place. Probably the latter.

[10] Wells, *Southern Presbyterian Worthies,* p. 19.

organized Lancaster church. Soon the old mother church of Waxhaw and the church of Six-Mile Creek were added to his charge. The minister gained the reputation of 'being a little fast' as he covered his circuit on his fleet horse, Red Rover! His preaching, wrote John Wells, was 'plain, practical, and pungent . . . With his ministry there came a deepening of religious experience. Christ became more precious. Salvation became a richer blessing. The glory of God became more and more the chief end of his life.'[11]

Years later, in his inaugural address as professor of theology at Columbia Seminary, Thornwell said:

> When, a little more than twenty-two years ago, I was set apart by the imposition of hands to the general functions of the ministry and the special duties of a pastor, I felt that my position was a solemn one, and the text from which on that occasion the usual sermon was preached, 'Who is sufficient for these things?' exactly expressed my sense of the magnitude and grandeur of the duties I had assumed. The cure of souls is a burden; however, like the Redeemer's burden, it is lightened to those who sincerely and humbly seek His glory. It is a burden—a burden upon the conscience and a burden upon the heart—but still a burden of that peculiar kind that he who has once borne it would rather bear it on forever than be released from it.[12]

On December 3, 1835, the young pastor married Nancy White Witherspoon, the daughter of Lieutenant Governor James H. Witherspoon of South Carolina and the great-niece of Dr. John Witherspoon of Princeton. Nancy was twenty-seven at the time of her marriage to James, who was then

[11] Wells, *Southern Presbyterian Worthies*, pp. 19-20.
[12] Thornwell, *Collected Writings*, 1:573.

twenty-three. She was described as 'tall, and of a large frame, with unusual force of character . . . firm as a rock and yet kind and loving.'[13] A later acquaintance found her 'simple, kind, and yet highly refined in her manner.'[14] John Wells wrote that 'her influence molded [her husband's] character and made it much more symmetrical. His undue sensitiveness and moodiness of temper left him, largely through her helpful love and sympathy.'[15]

South Carolina College attempted to recover its standing among the state's Christians after the Cooper years. In 1835 Robert W. Barnwell was elected president, and Stephen Elliott became chaplain and professor of the evidences of Christianity and sacred literature. Both men were committed Christians, having been converted through the preaching of Daniel Baker in Beaufort, South Carolina, in 1831. The college trustees noted Thornwell's promise as a teacher and invited him to join the faculty in November 1837 as teacher of literature, rhetoric, and metaphysics. Thornwell felt that he 'had undertaken an arduous trust,' standing 'in relations of grave responsibility to the Church and to the State.'[16]

One of Thornwell's colleagues at the college was dismayed that 'a theological firebrand' who was a 'nineteenth century Jonathan Edwards' would be teaching the students

[13] Kelly, *Preachers With Power*, p. 65.

[14] The quotation is from Alexander T. McGill, who taught at Columbia Seminary during the winter of 1852-53, during which time he met Mrs. Thornwell. See Margaret DesChamps Moore, 'A Northern Professor Winters in Columbia, 1852-1853,' *South Carolina Historical Magazine* (October 1959), p. 191. It was said that Nancy Witherspoon Thornwell was 'noted for her common sense' as 'her great husband, James Henley Thornwell, [was] noted for his uncommon sense.' Margaret Adams Gist, *Presbyterian Women of South Carolina* (Published by Woman's Auxiliary of the Synod of South Carolina, 1929), p. 305.

[15] Wells, *Southern Presbyterian Worthies*, p. 20.

[16] Thornwell, *Collected Writings*, 1:573.

and influencing them toward his 'hyper-Calvinism.'[17] Thornwell did indeed shape the lives and thought of many of his students.

Thomas E. Peck grew up in Columbia, where he was taught 'the principles of the Calvinistic system' by his widowed mother.[18] But it was later as a student at South Carolina College that 'he came under the saving power of the gospel' through the teaching and preaching of Dr. Thornwell.[19] Peck graduated from South Carolina College in 1840 and began studies at Columbia Seminary but, after two weeks, was forced to leave because of illness. He continued his theological studies, however, under the guidance of Thornwell. Thornwell was called to Second Presbyterian Church in Baltimore, recently vacated by his friend Robert J. Breckinridge, and gladly accepted. When he was delayed by the efforts of the state college and the Presbyterian Church to keep him in South Carolina, he sent Thomas Peck, not yet twenty-four years old, to fill the pulpit until he arrived. The college trustees appealed to Charleston Presbytery, of which Thornwell was a member, to refuse to release him to the Baltimore church.[20] Not only was he the representative of the Presbyterian Church at the college, without whose support, they stated, 'the institution cannot exist,' but he had 'acquired that moral influence over

[17] Daniel Walker Hollis, *University of South Carolina*, 2 vols. (Columbia, S.C.: University of South Carolina Press, 1951), 1:187.

[18] White, *Southern Presbyterian Leaders*, p. 454

[19] *Writings of Thomas E. Peck* (Edinburgh: The Banner of Truth Trust, 1999) 1: vi. Iain H. Murray's introduction and C. R. Vaughan's brief life of Peck are both included in the three-volume *Writings of Thomas E. Peck*.

[20] Charleston Presbytery was formed by Harmony Presbytery in 1823 after the merger with the Congregational Association of South Carolina. It was known as Charleston Union Presbytery until 1839, when it was renamed Charleston Presbytery with the transfer of Richland County from Harmony Presbytery.

the students which is superior even to the law.'[21] At the direction of the presbytery, Thornwell remained at South Carolina College, and the Baltimore church appointed Thomas Peck as its pastor. Peck served two churches in Baltimore and then 'took up the great work of his life at Union Theological Seminary,' teaching first church history and then theology after Robert Lewis Dabney's departure to Texas.[22]

Christopher Philip Gadsden, from an important Episcopal family in Charleston (his uncle was bishop of the diocese), studied at South Carolina College. Up to that time, although moral and principled, he had not shown much interest in the things of Christ. During his sophomore year, 'while sitting under the powerful ministry of Dr. Thornwell,' he made a 'complete surrender of his heart to God, and public profession of the gospel of Christ.' Thornwell recognized in Gadsden the promise of a bright and useful career, and the young student 'responded with a cordial appreciation of the genius and piety of his distinguished instructor, which ripened into a life-long friendship.' Gadsden became an effective and beloved pastor in Charleston, serving a number of Episcopal churches, including the famous St. Philips. His theological views were shaped by 'the powerful presentation of that scheme of doctrinal truth of which Dr. Thornwell was so eloquent and uncompromising an expounder.' Gadsden held firmly to Calvinism throughout his life, believing it to be 'most consonant with the creed of the Reformers and with the acknowledged standards' of the Church of England. A low church, evangelical Episcopalian, he so respected the views of those who disagreed with him, in his Episcopal Church and

[21] Daniel Walker Hollis, *University of South Carolina*, 1:161-2.

[22] *Writings of Thomas E. Peck*, 1:vii.

outside it, that they honored and loved him. Just before his death in 1871, prayer was offered for Gadsden by Christians of every name, Protestant and Catholic, in Charleston, including, it was said, two thousand black people whom he had loved and served in his ministry.[23]

Thornwell was now widely recognized as a scholar of distinction. In 1845, three colleges—Jefferson, Hampden-Sydney, and Centre—within the same week conferred upon him the degree of doctor of divinity. He greatly enjoyed teaching at the college, but 'his ordination vow' troubled him. He had 'covenanted,' he said, 'to make the proclamation of God's grace to sinners the business of his life.' He resigned in 1839 to accept the pastorate of Columbia's First Presbyterian Church, stating that he believed that 'the pastoral office is the most important of all other offices' and he could no longer occupy a position in which he was not 'permitted to discharge the duties of a pastor.'[24]

On January 1, 1840, Thornwell was installed as pastor of First Presbyterian Church. Seminary student Benjamin Morgan Palmer described the new pastor: he had 'a thin, spare form, with a slight stoop in the shoulders . . . with soft black hair falling obliquely over the forehead, and a small eye, with a wonderful gleam when it was lighted by the inspiration of his theme . . . From the opening of the discourse, there was a strange fascination, such as had never been exercised by any other speaker.' At the installation service Palmer asked a neighbor, during one of the speaker's pauses, 'Who is this preacher?' 'That is Mr. Thornwell,' came the impatient answer, 'Don't you know him?'[25] Thornwell would soon

[23] James H. Elliott, *In Memoriam: Tributes to the Memory of the Rev. C. P. Gadsden* (Charleston, S. C.: Forgartie's Book Depository, 1872), pp. 5-6.

[24] Palmer, *Thornwell*, pp. 127, 153.

[25] Palmer, *Thornwell*, p. 154.

become the most powerful influence in the young seminarian's life.

Late in 1840, Stephen Elliott, chaplain and professor of apologetics and Bible at South Carolina College, was elected bishop of the Episcopal Diocese of Georgia. All eyes of the college board were turned at once to Thornwell, and he was elected as Elliott's successor. There was statewide pressure for him to accept the position in which he would influence many of South Carolina's future leaders. As chaplain he would preach every Sunday, not to a local congregation but to the students of the state's college. Not everyone was thrilled that Thornwell was invited to take such a prominent place in the college. Some worried about the influence of this 'militant Presbyterian.'

Thornwell struggled with his decision and finally told First Church:

> The general principle upon which I acted—and I think that the principle will commend itself to your judgment—was this: that the dispensations of Providence are intended for our guidance and direction, whenever they do not come into collision with the express and implied precepts of the Word of God. In all other cases they are designed to try us, but in these to lead us, being unambiguous intimations of the Divine will. In the present instance you are familiar with the facts, and can apply the principle . . . Guided by this principle, and from a spirit, as I trust, of obedience to God, I consented, after a long and painful struggle, and after much earnest prayer, to accept the appointment which was unanimously tendered to me. I can truly say, with Paul, that 'I go bound in the Spirit.'[26]

[26] Palmer, *Thornwell*, p. 218.

The people of the church were stunned and saddened. Dr. Thornwell had been their pastor for only a year, and he had impressed them as had no one else. Benjamin Palmer later wrote, 'Never before or since was the gospel preached to them with the eloquence and power with which it fell from his lips; and in the agony of their great loss, the question was upon every tongue, "What shall the man do that cometh after the king?"'[27] William Boggs, who, like Palmer, would one day become pastor of First Presbyterian Church, reported that the disappointment of some was so great when Thornwell resigned that they 'felt they could not listen to another minister.'[28]

[27] Palmer, *Thornwell*, p. 155.
[28] 'Centennial Sermon of William E. Boggs.'

6

BENJAMIN MORGAN PALMER

THE Columbia Seminary students persevered in their demanding studies and worked tirelessly in ministry and missions in and around Columbia—in the city jail, the state penitentiary, the cotton mills, and Sunday schools, some of which were formed into churches. A steady stream of graduates served as pastors, mainly in Southern churches from the Carolinas to Texas. In 1836 A. R. Banks went to Arkansas to work for a year as an itinerant preacher. It was not an easy assignment, traveling by horseback 'through wild and unknown regions, swimming creeks and rivers, sleeping under trees with a saddle for a pillow and a saddle blanket for a bed.'[1] But Banks stayed on for almost thirty years, working as a missionary and educator and organizing more than twenty churches. Banks's classmate W. L. Gray also went to the West and settled in Mississippi, where he was a pastor for the rest of his life, about forty years. Joseph D. Porter finished the seminary in 1848, preached in Alabama for some years, and went on to Texas, 'building up decaying churches, searching out isolated saints, and preaching at many points never before visited by a Presbyterian minister.'[2] On his way to a presbytery meeting in 1879 he was taken ill and died

[1] Thompson, *Presbyterians in the South,* 1:185.
[2] *Memorial Volume,* p. 349.

by the roadside. William Banks of the class of 1840 became pastor of the Catholic Presbyterian Church in Great Falls, South Carolina.[3] In his twenty-nine years in this church he brought eleven young men into the ministry and sent out five 'colonies' that settled in states in the Deep South and formed churches.[4]

Mission work among Native Americans in the South was not forgotten. Andrew M. Watson of the class of 1851 served for a time at the Choctaw and Chickasaw mission, as did Candor J. Silliman, who graduated in 1853. Silliman grew up among the Choctaws, to whom his parents were missionaries. J. H. Colton of the class of 1862 also served as a missionary to the Choctaw people.

Some graduates became foreign missionaries. One of these was Samuel Robbins Brown. Brown was born in East Windsor, Connecticut, on June 16, 1810, a little over a hundred years after Jonathan Edwards' birth in that place.[5] He was thirteen days old when the first American foreign missionary society, the American Board of Commissioners for Foreign Missions, was formed. When Samuel's mother, a devout Christian and hymn writer, heard the news, she took her baby boy in her arms and dedicated him to God to take the gospel to distant lands. One of Samuel Brown's closest childhood friends was James Merrick, who, after graduating from

[3] The families that organized the church in 1759 were emigrants from different branches of the Presbyterian church in Ireland—Presbyterians, Associate Presbyterians, and Reformed Presbyterians. They called their church 'Catholic Presbyterian' because they agreed to have one church that would become the property of the denomination of its first minister.

[4] *Memorial Volume,* p. 228.

[5] See William Elliot Griffis, *A Maker of the New Orient: Pioneer Educator in China, America, and Japan. The Story of His Life and Work* (New York: Fleming H. Revell, 1902).

Columbia Seminary, became a missionary in Persia. When Samuel Brown completed studies at Yale College, a friend offered to pay his expenses at Princeton Seminary. But Samuel Brown decided to work for a time to repay his father for the cost of his college studies and to gain experience before beginning his theological study. He lived in New York City for several years, until he was advised by his doctor to go to a warmer climate to recover from a severe case of pneumonia. He 'looked southward for healing in the region of the palmetto tree' and entered Columbia Seminary. He supported himself by teaching music in Columbia. Among his pupils was Martha Bulloch, who became the mother of the twenty-sixth president of the United States, Theodore Roosevelt.

'Two years of life in this genial southern climate found Samuel Brown fully restored to health'; so he decided to return to the North to be closer to his fiancée Elizabeth Bartlett, the minister's daughter at East Windsor, and to complete his theological study at the newly formed Union Theological Seminary in New York City. Samuel and Elizabeth were married on October 10, 1838. A few days later, on October 13, Samuel was ordained to the Christian ministry, and on October 17 he and his bride boarded the ship *Morrison* for their voyage of 125 days around the Cape of Good Hope to Macao. After seven years of missionary work in Canton, China, Samuel and Elizabeth returned to the United States because she was in poor health. He served as pastor of a Dutch Reformed church near Auburn, New York, and helped found Elmira College, the first women's college chartered as such in the United States. He then accepted a call to go to Japan as a missionary in 1859. The *Biographical Dictionary of Christian Missions* states that Brown 'combined rich talent with breadth of education and years of ministerial experience in the United States and China before arriving in Japan.'[6] When the first Protestant church in Japan was organized March 10, 1872, in Yokohama, Dr. Brown took part in baptizing nine young men, ordaining an elder and deacon, and administering the Lord's Supper. The first Japanese Protestant theological seminary began in his home in Tokyo in 1878. Brown, who died in 1880, often said, 'If I had a hundred lives, I would give them all for Japan.' A colleague wrote: 'When the plan of God for these great Eastern nations is fully unrolled, [Samuel] Robbins Brown will not be ashamed.'[7]

Other Columbia graduates were called to foreign mission work. T. L. McBryde of the class of 1839 served for a short time in Singapore. William Curdy Emerson, a graduate of 1841, went to Brazil with the South Carolina colonists who emigrated there after the Civil War, as did J. R. Baird of the class of 1844. A special connection with China began when Richard Way, a native of Liberty County, Georgia, and his wife, the daughter of a pastor of the old Midway church, founded the Ningpo mission station. Richard Way graduated from the seminary in 1843; J. W. Quarterman, the brother of Mrs. Way, graduated in 1845, joining his sister and brother-in-law at Ningpo, where they planted what was possibly the first Protestant church in China.[8] J. W. Quarterman died of smallpox in China in 1857. He translated the catechism of C. C. Jones into Chinese; it was used in Chinese mission schools for many years. Marcus M. Charlton graduated in 1854 and went to India, where he served for twenty-five years.

[6] Gerald H. Anderson, ed., *Biographical Dictionary of Christian Missions,* p. 96.

[7] LaMotte, *Colored Light,* p. 86.

[8] Kenneth Scott Latourette, *A History of Christian Missions in China* (Taipei: Ch'eng-wen Pub. Co., 1929), p. 248.

* * * * *

Columbia's First Presbyterian Church recognized the 'urgent necessity' of having a full-time pastor. Dr. Thornwell had resigned two years earlier; John Breckenridge, C. C. Jones, and other prominent Presbyterian ministers had declined calls from the church. At the end of 1842 the session 'cordially and unanimously' nominated twenty-five-year-old Benjamin Palmer, and the congregation elected him as their pastor. Mr. Palmer, minister at the First Presbyterian Church of Savannah, accepted the call and moved to Columbia in January 1843.

Benjamin Morgan Palmer was born in 1818 in Charleston. His father, Edward Palmer, a Congregational minister who traced his ancestry back to William Palmer of Plymouth Colony, served churches in the Low Country of South Carolina. Benjamin's mother, Sarah, was the daughter of a Connecticut sea captain who commanded the packet *Georgia,* which sailed between Philadelphia and Charleston. Benjamin grew up a devoted South Carolinian. Even late in life—after nearly fifty years in New Orleans—he would often say, 'I am a South Carolinian, you know,' so as to explain some strongly held opinion or distinctive course of action! In his early teens, Benjamin was sent to Amherst College in Massachusetts. There he became part of a small group of Southern students 'nestled like birds in a nest,' he wrote, 'in that far off New England clime.'[9] Becoming unhappy with the anti-Southern feelings at Amherst aroused by the abolitionist movement and the nullification controversy, he left the college abruptly without seeking the advice of his parents. For a few years he

[9] Wells, *Southern Presbyterian Worthies*, p. 142.

taught school in villages near Charleston. Despite his parents' faith, Benjamin was not a Christian. He felt that he had been treated badly by Christian people. 'I was irreligious,' he wrote, 'nay, worse than that I was hostile to religion, in decided hostility to God and the Gospel.'[10] In 1836, when he was eighteen years old, Palmer was led to accept Christ through the personal witness of a cousin, the Reverend I. S. K. Axson, who was one of the earliest graduates of Columbia Seminary.[11] 'My cousin,' Axson said to Palmer one night, 'you are growing up fast to manhood; is it not a good time to give yourself to the Savior, when you are soon to choose the course in life which you shall pursue?' That very night Benjamin 'took the solemn vow,' as he later put it, that he would make the salvation of his soul 'the supreme business' of his life.[12] He completed his studies at the University of Georgia and, though at first inclined to become a lawyer, he soon became convinced that 'the Great Head of the Church had called him to be a preacher of the Gospel of the grace of God.'[13]

Benjamin Palmer entered Columbia Seminary in January 1839. A story was told at the seminary that when a speaker for a temperance meeting in Columbia failed to show up, young Palmer volunteered to give an address. He so impressed his hearers that some women in the city paid his way to become a student at the seminary. At that time, wrote John Wells, 'the material equipment of the Seminary . . . was most meager.'[14] There were only two professors, Dr. Howe and Dr.

[10] Wells, *Southern Presbyterian Worthies*, p. 143.

[11] Axson was later long-time pastor at the Independent Presbyterian Church of Savannah, Georgia. See David B. Calhoun, *Splendor of Grace: Independent Presbyterian Church 1755-2005* (Greenville, S.C.: A Press, 2005), pp. 183-250.

[12] Wells, *Southern Presbyterian Worthies*, p. 143.

[13] Thomas Cary Johnson, *The Life and Letters of Benjamin Morgan Palmer* (Richmond, Va.: Presbyterian Committee of Publication, 1906), p. 63.

[14] Wells, *Southern Presbyterian Worthies*, p. 144.

Leland. The greatest influence on the young seminarian was James Henley Thornwell, who, soon after Benjamin came to Columbia, moved from his post at South Carolina College to the pastorate of First Presbyterian Church. The next year Benjamin transferred his membership from the Congregational church in Beaufort to First Presbyterian Church in Columbia. Put to work immediately, he was given the task of reopening 'the colored Sunday School.'

While a college student, Palmer was 'accused . . . of always being in love,' but in Columbia he found the love of his life.[15] He began to spend time with Mary Augusta McConnell, the stepdaughter of Dr. George Howe. George Howe's first wife died on September 18, 1832, and was buried in the First Presbyterian churchyard. Four years later Dr. Howe married a widow, Sarah Ann Walthour McConnell of Liberty County, Georgia. As a consequence of his marriage, Howe established a connection to the Midway Church and Liberty County people and also became a slave owner. Dr. Howe was at first dismayed by Benjamin's friendship with his stepdaughter. 'Miss Augusta,' he thought, 'could do better than to marry a poor seminarian!' Palmer, however, persisted, and when he began to show great promise as a preacher, Dr. Howe decided that the match might not be so bad after all. Augusta and Benjamin were happily married on October 7, 1841—by Dr. Howe.

A few days after their wedding, the young couple made their journey to Savannah, where Benjamin was called to the First Presbyterian Church. They traveled in a buggy presented to them by Dr. Howe as a wedding gift. Their clothes and Benjamin's small library were packed in one small trunk. He had ten dollars in his pocket. Although both, especially

[15] Johnson, *Palmer*, p. 70.

Augusta, were sad to leave family and friends in Columbia, they enjoyed some fall colors and beautiful October weather. Thomas Cary Johnson described their journey:

> He was twenty-three, she was three or four years younger. They were not poor. God had richly endowed them with health and strength, and genius, and energy and character. They went to a sufficient if modest, living; to a position of honor and esteem which God would enable them to fill. So on over the country roads toward Savannah they drove, close to nature, sympathizing with it, a part of it, close to each other, conscious also of being the children of God. They reached the city safely.[16]

Palmer was ordained and installed on March 6, 1842. He was there only a few months when the call came from Columbia. For the next eleven years Palmer served as the minister of the First Presbyterian Church of Columbia. His congregation included members of government, lawyers, doctors, and teachers, including James Henley Thornwell, his predecessor in the pulpit who was now president of South Carolina College. There were also students from the college, among whom were the future leaders of the state, and seminary students, who would go out to serve churches throughout the South. Among the church's elders were William Law, a great friend to Columbia Seminary, and G. T. Snowden, the spiritual son of Dr. John B. Romeyn of New York, who was tutored in the faith by John Holt Rice of Richmond, another friend of the seminary.[17]

[16] Johnson, *Palmer,* p. 75.

[17] John B. Romeyn was pastor of the Presbyterian Church in Albany, New York, and Cedar Street Presbyterian Church in New York City, where he preached to one of the largest congregations in the city. John Holt Rice, who studied theology with Archibald Alexander, organized the First Presbyterian Church of Richmond, Virginia, and in 1824 became president of the Theological Seminary at Hampden-Sydney

Palmer's first sermon as pastor of First Presbyterian Church, preached on January 29, 1843, came from the words of Balaam to Balak in Numbers 22:38—'Lo, I am come unto thee: have I now any power at all to say anything? The word that God putteth in my mouth, that shall I speak.' The young minister set forth two main points. First, true ministers of the gospel are called to their office by God himself and their fields of labor are especially designated by him. Second, all true ministerial ability and authority are derived from God. Palmer told his people that the minister of the gospel is 'a messenger from God to speak only the word that is put into his mouth.' He may 'not invent or add anything to the message. His sole care must be to inquire what God the Lord will say. The pastoral commission is no contract formed merely for the pleasure and amusement of the hearers,' Palmer said. 'The pastor is not called upon to cater to the various tastes which may perchance prevail among his auditors; his duty is to study God's Book, to present its promises, to recite its warnings, to declare its judgments.'[18]

Palmer was installed on May 7. The First Presbyterian session minutes described the service as

> deeply solemn and interesting. Rev. Edward Palmer, Father of the Pastor elect, preached the Sermon. Rev. Dr. Howe, Moderator of Presbytery, presided and proposed the constitutional questions. Rev. B. Gildersleeve gave the charge to the Pastor and the Rev. Professor Thornwell the charge to the people, after which the Elders and Temporal Committee as representatives of the church and congregation gave their hands to the Pastor in token of their regard and cordial reception of him as appointed over them in the Lord.

(later Union Theological Seminary in Virginia).

[18] Johnson, *Palmer*, p. 89.

The young pastor of First Presbyterian Church quickly established a reputation as 'a prince in the pulpit.'[19] Palmer prepared his sermons by studying the Hebrew or Greek text, comparing various translations, and consulting a few commentaries. He then, according to his biographer, put a cigar in his mouth and walked back and forth across his study floor. As he wore away the weavings of his carpet, he was weaving 'the threads of mighty discourses.' Again and again he thought through the sermon outline but did not memorize the words, 'meaning to body forth his sermon in any words given him at the moment of delivery.'[20]

Palmer was not imposing in appearance—small-framed, with heavy lips and eyebrows—but hearers often commented that when he began speaking he was almost transformed.[21] William Boggs said that action was 'the characteristic element' of Palmer's preaching. 'Not acting, but action. And thus the great truths of the Bible were poured in upon the hearer's soul by the two great avenues of "ear-gate" and "eye-gate".'[22] Douglas Kelly describes the four major features of Palmer's preaching: (1) he drew his sermons from the biblical text; (2) he held his hearers' interest; (3) he possessed profound sympathy allied to a realistic pastoral insight; and

[19] See Kelly, *Preachers With Power*, 'Benjamin Morgan Palmer: Capturing the Heart of New Orleans,' pp. 87-88.

[20] Johnson, *Palmer*, p. 91.

[21] There is a story of Dr. Palmer's address at Washington and Lee College on June 27, 1872. Among the distinguished men on the platform were Mr. John Randolph Tucker and Commodore Matthew Fontaine Maury. When Palmer began to speak, Commodore Maury turned to Mr. Tucker and remarked, 'He is the ugliest man I ever saw, sir.' After about ten minutes, Maury remarked to Tucker again, 'He is getting better looking, sir.' When Palmer was about two thirds of the way through his address, Maury—now hardly able to sit quietly under the impact of the preacher's words—said to Tucker, 'He is the handsomest man I ever saw, sir.' Johnson, *Palmer*, p. 362.

[22] 'Centennial Sermon of William E. Boggs.'

(4) his life and preaching were characterized by total commitment to the Word of God.[23]

First Presbyterian Church senior pastor Glen Charles Knecht, in a sermon preached on March 23, 1986, marking the bicentennial of the city of Columbia, summarized the Columbia ministry of his predecessor. Benjamin Morgan Palmer 'was a great Puritan who came from an ancestry of preachers, and stepped like a prince into this pulpit, full of eloquence, and into the streets and homes full of compassion and sympathy.'

As Dr. Knecht said, not only was Palmer a great preacher, he was a pastor 'full of compassion and sympathy.' When the Palmers' first child, a beautiful little blond-haired boy, was twenty months old he became very sick. 'Every trace of infantile beauty was effaced,' his father wrote; 'only the golden curls floated over the pale brow; and the brilliant eyes which strangers in the street stooped to gaze upon, burned now with a feverish luster.' Sitting by the bed of his dying son, Palmer prayed for strength to submit to God's will. At last the hope of the covenant of grace that was present in the child's baptism broke through Palmer's gloom and he was comforted 'with the strong comfort of believing that the promise of the covenant was assured to his seed forever.' From then on, Dr. Palmer possessed to an even greater extent the ability 'to comfort them which are in any trouble with the comfort by which he himself was comforted of God' (2 *Cor.* 1:4). He was 'marvelously gifted in writing letters of consolation,' as he did to the mother of Thomas Peck after her son's death. 'There are few who can draw closer to you than I,' he wrote, 'as with the tenderness of a son I share with you the burden of sorrow—

[23] Kelly, *Preachers With Power*, pp. 106-18.

and then lift with you the hallelujah of praise.'[24] Near the end of his life, Dr. Palmer published *The Broken Home; or Lessons in Sorrow,* in which he had written about his family—a son, four daughters, and his wife—who one after another had been taken from him. Palmer wrote: 'From the simple desire of comforting those who mourn, this story of repeated bereavements is here told . . . Long treasured memories are now scattered upon the winds, with the prayer that they may help to bind up the broken-hearted.'[25]

The Columbia church prospered under Palmer's ministry. In a report to Charleston Presbytery less than a year after he became pastor, Palmer wrote that sixteen people had joined the church and that there was

> a greater degree of external harmony and an increasing attendance upon the preaching of the word. Sabbath school, both class and Catechetical instruction, is faithfully attended to and the colored people connected with the congregation receive a proper share of the pastor's attention. There is a weekly Lecture for their especial benefit, which is well attended, and a Sabbath School on the plan of oral instruction in which they are taught the doctrines and duties of our religion.

[24] Wells, *Southern Presbyterian Worthies*, pp. 163-64.
[25] Wells, *Southern Presbyterian Worthies*, pp. 167-68.

7

THE *SOUTHERN PRESBYTERIAN REVIEW*

THE *Biblical Repertory and Princeton Review*, founded by Charles Hodge of Princeton Seminary in 1825, ably represented conservative Presbyterianism and quickly became one of the leading theological journals in the English-speaking world. The Synod of South Carolina discussed the need for a theological journal for the southern part of the Presbyterian Church 'to subserve the cause of Christ, and to promote sound learning and doctrinal knowledge among us.'[1] The *Southern Presbyterian Review* was founded in 1847 and was conducted by 'an association of ministers in Columbia, S.C.': James Henley Thornwell, professor in South Carolina College, and the South's leading theologian; Benjamin Morgan Palmer, young pastor of Columbia's First Presbyterian Church; and George Howe, senior professor at Columbia Seminary. There were 'giants there, in those days,' wrote Dr. Palmer's biographer; 'they had messages from the Lord to their brethren, which they burned to deliver.'[2]

The editors—Thornwell, Palmer, and Howe—stated that the publication was 'devoted mainly to the exposition and defense of the doctrines and polity of the Presbyterian Church,' but they expressed the hope that it would appeal to

[1] *Manuscript Minutes of the Synod of South Carolina 1845-1873*, p. 264.

[2] Johnson, *Palmer*, p. 126.

all 'who love the truth as it is in Jesus.' Not only theological and biblical topics were envisioned for the *Review,* but also articles on 'sanctified science and literature.'[3]

The editors gave themselves to the task of getting the new publication underway. Dr. Thornwell wrote to Dr. Robert J. Breckinridge, recently elected president of Pennsylvania's Jefferson College, on September 25,1846, 'I have no idea that we can get subscribers in your region, but I hope that we can get articles. You must write. Can you not get Drs. Green and McGill [of Princeton Seminary] to write?'[4] On November 6, Thornwell reported to Breckinridge that the *Review* now had four hundred subscribers and would begin if it could reach five hundred. 'We intend to make it a free journal,' Thornwell wrote; 'we shall not, like Princeton, put an extinguisher upon any candle that emits any light.' Dr. Thornwell believed that the names of authors of articles normally should be given. 'No man ought to write who is not willing to be responsible for what he says,' he commented.[5] Later the editors stated that they did not endorse every opinion of each writer, pointing out that there were minor differences among the editors themselves. Free discussion is important 'to the interests of truth, if kept within just limits,' they wrote. They were aware, however, that these limits must be strictly observed. 'Editors would be worthy of censure,' they wrote, 'should they allow opinions to be expressed subversive of any doctrine of the Gospel.'[6]

The first issue of the *Southern Presbyterian Review* appeared in June 1847. Its lead article, by Dr. Thornwell,

[3] *Southern Presbyterian Review* (July 1847). On back cover.

[4] Palmer, *Thornwell,* p. 296.

[5] Palmer, *Thornwell,* p. 296. It was not until January 1879, however, that articles generally were signed with the names of the authors.

[6] *Southern Presbyterian Review* (April 1863). On back cover.

entitled 'The Office of Reason in Regard to Revelation,' was a careful statement of what reason can and cannot do in theological matters.

Dr. Palmer contributed an article to the first issue on 'The Relation between the Work of Christ and the Condition of the Angelic World.' He stated that 'the scheme of grace revealed in the Bible' not only provided salvation for a great multitude of mankind but confirmed in their holiness the unfallen angels. 'We have only to look upon the different orders of worshippers in the heavenly temple and witness the whole hierarchy bending before the throne to be overwhelmed with the mystery of divine grace,' Palmer wrote.

Article three, thirty-nine pages on 'The Baptism of Servants' by George Howe, challenged Southern Christians to greater efforts toward the evangelization of the slaves. 'The day has come,' the author wrote, 'for more energetic action, more ample instrumentalities, more self-denying labor to bring them to a knowledge of Christ, who hath made of one blood all nations of the earth.'

There were two other articles in this first issue: an exposition of Matthew 16:18,19 and a spirited defence of Puritan leader Oliver Cromwell against the popular 'slander' of him as 'an arch hypocrite and usurping tyrant.' Twelve book reviews concluded the offerings of the first issue, including a brief notice of a new edition of the Hebrew grammar of Gesenius, and a sermon commemorating the 150th anniversary of the founding of the Congregational church at Dorchester, St. George's Parish, South Carolina—the church of the congregation that mostly moved to Liberty County, Georgia, and founded Midway Church.

The second issue of the *Review* contained an article on the General Assembly of 1847 by Dr. Thornwell. Thereafter, this valuable feature, giving Thornwell's or John Adger's report on the assembly, appeared regularly. Adger, former missionary to Armenia, was pastor of a church for black people in his native Charleston. In addition to his General Assembly articles, John Adger contributed to many of the issues of the *Review* with writings on church government, missions, call to the ministry, sacraments, eldership, church finance, ordination, and slavery and the slave trade.

Dr. Thornwell was the major contributor to the *Review*. A large part of the four volumes of his published works appeared first in its pages—including articles on Roman Catholic baptism, the eldership, miracles, the Christian pastor, the priesthood of Christ, revelation and inspiration, public instruction in South Carolina, and Paul's preaching at Athens.

Between 1847 and the end of his Columbia pastorate, Dr. Palmer contributed more than three hundred pages to the *Review* and continued to write for it after he moved to New Orleans. His articles covered a wide range of topics: issues of church and state, doctrinal studies such as the imputation of sin, polemical writings on Mormonism and other threats to evangelical Christianity, and matters of general interest such as a study of the English language. In an 1848 issue of the *Review,* Palmer presented an article with the title 'A Plea for Doctrine as the Instrument of Sanctification.' He wrote,

> It probably falls within the experience of every pastor to see the gathering frown, the averted shoulder, and the drooping head, as soon as certain doctrines are announced as the theme for discussion. It does not excite our surprise that the world of the ungodly should manifest this displeasure: for the same 'carnal mind' which is enmity against God, is enmity likewise against the truth of God. But that professing Christians should engage in this unholy crusade against doctrinal

> religion, and that even ministers of the Gospel should sigh over the earnest proclamation of its truths, and accuse the faithful witness of 'daubing with untempered mortar,' is certainly a most afflictive and atrocious scandal.

Palmer attributed the cause for this sad decline to 'some latent skepticism [toward] the doctrines themselves,' to 'timid concessions to the clamors of the ungodly,' to 'the fear of losing church members' if doctrine is preached, to 'indolence and sluggishness of mind,' and to 'the belief . . . that doctrine is not necessary to sanctification.' The Columbia minister then showed how doctrine is necessary for progress at every stage of the Christian life. He concluded with a strong recommendation for study of the Westminster Confession and Catechisms as an instrument of sanctification. 'Next to the Bible, from which all that relates to God and the soul must be drawn,' he stated, 'there are no books we would sooner recommend for an experimental and devotional use than the Calvinistic Standards.' He suggested that Christians put ninety-nine percent of the current devotional literature into the fire 'and thoroughly digest [the] Shorter Catechism, and [they] will come forth stronger, brighter, happier Christians'![7]

Dr. Howe's contributions to the *Southern Presbyterian Review* included biblical themes ('The Mark of Cain and Curse of Ham'), historical matters ('The History of Presbyterianism in South Carolina,' 'Jean Calais, Martyr of Toulouse,' and 'The Scotch-Irish'), and issues of current importance ('The Unity of the Race,' and 'The Raid of John Brown and the Progress of Abolition').[8]

[7] Benjamin Morgan Palmer, 'A Plea for Doctrine as the Instrument of Sanctification,' in *Southern Presbyterian Review* (July 1849), pp. 32-35, 51.

[8] W. Duncan Rankin, ed., *An Index to the Southern Presbyterian Review* (Greenville: Reformed Academic Press, 1995), pp. 21-24 of Author Index. The first complete index of the Southern Presbyterian Review was produced by Professor W.

Of the many others who contributed to the *Southern Presbyterian Review,* none were so regular as Thomas Smyth, pastor of the Second Presbyterian Church of Charleston, South Carolina, from 1830 to 1870. A native of Ireland, Smyth graduated from Belfast College in 1827 with a brilliant record, studied for a year at Highbury College in London, and then emigrated with his family to New Jersey, where he enrolled in Princeton Seminary. He refused to leave his Charleston church for a position on the Columbia Seminary faculty but served on its board and loyally supported the seminary in its work to train a competent and godly ministry. 'With voice, pen and purse he aided in upbuilding this school of the prophets,' wrote Henry Alexander White.[9] Dr. Howe said that he had many conversations with Dr. Smyth and that two objects were 'near his heart as to the Seminary.' One was to provide 'a fund for the gradual increase and the preservation of its Library and to pay a salary to its Librarian.' The other was to found 'a Lectureship like that which produced the Boylean and the Hulsean Lectures.'[10] Dr. Smyth was a prodigious reader and a prolific author. During the summer of 1859, for example, Smyth read Pascal's *Thoughts,* Buckland's *Elements of Geology,* Guyot's *Earth and Man, Natural History of Trees, Natural History of Birds,* Macaulay's *Reformation,* Goethe's *Poems,* Bunyan for devotional material, McCosh for philosophy, and several theological

Duncan Rankin and his student assistants at Reformed Theological Seminary, Jackson, Mississippi. On Sunday morning, February 5, 1995, a presentation copy was given to Dr. Glen C. Knecht, senior pastor of First Presbyterian Church, Columbia, South Carolina, by Ligon Duncan III, professor at Reformed Seminary.

[9] White, *Southern Presbyterian Leaders,* p. 264.

[10] *Memorial Volume,* p. 148. The Boyle Lectuures began in 1692 and the Hulsean Lectures were established at Cambridge in 1777. The design of both was to support the truth of Christianity.

and exegetical works. Few matched Thomas Smyth in the volume or range of his published writings—including books challenging the claims of the Oxford Movement, supporting Presbyterianism, and asserting the unity of the human races. He wrote articles on missions, Sunday schools, the American Tract Society, the Young Men's Christian Association, the Charleston Orphanage, and other charitable institutions. His devotional books—such as *Solace for Bereaved Parents, Why Do I Live?* and *Well in the Valley*—were widely read. He produced a *Soldier's Prayer Book* and *Soldier's Hymnal.* J. W. Flinn, Smyth's son-in-law and an 1875 graduate of Columbia Seminary, edited Smyth's works and published them in ten thick volumes that included his *Autobiographical Notes.*[11]

Dr. Smyth's *Review* articles, beginning in September 1848 with 'Call to the Ministry—its Nature and Evidence,' included 'The Necessity and Importance of Controversy,' 'the Doctrine of the Trinity,' and writings defending Protestantism, the South, secession, and the Southern cause in the War between the States.[12] In 1868 Smyth wrote an article favouring the use of instrumental music in public worship—a view strongly opposed by his brother in-law John Adger and his long-time friend John Girardeau.

Numerous articles from John Leighton Wilson's pen appeared in the *Review,* on Africa, home and foreign missions, 'The Certainty of the World's Conversion,' 'Religious

[11] Louisa Cheves Stoney, ed., *Autobiograhical Notes, Letters and Reflections by Thomas Smyth, D.D.* (Charleston, S.C.: Walker, Evans and Cogswell, 1914), pp. 520-21. J. W. Flinn, ed., *The Collected Works of the Rev. Thomas Smyth, D.D.,* 10 vols. (Columbia, S.C.: R. L. Bryan, 1908). See Clarke, *Our Southern Zion,* pp. 157-58.

[12] Rankin, *Index,* pp. 39-41 of Author Index. The majority of these articles are in *The Collected Writings of Thomas Smyth* (Columbia: R. L. Bryan, 1908-1912).

Instruction of Colored People,' 'Schemes of Benevolence,' and 'Sustenation.'

Readers eagerly anticipated the next issue of the *Southern Presbyterian Review,* with its predictable mixture of theology, scriptural exposition, church history, and extended discussions of contemporary issues, as well as book notices and scholarly reviews. In 1855, after seven years of publication, the editors announced that the *Review* had experienced 'considerable flux of patronage.' 'It would be indecent in us to say a word designed to solicit patronage,' they stated, but added, 'The 4,800 pages of diversified matter, already laid before the world, are our proper credentials.' Nineteen agents for the *Review,* located in the Southern states from Texas to Virginia, and in Philadelphia, were listed.

The *Review* was edited by a board until 1861, when it ceased publication because of the Civil War, and by Dr. James Woodrow from 1866 to 1885, when it ended its illustrious career. The *Southern Presbyterian Review* was 'the most high-powered religious journal in the Old South,' according to Timothy Dwight Bozeman.[13] Ernest Trice Thompson writes that it was the one 'quarterly journal of high distinction' within the bounds of Southern Presbyterianism.[14]

[13] Timothy Dwight Bozeman, 'James Henley Thornwell: Ancient and Modern,' *Affirmation: Union Theological Seminary in Virginia,* 6 (Fall 1993), p. 59.

[14] Thompson, *Presbyterians in the South,* 1:453.

8

'A DOOR OPENED'

THE railroad reached Columbia in 1842. The *Robert Y. Hayne*, named in honour of South Carolina's governor from 1832 to 1834, began passenger service to Charleston on June 20. By mid-century the state had almost a thousand miles of track, with Columbia at the center. The *Daily Telegraph* was launched on October 18, 1847, the first successful newspaper of inland South Carolina. A visitor to Columbia in the early 1850s wrote enthusiastically, 'Columbia [is] out in its spring attire of roses and floral gems. Oh! It is a lovely and lovable place.'[1] The 'low and pleasing hills' around Columbia and the river scenery impressed visitors—as did the 'perfect' hospitality of the townspeople. Many were highly educated and possessed to a great degree 'the charming manners of an aristocratic society.' The area was touted as 'a healthy region' because of its sand and pines. The sand, it was thought, absorbed 'moisture so as to dry the atmosphere,' and the pine trees took out 'malarious elements, so that in this region persons having weak lungs in early years have lived a comparatively long and vigorous life.'[2] The climate was hot

[1] *A Columbia Reader, 1786-1986* (Columbia, S.C.: Institute for Southern Studies and the South Caroliniana Library), p. 44.

[2] John A. Broadus, *Memoir of James P. Boyce, D.D., LL.D.* (New York: A. C. Armstrong and Son, 1893), p. 84.

and sultry in the summer, but the rest of the year, most Columbians thought, made up for it.

South Carolina College had become the premier institution in the South and perhaps as fine as any in the nation, with impressive teachers and distinguished alumni. Elliott, Lieber, Pinckney, Legare, and Harper colleges had been built around the 'Horseshoe.' There the striking library, designed by the well-known South Carolina architect, Robert Mills, who had designed the grand house that was the home of Columbia Seminary, added impressively to the college campus. James Henley Thornwell was professor and chaplain at the college. Thornwell was well aware of what he called his 'double office.' It was his custom, he wrote, 'to make the pulpit and the lecture-room subservient to each other.'[3] He preached to the graduating class of 1844 a sermon on 'The Necessity of the Atonement.' Christopher P. Gadsden, a member of that class, said that Thornwell's sermon did more to shape his theology than anything apart from the Bible. Gadsden, who became an evangelical Episcopal minister in Charleston, was chairman of a student committee that arranged for publication of the sermon. John Lafayette Girardeau told Thomas Law, evangelist of Charleston Presbytery, that Thornwell's sermon on the atonement was the major influence in his theological thinking. In the spring of 1851 Dr. Thornwell preached a series of sermons to the faculty and the two hundred students of the college, taking as his text the words from Philippians 4:8: 'Whatsoever things are true . . . think on these things.'[4] Thornwell's sermons on truth dealt with ethics and morality but he did not preach

[3] James H. Thornwell, *Discourses on Truth* (New York: Robert Carter & Brothers, 1855), p. vi.

[4] See David B. Calhoun, 'Thornwell on Truth,' *Presbyterion* (Fall 2002), pp. 65-76.

moralism. In his first sermon Thornwell told the students that 'all your present excellencies are dead works . . . The first step in real moral improvement is faith in the Son of God. When that step is taken, we begin to live; until then, we are dead in trespasses and sins.'[5] These notable sermons were preached in the chapel, located in the college's oldest building.[6] When the sermons were published, Thornwell dedicated the book 'to the students of the South Carolina College, whose high character for truth reflects the greatest honor upon themselves and the State.'

Columbia Seminary was an important center of theological scholarship and Reformed orthodoxy, with great influence on the intellectual and moral life of the city and state. Its library slowly became one of the best theological libraries in the United States—eventually holding some eleven thousand volumes from the outstanding personal collection of Thomas Smyth.[7] The number of students fluctuated from year to year. There were only six students in the class of 1838, fifteen in the class of 1841, in 1843 just two, twelve in that of 1849, but only four in the class of 1850.[8]

Groves H. Cartledge came to the seminary in January 1846. A school teacher in Macon, Georgia, Cartledge met Dr. Leland at the first meeting of the Synod of Georgia in 1845 and decided to go to Columbia to take a course in Hebrew

[5] Thornwell, *Discourses on Truth*, pp. 53.

[6] The 1805 building, at first called 'South,' was later named Rutledge College. Although severely damaged by fire in 1855, Rutledge was rebuilt essentially as it had been. The central section of Rutledge still contains the chapel.

[7] Thomas Smyth was himself author of a number of books, including *Ecclesiastical Republicanism, Presbytery and Not Prelacy,* and *Unity of the Human Races,* all of which were published on both sides of the Atlantic. When Smyth died in 1873, the seminary board created a lectureship in his honor and planned for the publication of his works.

[8] Thompson, *Presbyterians in the South,* 1:508.

at the seminary. Dr. Leland and Dr. Howe were the only professors at the seminary, but Dr. Thornwell was professor at South Carolina College and Dr. Palmer was pastor of First Presbyterian Church. Because of health problems Cartledge stayed for only a few months, but his time in Columbia made a deep impression upon the young teacher. When he was later preparing for licensure, he found so much sin in his life, he wrote, that he felt 'wholly unworthy to enter the sacred calling.' In despair he went out one night alone to meditate and pray. He threw himself down on his face in the middle of a corn field and began to confess his sins and pray. He wrote in his autobiography,

> Suddenly, everywhere around me the light seemed to shine as brightly as day, and I seemed to see Jesus on the cross, and thought I heard him say, 'I am bearing your sins, and dying as you deserve to die, that you may be justified and saved for my sake.' Immediately my soul was filled with peace and joy ineffable, and I lay upon the ground, I know not how long, praising God the Lord for his amazing goodness and mercy to a miserable sinner like me. Of course, I saw no real, outward light that night. The light was in my own heart and mind. I had believed in Jesus as my Savior long before, but never till then had I such a clear and satisfying view of the plan of salvation.[9]

Groves Cartledge was pastor of two Presbyterian churches near his birthplace in northeast Georgia for over forty-seven years. He also helped at least a dozen nearby Presbyterian churches. Before he died on July 5, 1899, he prepared a paper

[9] Thomas D. Cartledge and Samuel J. Cartledge, eds., *Autobiography of Rev. Groves H. Cartledge* (Montreat, N. C.: Historical Foundation of the Presbyterian and Reformed Churches, 1960), reprinted from *Sermons and Discussions by Rev. Groves H. Cartledge* (Richmond, Va.: Whittet and Shepperson, 1903), pp. 12-13.

giving directions for his funeral service. He wrote:

> Let the twenty-third Psalm be read and commented upon. That has been my belief and my experience for nearly sixty years. In August, 1834, I took the Lord Jesus to be my Lord and Saviour, and as my Shepherd he has led me, fed me, and kept me; and I have not wanted any good thing, not even chastisement and correction.

He left a final message to the people of his churches:

> Let me beg you once more to love him more fervently, to trust him more implicitly, and to serve him more earnestly and faithfully . . . Meet me in heaven, and bring all your children with you.[10]

Groves Cartledge's sons, Thomas D. Cartledge and Samuel J. Cartledge, studied at Columbia Seminary and became Presbyterian ministers. A grandson, Samuel A. Cartledge, graduated from Columbia Seminary in 1929 and, two years later, was made professor at the seminary.[11]

* * * * *

Charles Colcock Jones returned to the Columbia Seminary faculty in 1848 (he had served on the faculty in 1837 and

[10] Cartledge, *Autobiography*, pp. 18-19.

[11] Samuel A. Cartledge's views on the Bible raised concern among conservatives about the theological soundness of Columbia Seminary in the 1940s. Dr. Charles Woodbridge, pastor of Savannah's Independent Presbyterian Church, wrote to Columbia Seminary president, J. McDowell Richards, that Dr. Cartledge did not 'hold to the Presbyterian point of view of the inspiration of the Scriptures.' Woodbridge asserted that 'Dr. Cartledge's *Conservative Introduction to the Old Testament* was more dangerous than an out-and-out liberal book, for it suggested repeatedly that a person may hold liberal views and still call himself a conservative. That is deadly as well as untrue.' Richards defended the orthodoxy of Dr. Cartledge and the seminary, but admitted that Dr. William Childs Robinson of the Columbia faculty had similar misgivings. Calhoun, *The Splendor of Grace*, p. 387.

1838). This time he was ready and even eager to come to Columbia, but first he and his wife faced the daunting task of leaving in good care their three plantations and three others they were responsible for and the more than 160 slaves who lived on them.

In September the Jones family, including three children and five servants, travelled from Savannah by steamer to Charleston and from Charleston to Columbia by train. They lived for a few days with Dr. and Mrs. Howe, who received them all 'as relatives.' Charles found Columbia 'much improved.' The Jones's two boys, Charlie and Joe, entered South Carolina College, and their daughter, Mary Sharpe, went to a private school in town. Charles was soon busy preparing and teaching his courses in church history and polity. He began to write his book *History of the Church of God during the Period of Revelation*. He and Mary enjoyed being with the seminary students, two of whom were former tutors for their children and took their meals with them. 'Almost any evening,' Charles noted, 'some of the students drop in and take a cup of tea with us.'[12]

Benjamin Palmer was the pastor of First Presbyterian Church, and James Henley Thornwell was at South Carolina College. Both Palmer and Thornwell frequently lectured at the seminary, and Charles regarded them as among his closest colleagues in Columbia. Charles's classes were successful and there was a large entering class at the seminary, but he was restless, as he always was when he was not directly engaged in work with the slaves. Then some things happened that Jones interpreted as showing him God's will for his next step.

On April 17, 1850, Jones wrote to Colonel William Maxwell, a plantation owner in Georgia and long-time friend, that

[12] Clarke, *Dwelling Place*, p. 267.

their 'faithful old friend and servant Jack' had died. 'I was with him night and day, and am worn down with anxiety and watching,' Jones wrote. The mind of the old servant who was 'one of the family . . . was clear and stayed on the Saviour to the last.' Dr. Jones had 'all the family called, white and black; and as each one came up, Jack took them one by one by the hand and charged them in the Lord and commended them to God.'[13]

The day after Jack died, the Jones's house in Columbia was completely destroyed by fire. In the home of a friend, Dr. Jones thanked God for saving them from the fire and said to Dr. Howe, who had come to be with them, 'We must now give thanks to God.' He asked Dr. Howe to pray, which he did 'in a most earnest and affecting manner; and our hearts were relieved at a throne of grace!'[14] Much help came from 'the good people of Columbia.' All Dr. Jones's 'clerical brethren' expressed their great sorrow, especially in the loss of his 'library and papers, lectures, sermons, *etc.*, of every kind—the accumulation of some twenty years or so.'[15] Two years later, in a letter to her son Charles, Mary Jones wrote: 'In remembering the many precious things which lie in one common grave in Columbia there is nothing that I oftener think of with regret than your father's missionary journals. They would have been to his children an invaluable legacy of rich Christian experience—a record of toils and labors that I have never seen equaled by anyone.'[16]

Adding sorrow to sorrow, two days later old Jack's wife, Marcia, died. Jones found comfort in reading George Whitefield's sermons—one on afflictions in particular. Whitefield

[13] Myers, *A Georgian at Princeton*, pp. 4-5.
[14] Myers, *A Georgian at Princeton*, p. 10.
[15] Myers, *A Georgian at Princeton*, p. 11.
[16] Myers, *A Georgian at Princeton*, p. 330.

said that 'he never bore the Cross but he always found it lined with the love of God.' 'How beautiful!' Jones said, 'and to God's own people how true.'[17]

As Mary and Charles grieved over their losses, a letter came from the Presbyterian Board of Missions in Philadelphia inviting Dr. Jones to become its secretary, succeeding Charleston native William A. McDowell who had served since 1835. Jones had been chosen for this position by the unanimous vote of the General Assembly. For some weeks Dr. and Mrs. Jones struggled to decide what they should do. On May 30 Jones wrote to his wife, who had gone to visit their plantations in Georgia, that he was willing to stay in Columbia, go to Philadelphia, or return to Liberty County and his old work with the slaves. Dr. Howe did his best to convince Jones to stay at the seminary. Mary Jones wrote to her husband that to do anything that would be harmful to the seminary was very painful to her. 'I love it in its every interest,' she wrote. 'My dear friend Mrs. Howe I am warmly attached to, and to the doctor and their children, and Dr. and Mrs. Leland and their family; and for each of the students I feel a strong personal regard, and very strong attachments to numerous friends endeared in joy and sorrow.'[18]

Dr. Jones wrote to many friends, including his beloved professor at Princeton, Archibald Alexander, seeking advice. He wrote to William McDowell, 'My friends are divided; yet the weight is for Philadelphia.'[19] The seminary students believed that Jones would go. He asked Dr. Leland, 'What if a person should conclude to go?' Leland replied, 'We should lose a great deal, and they would gain a great deal; and that

[17] Myers, *A Georgian at Princeton*, p. 52.
[18] Myers, *A Georgian at Princeton*, p. 25.
[19] Myers, *A Georgian at Princeton*, p. 42.

would be all.' Jones said, 'Well, it is strange to me. I cannot see that either way.'[20] Finally, on July 10, 1850, Jones wrote to the Presbyterian Board of Missions accepting their position—believing it 'to be a call from God so far as I have been enabled to discern His will through His providences towards myself and family, and through the opinions of relatives and Christian brethren and the church generally.'[21]

In June 1851 C. C. Jones paid a brief visit to Columbia, where Dr. and Mrs. Howe gave him 'the most cordial welcome imaginable.' Dr. Leland called on him, as did Dr. and Mrs. Palmer. Jones addressed the seminary students in the chapel. He found the town 'looking beautiful' and left after his short but 'delightful visit.' He wrote to his wife that 'the first thing my eyes rested upon on coming up to the depot in Columbia was Jack and Marcia's grave; and I rode there and looked at it the last thing before I came away . . . I shed tears over them. Jack is identified with all our married life and with our children from their infancy!'[22]

* * * * *

[20] Myers, *A Georgian at Princeton,* p. 49.

[21] Myers, *A Georgian at Princeton,* p. 53.

[22] Myers, *A Georgian at Princeton,* p. 184. Charles had a tombstone placed over the graves of Jack and Marcia. It read:

John Anderson Jones
A Servant of God
A. 60
And Marcia his Wife
A. 55
Of Liberty County. Ga.
Died
April 17th and 20th 1850
Our Kind and Faithful Friend
John 6:39-40

On December 5, 1850, Mary Jones wrote from Philadelphia to her son Charles at Princeton College that a letter from 'Aunt' Howe in Columbia sent love to Charles and his brother, Joseph, and reported that the seminary in Columbia 'is in a flourishing state; thirty students present, and Dr. McGill of this state elected by our Synod of Georgia to fill your father's place.'[23]

Of Scotch-Irish descent, Alexander McGill was born in Pennsylvania in 1807 and trained in the Scottish Seceder tradition. He graduated from Jefferson College at the age of nineteen and remained there as a tutor of Latin for two years. Seeking a milder climate for his health, he went to Milledgeville, Georgia, where he was principal of an academy. He studied law and received several important appointments from the Georgia legislature, including the work of surveying the lands of the Cherokee Indians before their removal to the West. Visiting Missionary Ridge, Tennessee, McGill was so impressed by the good work of the missionaries that he decided to enter the ministry himself.

Alexander McGill studied at the seminary of the Associate [Presbyterian] Church in Canonsburg, Pennsylvania, and was ordained in 1835. After several years of ministry in the churches of that denomination, he accepted a call from the Second Presbyterian Church (Old School) of Carlisle, Pennsylvania. In 1842, McGill became a professor at Western Seminary at Allegheny Town in western Pennsylvania—teaching church history and church government and, later, biblical literature.

While he taught at Columbia Seminary during the winter of 1852-53, McGill lived in the 'hospitable home of Dr.

[23] Myers, *A Georgian at Princeton*, p. 103.

Howe.' He was impressed with Howe's 'learning, piety, candor, and good sense.' Dr. Howe, McGill said, combined 'the simplicity of a child' with 'greatness of mind.' McGill appreciated the Christian devotion of the seminary professors and students. Years later he wrote: 'This was manifested peculiarly in the devout attention of all together, at the daily exercise of worship, in the prayer hall; a particular ornament of godliness, in which, it has never been excelled by any other Theological Seminary I have known or heard of.' McGill remembered especially Dr. Leland's reading of the Bible. With his 'majestic form and mellow voice,' McGill wrote, he read the Scripture 'with tones and emphasis which no commentary could rival in pressing every shade of thought contained on the ear and the heart' of his hearers. Young Bazile Lanneau, who was tutor in Hebrew, took his turn with the professors in leading prayers for the week, 'with singular pathos and heavenly unction which cannot be forgotten.'

Not only was McGill impressed by the seminary, he loved the city. On February 3, 1853, he wrote to his wife, who had stayed in the North:

> One thing is nearly certain to my mind, that, if you come to Columbia, you will not be willing to leave it again. It is just the place for you. Its charming walks and gardens, delightful circles of female society, balmy climate, fattening foods, and ebony hands to dress it, will take such a hold of your local attachment that you will refuse to move, anymore. Are you then prepared, to become permanently identified with the South in general, and South Carolina in particular?[24]

Like his fellow Northerners George Howe and Araon Leland before him, and Joseph Ruggles Wilson and William

[24] Margaret DesChamps Moore, 'A Northern Professor Winters in Columbia, 1852-1853,' *South Carolina Magazine* (October 1959), pp. 183-92.

Swan Plumer who came later, Alexander McGill found the South congenial in its culture and attitudes. Either his wife was not ready to move to Columbia or McGill had second thoughts, because after one school year at Columbia he returned to Western Seminary. In 1854 he was elected to the faculty of Princeton Seminary by a unanimous vote of the directors. He never forgot his time in Columbia. In 1881, on the occasion of Columbia Seminary's semi-centennial, McGill wrote, 'It was, indeed, a privilege to be there, and that sacred school was a revival of religion for me all the time I communed with teachers and scholars at Columbia.'[25]

* * * * *

Students came to Columbia Seminary from such Northern schools as Princeton, Dartmouth, Yale, and Middlebury, as well as from the colleges of the South. In 1854 and 1855 two new buildings were added to the campus, called Simons Hall and Law Hall for two generous women—Eliza Lucilla Simons of Charleston and Agnes Law of Columbia—who each gave $5,000 to the seminary. Simons Hall was furnished by friends in the city of Charleston. Law Hall was named for Agnes Law and her husband, for many years the treasurer of the seminary. In his will Mr. Law left money to the seminary for several scholarships. Other improvements to the campus were planned, but local workmen were engaged in building the new State House in Columbia. The desire to create a common hall for student dining had to be, for a time, abandoned. The students found their meals in 'approved families' in the town, paid for by the seminary. The seminary converted the former

[25] *Memorial Volume,* pp. xx-xxi.

stables and carriage house into a chapel. Dr. Howe wrote, 'We were comforted by remembering that our Savior was said to have been born in a stable and cradled in a manger; and so sweet have been our seasons of religious instruction and enjoyment in that place often since, that we have forgotten that it ever was a stable at all. We have "looked", sometimes, almost like John in Patmos, "and behold a door opened" unto us also "in heaven".'[26] In 1856 the valuable library of Thomas Smyth, over eleven thousand volumes, was purchased. Others contributed books through the years, including the Rev. John Douglas, a graduate of the seminary and a long-time director. Douglas was pastor of the Presbyterian church on James Island from 1846 to 1864, serving 'blacks and whites,' according to the *Ministerial Directory of the Presbyterian Church, United States*. 'Besides the books that would appeal to a bibliophile, or volumes that might be sought by a lover of learning, there was a notable collection of Puritan literature,' according to one history.[27] Through the generosity of John Adger, the seminary's debt on the Smyth library purchase was paid and a small library fund was created.

[26] *Memorial Volume,* p. 148. The chapel was later used for a training school for teachers, named Winthrop College, which moved in 1895 to Rock Hill, South Carolina. The old seminary chapel was taken down and reconstructed brick by brick on the Rock Hill campus in 1936. Later an exact replica was built in Columbia on the original site.

[27] Jones and Mills, *The Presbyterian Church in South Carolina,* p. 429.

9

'THE GLORY OF THE LORD RISEN UPON IT'

AS pastor of the First Presbyterian Church, Dr. Palmer had many ties with the seminary in which he had been trained for the ministry. The seminary students worshipped at the church, and heard him preach. Palmer taught them, Thomas Cary Johnson wrote, 'by doing it, how to open God's word to the people.'[1] Palmer was also frequently called upon to lecture or speak at the seminary. The gifted young Bazile Edward Lanneau, who was related to Palmer and lived in the Palmer home while a student at the seminary, wrote to his parents on July 16, 1852:

> The anniversary of the Society of Enquiry [the missionary organization at the seminary], on Monday evening, was . . . quite interesting. In Dr. McGill's absence, they fell back upon our fluent kinsman, who, with his usual readiness of concoction and utterance, gave us a free and easy, plain and powerful talk on the subject of preaching.[2]

* * * * *

First Presbyterian Church was soon to have a splendid new building. The old church building was moved by mule power

[1] Johnson, *Palmer*, p. 85.
[2] Johnson, *Palmer*, p. 136.

to the center of an adjoining street, and the congregation continued to meet there until the new church was completed. The last service in the old building took place on October 2, 1853. Samuel Wells Leland (son of seminary professor Aaron W. Leland), a young doctor in the Mill Creek community nine miles south of Columbia, wrote in his diary: 'As there was to be preaching in the old Presbyterian Church of Columbia for the last time, I made an effort and attended. The services were very solemn, the sacrament of the Lord's Supper was administered.'[3]

The new building, an English Gothic Revival structure of rose stucco, with arched stained-glass windows, vaulted ribbed ceilings, tracery work, and a graceful steeple, gave the Presbyterians a lovely, impressive church. A center aisle and two side aisles lined the box pews. Chandeliers with seven lights each were suspended above the center aisle. The large marble pulpit was prominent and a plain communion table stood directly below the pulpit at the end of the center aisle. The building cost $35,000.

The new church was dedicated on October 9, 1853. Dr. Palmer's sermon on the 'Warrant and Nature of Public Worship,' from John 4:23, 24, was a powerful presentation of the Protestant view of public worship. He closed with the words:

> As for this building, beautiful as it may be in our eyes, let it please us to call it only a plain Presbyterian meeting-house. The glory we see in it, let it not be the glory of its arches and its timbers; not the glory of its lofty and graceful spire, pointing ever upwards to that home the pious shall find with God; not the glory of this chaste pulpit, with its delicate tracery, and marble whiteness, not the glory found in the

[3] John M. Bateman, 'History of First Presbyterian Church,' pp. 14-15.

eloquence or learning of those who, through generations, shall here proclaim the gospel; nor yet the glory traced in the wealth and fashion, refinement and social position of those who throng its courts. But let its glory be The Glory of the Lord Risen Upon It! Let its glory be the promises of the covenant engraved upon its walls, which are yea and amen in Christ Jesus. Let its glory be found in the purity, soundness, and unction of its pastors; in the fidelity and watchfulness of its elders; in the piety and godliness of its members. Let its glory be as a birthplace of souls, where shall always be heard the sobs of awakened penitence, and the songs of newborn love. Let its glory be the spirituality of its worship, its fervent prayers, its adoring praise, and the simplicity and truth of its ordinances and sacraments. Let its glory be the communion of saints, who here have fellowship one with another, and also with the Father, and his son Jesus Christ. Let its glory be as the resting place of weary pilgrims, toiling on toward the heavenly city—the emblem of that Church above—'Where congregations ne'er break up, And Sabbaths never end.'

And now 'To the only wise God, the King, eternal, immortal and invisible,' to God 'glorious in holiness, fearful in praises, doing wonders,' to God who 'is a spirit, infinite, eternal and unchangeable, in His being, wisdom, power, holiness, justice, goodness, and truth'—to God the Father almighty, the maker of heaven and earth; to God the Son, the brightness of the Father's glory, and express image of His person; to God the Holy Ghost, proceeding from the Father and the Son, to the service and glory of the adorable and incomprehensible Trinity—we solemnly dedicate this building, with all that appertains to it.[4]

Dr. Samuel Leland was back in town for this important day and described the service: 'My father prayed and Dr. Palmer

[4] Johnson, *Palmer*, p. 124.

the pastor preached. The church was filled to overflowing. All sects were represented; even Jews, Roman Catholics and infidels were there. The discourse was a powerful one; on the warrant and nature of public worship. Roman Catholics and High Church Episcopalians were very much offended by the closing remarks.'[5] In concluding his sermon, Dr. Palmer had insisted that as Protestants, Presbyterians do not view church buildings as sacred and had stressed the spirituality of Reformed worship. He described the new building as 'only a plain Presbyterian meeting-house.' It was, however, 'consecrated to the worship of God,' he said; and, accordingly, the session would guard its use with great care, regularly turning down requests for 'orations' and other functions not in line with its spiritual purpose.

* * * * *

Not surprisingly, the First Church pastor, Dr. Palmer (Oglethorpe University conferred the degree of doctor of divinity upon him in 1852), was called to a number of the country's major churches—in Charleston, Baltimore, Cincinnati, and Philadelphia—and to several seminaries. Worried Southern commissioners to the 1853 General Assembly called a meeting to express their opinion that Dr. Palmer should not leave the South. In 1854 he was elected professor of ecclesiastical history and church polity at Columbia Seminary, where he had been lecturing for several years. Things had reached a crisis at the seminary. There were few students, and two major faculty positions—theology and church history—were vacant. The directors acted decisively. They nominated Palmer

[5] *A Columbia Reader*, p. 36.

for church history and polity and James Henley Thornwell for theology. Robert J. Breckinridge, president of Danville Theological Seminary in Kentucky, wrote enthusiastically to Thornwell, 'If you and Palmer enter Columbia, that Seminary must immediately occupy the very first rank . . . No seminary in this country can compare with [it].'[6]

When Palmer accepted the seminary position, the session, knowing that it was hopeless to appeal to either presbytery or synod to prevent his leaving, attempted to convince him to stay at the church by calling him and Dr. Thornwell to fill the pulpit jointly. Dr. Palmer decided, however, to leave the pastorate for the seminary. Mrs. Palmer predicted that her husband would not stay long at the seminary. To those who pushed him in this direction she said, 'you will soon lose both pastor and professor. Your new-made professor must be a pastor; you have, in taking him out of this church, made it inevitable that he shall soon accept a call to another church.'[7]

Dr. Palmer's ministry at First Presbyterian had lasted for thirteen years—from January 1843 to December 1855. The new church building had become a landmark in Columbia. 'A great preacher, in a great pulpit, in a great city . . . filled that church to the doors,' wrote John Wells, 'and preached with matchless power and ever-broadening influence.'[8]

Benjamin Palmer remained at the seminary for only a year. He soon found—what his wife knew—that he had to have 'a preaching place.' During 1856, he supplied the Presbyterian church at Orangeburg—a congregation 'too feeble' to support a pastor—and taught his classes at the seminary, but he was not happy. 'Academic life does not suit me,' he wrote to

[6] Palmer, *Thornwell*, p. 385.
[7] Johnson, *Palmer*, p. 149.
[8] Wells, *Southern Presbyterian Worthies*, p. 150.

John Adger, 'as I have neither the taste nor the learning for it, and as a professor [I] am only a wretched sham.'[9] Palmer was convinced of the importance of church history in the seminary but felt that he was too old to 'go through all the drudgery of microscopic investigation, to be fit for an office which I must vacate by death as soon as the qualifications for it have been attained.'[10]

Palmer's students, however, were impressed with his classes, admired his Christian walk, and consulted him regularly with their problems and spiritual needs. W. T. Hall, later a professor at Columbia Seminary, was a student of Palmer's. He wrote that Dr. Palmer was the best teacher the students had until Dr. Thornwell arrived. If Palmer had chosen to devote his life to teaching, Hall added, 'he would have made a great reputation and have been a pillar in the Seminary.'[11]

But Palmer was convinced that his true sphere was not in the classroom; his heart lay in the pastorate. Despite strong agitation in Columbia Seminary, the Presbytery of Charleston, and the Synod of South Carolina to keep him within their bounds, the church courts finally relented and allowed him to accept a call from the First Presbyterian Church of New Orleans. In the words of Thomas Cary Johnson, 'Thus nobly did the noble Synod of South Carolina dismiss one of her noblest sons, whom she had so longed to keep, to his great field of the Southwest.'[12] Palmer preached a farewell sermon at First Presbyterian Church in Columbia and, still in his early prime, departed for his new charge. Before many years his Columbia friends would see him again, but not in the best of times.

[9] Johnson, *Palmer*, p. 161.
[10] Johnson, *Palmer*, p. 162.
[11] Johnson, *Palmer*, p. 155.
[12] Johnson, *Palmer*, p. 166.

10

DR THORNWELL AT THE SEMINARY

Southern Presbyterians were convinced that Columbia Seminary needed the services of James Henley Thornwell, now the president of South Carolina College. John Adger explained: 'The friends of the Seminary knew well what a sacrifice they were demanding of the college, but the Presbyterian Church had lent him to the State for a long time, and they now stood in great need of his services in the education of their rising ministry.'[1] To raise the funds to bring Thornwell to the seminary, the energetic Dr. Palmer travelled to Savannah, where earlier he had been pastor at First Presbyterian Church, and to Augusta, Montgomery, Mobile, and back home to New Orleans. 'The thing begins to look feasible,' he wrote on March 24, 1855, 'and notwithstanding the hard times, we are quietly pushing the endowment forward.'[2] The next year Thornwell, at the age of forty-four, left the presidency of the college to become professor of theology at the seminary. In his biography of Thornwell, Benjamin Morgan Palmer laments that 'the Church did not have the wisdom to effect that change in his position at least five years

[1] John B. Adger, *My Life and Times* (Richmond, Va.: Presbyterian Committee of Publication, 1899), p. 216.

[2] Johnson, *Palmer*, p. 137.

earlier,' so as to give Thornwell time to complete a systematic theology and publish it.[3]

Torn all his life between the church, the college, and the seminary, Thornwell served all three. He was twice pastor of Columbia's First Presbyterian Church. Twice he served South Carolina College, first as professor and chaplain, then as president, shaping 'the life of an important institution as well as the intellectual life of society.'[4] From his entrance as a student until his death Thornwell was connected with the college, except for short intervals adding up to a little more than five years. During his three years as the president of South Carolina College, he had raised entrance requirements, reinforced classical studies, replaced oral with written examinations, and effectively defended state-supported education. Chapter 9 of Daniel Walker Hollis's history of the University of South Carolina has the title 'Thornwell and the Status Quo,' but it was a 'status quo' that most South Carolinians wanted. Hollis admits that Thornwell's 'administration was regarded in all quarters as highly successful.'

Preacher, teacher, editor, leader—Thornwell was a major force in the life of the city. When a long-standing feud between the college students and the city's policemen erupted, armed citizens and students faced each other. Appeals for calm failed until someone had the good sense to summon Dr. Thornwell from the seminary. Rushing to the scene, he promised to personally investigate their grievances and urged the students to return to their rooms. Then, shouting 'College! College!' he led the agitated young men back to the campus. According to Daniel Hollis, 'Probably nobody else in the State could have done it.'[5]

[3] Palmer, *Thornwell*, p. 382.
[4] Leith, *Probing the Reformed Tradition*, p. 424.
[5] Hollis, *University of South Carolina*, 1:199.

Although Thornwell did not become a faculty member at Columbia Seminary until 1856, he had a long and close relationship with the seminary. In 1838 he became a director, and was the 'regular' substitute for the Columbia Seminary professors when they were sick or absent.

On October 13, 1857, almost two years after he began to teach at the seminary, Thornwell gave his inaugural address at First Presbyterian Church in the presence of the directors of the seminary, members of the Synod of South Carolina, and people of the church and city. He set forth his task:

> The office of a teacher in a school which aims to prepare a ministry for the whole Church and for a dying world, which aims to realize the ascension gifts of the Saviour in evangelists, pastors and teachers, until the whole body of Christ shall be gathered and the bride be adorned to receive her husband at His second coming in glory and majesty and power . . . Who is sufficient for this work? Fathers and brethren, not I! With profound impression of the truth I say it, not I! And like Moses, as I buckle on the armor of a graver warfare than I ever waged before, I utter from the heart the prayer of conscious weakness: 'If thy Spirit go not with me, carry me not up hence.'[6]

Thornwell ended his inaugural address with three short statements that summed up the work he had to do in teaching theology at the seminary. In the published sermon these appear as follows:

> (1) Is it not vast? God, Creation, Providence, Angels, Men, Heaven and Hell! (2) Is it not important? Other knowledges bring comfort, power, wealth—this is eternal life. (3) [Are there not] peculiar responsibilities of a religious teacher

[6] Thornwell, *Collected Writings*, 1:574.

> in this age? Irreligion is now a religion, a philosophy. An ignorant ministry will no longer do. God bless us, our seminary, his church and our work![7]

On the departure of Benjamin Morgan Palmer, Thornwell was invited to supply the pulpit at First Presbyterian Church; so after fifteen years he returned to the church as its regular preacher. In June 1856 the session of First Church nominated John Lafayette Girardeau as pastor, and Dr. Thornwell made an 'earnest address' in his favour at the congregational meeting. But a large majority of members was opposed to the election of a pastor at this time—and the session asked Thornwell to continue to preach.

The year 1856 brought great trials and sorrow to Thornwell. His mother died of typhoid fever in October, and two of his children were stricken with the same disease. When he returned from his mother's funeral, he found that his daughter had recovered, but Witherspoon, his 'lovely little boy,' nine years old, had followed his grandmother 'to the unseen world.' Thornwell wrote to a friend:

> These sad visitations, in such rapid succession, weighed down my spirits. I had no heart for my everyday work. But although I have suffered, and suffered keenly, and suffered, as I hope, never to suffer again, yet I can truly say that I was not conscious of the first emotion of rebellion against the Providence of God. I could trust Him in the deepest darkness which surrounded me. The gospel which I have long believed, and preached because I believe, was a very present help in time of trouble. I felt its truth, and was strengthened by its grace.[8]

Some weeks after the death of Witherspoon, Benjamin Palmer asked Thornwell what his opinion was as to the

[7] Thornwell, *Collected Writings*, 1:582.
[8] Palmer, *Thornwell*, p. 406.

salvation of children who die early in life. Thornwell believed that his little son gave evidence that he understood and accepted the gospel. He added that, 'independently of all this,'

> I believe the covenant which God has made with His people, and which is sealed to their faith in the baptism of their offspring, to be a real and precious thing; and where Christian parents have, in faith, laid hold upon this covenant, and have pleaded its promises on behalf of their seed, they may, when dying in these early years of childish immaturity, be laid, without a particle of apprehension or distrust, upon the bosom of that promise, 'I will be a God to thee, and to thy seed.'[9]

* * * * *

Dr. Thornwell attended the 1857 General Assembly at Lexington, Kentucky, and made a tour lasting more than two months through parts of Alabama, Mississippi, and Tennessee in behalf of Columbia Seminary. The Synod of Alabama joined the synods of South Carolina and Georgia in their support of Columbia Seminary. They adopted 'the Seminary as their own' and placed 'its name among those of the institutions which we call "ours", and which we are to cherish and care for, support, help, and encourage as our own.'[10] Early in 1858 Thornwell went to New Orleans to promote Columbia Seminary at the Synod of Mississippi meeting in that city. Dr. Palmer wrote that it was his 'unspeakable pleasure to receive the friend whom he loved into his home . . . and to hear his voice proclaiming the gospel of the grace of God . . . from his own pulpit.'[11]

[9] Palmer, *Thornwell*, p. 416.
[10] *Memorial Volume*, p. 150.
[11] Palmer, *Thornwell*, p. 431.

* * * * *

The Revival of 1858 touched churches on both sides of the Atlantic. Revival came to New York City following prayer meetings organized by a member of J. W. Alexander's Nineteenth Street Presbyterian Church. Similarly, revival came to Charleston after a long season of congregational prayer in the Anson Street Presbyterian Church under the leadership of John Girardeau. Following this extended time of prayer, Girardeau preached solid doctrinal sermons to large crowds. He later wrote:

> The most glorious work of grace I ever felt or witnessed was one which occurred in 1858 . . . in Charleston. It began with a remarkable exhibition of the Spirit's supernatural power. For eight weeks, night after night, save Saturday nights, I preached to dense and deeply moved congregations . . . About 120 white persons whose names are now on a list I still have, and many whose names I did not get, professed hope in Christ; and between 300 and 400 colored people; many more perhaps, for multitudes attended.[12]

For several weeks in the spring of 1858 there was preaching every night except Sunday in Columbia's First Presbyterian Church, 'in consequence of the awakened interest in religion which seemed to pervade the whole community.' The next year, during a meeting of the synod in Columbia, a motion was made to invite a delegation of Irish Presbyterian ministers who were touring the United States to visit the churches of the synod and tell them about the revival then in progress in Ireland. Thornwell moved that the motion be defeated, probably

[12] Blackburn, *Girardeau,* p. 80; C. N. Willborn, 'John L. Girardeau (1825-98)—Pastor to Slaves and Theologian of Causes: A Historical Account of the Life and Contributions of an Often Neglected Southern Presbyterian Minister and Theologian' (Ph.D. dissertation, Westminster Theological Seminary, 2003), p. 119.

because of the well-known tendency of these Scotch-Irish brethren to protest against slavery.

* * * * *

Dr. Thornwell returned from the 1859 General Assembly that met in Indianapolis to find his oldest daughter, Nannie, seriously ill. Within a week she died. Nannie was on the eve of her marriage, and her father had hurried home to bestow his blessing upon the bride and groom—Columbia Seminary graduate T. Dwight Witherspoon, who Thornwell said was 'eminently worthy of any heart or any hand.'[13] The invitations to the wedding had already been sent out. Dr. Palmer described the sad occasion:

> The bridal dress became the shroud; and just a little after the day when she should have plighted her vows before the altar, the very attendants who, in a different scene, should have 'rejoiced, hearing the bridegroom's voice,' with their white gloves lifted the bier, and bore it to the grave. In the peaceful Elmwood Cemetery, at Columbia, a marble slab bears the simple inscription of her name and age, with these appropriate words beneath: 'Prepared as a Bride Adorned for her Husband.'

'It was a sorrow from which the stricken father never fully recovered,' wrote Palmer.

> From this time his health became feebler, a tinge of sadness rested upon his countenance, the Christian graces became sweeter and softer every day, and it was evident to all that he was himself mellowing rapidly, to be gathered above with her who had gone.[14]

[13] Palmer, *Thornwell,* p. 441.

[14] Palmer, *Thornwell,* p. 440.

* * * * *

In February 1860, in order to retain the ministry of Dr. Thornwell but 'relieve him in a great measure of his pastoral and in part of his pulpit labours,' the session and the congregation of First Presbyterian Church called as its 'collegiate pastors' Thornwell and Francis P. Mullally. Thornwell was to share duties with Mullally for nine months, taking three months for rest in the summer. Mr. Mullally was ordained on May 4, and Thornwell and Mullally were installed as co-pastors of the church. John Girardeau preached the sermon on the text 1 Timothy 1:11: 'The glorious gospel of the blessed God, which was committed to my trust.' 'The incarnation, death, and resurrection of Jesus Christ, and the mission, supernatural influence and new creating energy of the Holy Ghost—all tending to secure the redemption of miserable sinners, to the glory of God's grace'—these, Girardeau told the crowded congregation, are the vital truths that render the gospel 'the glorious gospel of the blessed God.' Thomas Smyth, pastor of Charleston's Second Presbyterian Church, gave the charges. 'Oh, my dear Brothers, preach . . . Christ Jesus the Lord,' he told the two ministers. 'Preach this Gospel—this glorious Gospel of good news—first and last, every way and everywhere, in public and in private; in the pulpit and by the press; to the living and to the dying; to the lost and to the saved.' He continued:

> Let the spirit of the Lord be upon you that you may know how to speak a word to the weary, and of comfort to the afflicted, and of consolation to the bereaved; that you may be able to impart, out of a full soul, the comfort with which you have been comforted of God; to bind up the broken-

hearted; to give beauty for ashes, and the oil of joy for mourning, and the garment of praise for the spirit of heaviness; to weep with them that weep and rejoice with them that rejoice.

Supreme love to Christ will animate you with one absorbing passion—the love of souls—and concentrate and direct your energies in seeking their salvation. Like Paul, you will . . . rejoice to be offered upon the sacrifice of their faith. As in the case of Whitefield, this predominant passion, this enthusiasm, and even frenzy of love, will beam in your face, flow in your tears, breathe in your devotions, and vent itself in the impassioned eloquence of discourse. To this it will—as with Martyn, and Buchanan, and Heber—sacrifice ambition, emolument, honour, social comfort and domestic enjoyment. Infinitely and insatiably greedy of the conversion of souls as Alleine was, you will seem to your hearers as M'Cheyne did, 'as if dying to have them converted'; as if you felt it to be a greater pleasure, like Matthew Henry, 'to gain one soul to Christ than mountains of silver and gold to yourself'; and like Brainerd, 'care not where or how you live, or what hardships you go through, so that you may but gain souls to Christ.' Oh that you may so enter into this travail of soul that you may be able to say with holy Rutherford, 'My witness is above that your heaven would be two heavens to me, and the salvation of you all two salvations to me.'[15]

To the people of the congregation, Thomas Smyth said: 'May you go forward prospering and to prosper—a city set

[15] George Whitefield (1714-70) was one of the leading preachers of the Great Awakening. Henry Martyn (1781-1812), Claudius Buchanan (1766-1815), and Reginald Heber (1783-1826) were missionary leaders. Joseph Alleine (1611-81) was a Presbyterian and Puritan minister of England. Robert Murray M'Cheyne (1813-43) was the saintly pastor of St Peter's (Presbyterian Church) in Dundee, Scotland. Matthew Henry (1662-1714), English Presbyterian minister, wrote the famous Commentary on the Bible. David Brainerd (1718-47) served as a pioneer missionary to the American Indians. Samuel Rutherford (1600-61) was a pastor and theologian who was chosen one of the Scottish commissioners to the Westminster Assembly.

on a hill, a burning and a shining light, provoking all around you to love and liberality. May strength go out of this Zion, and may you arise and shine, the glory of the Lord having arisen upon you.' The impressive service was over. The congregation, stirred and thankful, congratulated one another on the church's prospects and filed by to shake the hands of their two pastors.

In May 1860 Thornwell was present at the General Assembly at Rochester, New York; it was the tenth and last assembly that Thornwell attended. He debated with Charles Hodge on the subject of church boards. Hodge's position approving of boards passed by a large majority, but Thornwell wrote to his wife, 'I think we had the best of the argument.' Thornwell had preached twice at Rochester and found the people 'very kind and hospitable.'[16]

Immediately after the assembly Thornwell went to New York and sailed for Europe. Nineteen years earlier, a journey to Europe had restored him to good health, and, as Palmer wrote, 'large hopes were cherished that he would again be toned up by a second trial of the sea, and the recreation of foreign travel.'[17] This time he was accompanied by a number of friends: his second daughter, a young bride, and her husband, the Rev. Robert B. Anderson; his nephew, John A. Witherspoon, a seminary student; the Rev. P. H. Thompson, a recent graduate of the seminary; and a close friend, the Rev. John Douglas, with his wife and niece. Thornwell's health seemed restored, but only temporarily. Burdened by his work and troubled for the South, he declined again. During the summer of 1861 he travelled to various places in the South,

[16] Palmer, *Thornwell*, p. 447.
[17] Palmer, *Thornwell*, p. 449.

seeking some restoration and relief. When he returned to his duties in the fall, his health was so shattered that he had to resign his postion as co-pastor in the First Presbyterian Church.

11

THORNWELL'S LEGACY: THEOLOGIAN

FROM 1856 until his death six years later, James Henley Thornwell was a professor at Columbia Seminary. 'Thornwell filled this post with brilliant distinction,' writes Douglas Kelly; 'he continued to be an outstanding preacher, teacher, writer, theologian, educator, ecclesiastical statesman, venerated public figure and husband and father.'[1] Thornwell's 'master work was as a theologian,' according to Thornton Whaling, 'for while he was a preacher, teacher, writer and ecclesiastic, he was always the theological preacher, teacher, author and ecclesiastic.'[2]

John Leith aptly describes Thornwell's theology as 'a development of the Reformed tradition that runs from Calvin through the Westminster Confession and Catechisms in the context of the Scottish Common Sense philosophy and of Southern culture.'[3]

Thornwell stood squarely in the Reformed tradition. He used John Calvin's *Institutes of the Christian Religion* as his primary text at Columbia Seminary. One of his students exclaimed that Thornwell found more in the *Institutes* than

[1] Kelly, *Preachers With Power*, p. 69.

[2] *Centennial Addresses*, p. 22.

[3] Leith, *Probing the Reformed Tradition*, p. 442.

Calvin did![4] Thornwell read Calvin's commentaries for his own spiritual refreshment as well as for biblical and theological learning. He wrote to a fellow minister in 1860:

> I have just finished Calvin's *Commentary on Genesis,* and cannot tell you how much spiritual refreshment and comfort I have derived from the light which his own experience and grace enabled him to throw upon the dealings of God with the ancient patriarchs. Every day enlarges my views, and deepens my convictions of the infinite riches of Divine wisdom and goodness.[5]

One of the great moments of Thornwell's life came when he visited Calvin's church in Geneva and stood at the site of his grave. He wrote to his wife, 'I felt the inspiration of his genius, of his learning, and of his piety.'[6]

Thornwell loved the Westminster Confession of Faith and Catechisms—intellectually, theologically, and devotionally. He believed them to be faithful expositions of the Word of God.[7] In his inaugural address at the seminary, Thornwell said:

> I am not ashamed of [the] Confession of Faith. I am not ashamed of the men who formed it, of the men who adopted it, of the noble army of martyrs and confessors who have sealed its doctrines by their blood . . . Ashamed of the Westminster Confession of Faith? . . . No never! I love it, sir, and love it with all my heart.[8]

Thornwell, however, did not believe that 'the goal of the full unfolding of the total contents of revelation had yet been

[4] *Centennial Addresses*, p. 19.
[5] Palmer, *Thornwell*, p. 445.
[6] Palmer, *Thornwell*, p. 458.
[7] Thornwell, *Collected Writings*, 4:442.
[8] Thornwell, *Collected Writings*, 1:576-77.

reached,' according to Thornton Whaling. There was 'rich ore in the Scriptures . . . which had not been adequately mined,' and Thornwell, through his brief life, 'worked with a single eye and with consuming intensity' at the task of more fully understanding the truth found in God's Word.[9]

Thomas Law was a student at the seminary when Thornwell began to teach there. 'His lectures on theology,' Law wrote, 'were always delivered with the utmost solemnity, reverence, and earnestness. They were like sermons from the pulpit, and the students felt their solemnizing, worshipful power as they heard him.'[10]

Thornwell defined theology as 'the science of the life of God in the soul of man.'[11] He belongs in 'the tradition of those who believe in order to understand,' explains John Leith.[12] Thornwell greatly appreciated Calvin's teaching that true knowledge of God includes love for God. Both Calvin and Thornwell stressed that theology is practical and theoretical; and although these elements may be distinguished, they cannot be disjoined. Theological knowledge knows by loving and loves by knowing. Both Calvin and Thornwell believed that our theological knowledge is always limited. 'The incomprehensibility of God,' Thornwell said, 'is the universal confession of all classes of divines . . . We must never forget that all cannot be explained. Our knowledge is a point, our ignorance immense. But we can know enough to glorify God, and to save our souls. We can know enough to make us sure that the unknown is full of glory and beauty.'[13]

[9] *Centennial Addresses,* p. 24.
[10] *Centennial Addresses,* p. 20.
[11] Thornwell, *Collected Writings,* 1:578.
[12] Leith, *Probing the Reformed Tradition,* p. 440.
[13] Thornwell, *Collected Writings,* 1:578, 582.

Thornwell held to a natural theology by which 'we must first know as men before we can know as renewed man.'[14] He eloquently wrote of the presence of God in nature—'an august temple which God dwells in and irradiates with his light; all created things a vast congregation of worshippers; and the glory of God, as it shines over all and upon all, is the burden of that mighty chorus of praise and doxology which is ever sounding in the ears of the Almighty from all above and all below.'[15]

Thornwell identified the organizing principle of theology as justification—for 'every Divine system of religion is only the answer which Divine wisdom gives to the question, How shall a moral creature be justified?'[16] Thornton Whaling said that Thornwell supported this assertion by 'the supreme and regulative place he assigned Adoption'—by which a servant becomes a son. Whaling explained:

> In the Covenant of Works the question relates to a righteous servant; in the Covenant of Grace to an unholy and condemned servant; but the end proposed in each case is the same, the change from the status of a servant to that of a son through adoption. From this point of view, Election is election 'into the adoption of sons'; Justification is a means devised by which the standing of the servant may be so assured that adoption to sonship shall certainly follow; Federal Headship again is a sublime means which the adoptive decree utilizes in order that the one who is represented shall receive this gracious benefit of the change from the status of servant to that of a son; Regeneration is the effective way in which the spirit of sonship is made real in those who have secured the adoption of sons.[17]

[14] Thornwell, *Collected Writings,* 1:37.
[15] Thornwell, *Collected Writings,* 1:467.
[16] Thornwell, *Collected Writings,* 1:580.
[17] *Centennial Addresses,* pp. 28-29.

Thornwell taught the history of theology at the seminary. He described how 'the first creeds were accepted as facts, and men lived upon the truth without having traced the deep philosophy which pervades it. It was a life, not a system.'[18] He believed that the theological 'productions of the Middle Ages are not without their value, and he who applies to them with a discriminating search will find many a jewel in the heaps of rubbish which cover it.'[19] He admired the logical precision of Protestant scholastic theology but protested that 'it gave no scope to the play of Christian feeling; it never turned aside to reverence, to worship or adore.'[20] It may be questioned whether Thornwell correctly understood the spiritual and even devotional content of at least some of the Protestant scholastics, but his objection to what he perceived there vividly illuminates his own deepest convictions.

Thornwell was a lifelong student of philosophy. As a boy he relished Locke's *Essay on Human Understanding* and Dugald Stewart's *Elements of the Philosophy of the Human Mind*. He owned the finest editions of Plato and Aristotle, and he read and quoted them in Greek. He lectured on metaphysics and the history of philosophy at South Carolina College. In his inaugural address when he became a professor at Columbia Seminary in 1857, Thornwell said: 'The great work of seminaries and theological professors now is to meet the altered aspects of infidelity; and not only to vindicate the external evidences of Christianity, but the internal, by showing the complete harmony of sound philosophy and theology.'[21]

[18] Thornwell, *Collected Writings*, 1: 579.
[19] Thornwell, *Collected Writings*, 1:579.
[20] Thornwell, *Collected Writings*, 1:34.
[21] Leith, *Probing the Reformed Tradition*, p. 442.

Thornwell was an adherent of the Scottish School of Common Sense Realism, as were most nineteenth-century American intellectuals. Holifield explains the central point of Scottish epistemology, as developed by Thomas Reid at Edinburgh and expounded by Dugald Stewart, as 'the conviction that the mind contained innate constitutive principles that enabled thinking men and women to describe the world accurately. Such principles were logically prior to sense experience; indeed they regulated and organized all experience.'[22] Thornwell agreed when he described theology as based on truth or facts arranged and classified according to the necessary laws of the human mind, but he also appreciated the limitations that the Scottish philosophy placed on knowledge. He noted that 'from Locke to Hamilton, English and Scotch philosophy has been for the most part a confession of human ignorance; from Leibnitz to Hegel, German philosophy has been for the most part an aspiration to omniscience.'[23] He agreed with the celebrated epigram of Sir William Hamilton: 'A learned ignorance is . . . the end of philosophy, as it is the beginning of theology.'[24]

Much has been made of the allegiance of early nineteenth-century American theologians to the idea of rationality. This is usually described as 'rational orthodoxy' with the emphasis on the word 'rational.' For many of these theologians, certainly for James Henley Thornwell, it should be more accurately described as 'rational orthodoxy,' with the emphasis on 'orthodoxy.' Philosophy did not shape theology; theology controlled and limited philosophy. The opposite of rationality for Thornwell was irrationality, not supra-rationality.

[22] Holifield, *The Gentlemen Theologians*, p. 63.
[23] Thornwell, *Collected Writings*, 3:85-86.
[24] Holifield, *The Gentlemen Theologians*, p. 118.

Christianity was not based on 'cunningly devised fables' (2 *Pet.* 1:16), as Thomas Paine claimed in his *Age of Reason* and Thomas Cooper taught for a few years at South Carolina College; but Thornwell never taught that Christianity was based on rationality. The last word was never philosophy but revelation, as contained in the Bible and admirably, though not perfectly, summarized in the Westminster Confession of Faith.[25] John Miller Wells writes about Thornwell, 'Knowing philosophy, as few men knew it, and with a cast of mind that was distinctly philosophic, he made it merely the handmaid of the Word. There must be a "thus saith the Lord" for every view held and for every position taken.'[26]

James Henley Thornwell was a major theologian and an astute philosopher. He was also a gifted preacher, although he did not see himself as such.[27] Thornwell wrote to young Thomas Peck, who was struggling to meet his own expectations as a preacher, 'My own performances in this way fill me with disgust. I have never made, much less preached, a sermon in my life; and I am beginning to despair of ever being able to do it.'[28] This sense of failure is one that is present at times, perhaps most of the time, in all preachers. Palmer reports the 'sketch' of a three-hour conversation that Thornwell had with one of the seminary students as they travelled by train from Columbia to Charlotte. Thornwell told the student that he frequently felt miserable after preaching, judging

[25] Paul K. Helseth in his *'Right Reason' and the Princeton Mind: An Unorthodox Proposal* (Phillipsburg, N.J.: P&R Publishing, 2010) presents compelling evidence that the Old Princetonians were not guilty of undermining their Reformed faith by their use of Common Sense Philosophy. Helseth's thesis applies equally to the Old Columbians.

[26] Wells, *Southern Presbyterian Worthies*, p. 40.

[27] See Kelly, *Preachers With Power*, Part Two, 'James Henley Thornwell: Logic on Fire,' pp. 61-83.

[28] *Writings of Thomas E. Peck*, 1:vi.

his sermon a failure. Once, he said, he had preached a sermon that was the poorest he had ever preached. He got on his horse and sneaked away. Some time later he came back to the same church. Two people joined the church that day 'who traced their convictions to that "abominable sermon", which, he still thought, was the poorest of his life.'[29]

Thomas H. Law, a seminary student who regularly heard Thornwell preach, greatly admired his sermons but admitted that 'his language was rather that of the schools than of the masses.' He could not reach the African Americans as his friend John Girardeau did. He failed in his efforts to preach to children. But to many, Thornwell was, above all, a great preacher.

As Thornwell warmed to his subject, it was said, 'a wonderful gleam' would light his small eyes, and impassioned words would pour from his mouth.[30] When Daniel Webster heard Thornwell preach in the South Carolina College chapel, he said that it was 'one of the finest exhibitions of pulpit eloquence' he had ever heard.[31] In 1856 Thornwell gave a notable sermon on 'The Sacrifice of Christ, the Type and Model of Missionary Effort' at the First Presbyterian Church of New York City for the Board of Foreign Missions of the General Assembly of the Old School Presbyterian Church. Robert Lewis Dabney called it 'a noble sermon.'[32] John Adger wrote: 'It was this sermon of which Dr. Addison Alexander, who was a hearer of it, remarked to a friend . . . that it realized his idea of what preaching should be.'[33]

[29] Palmer, *Thornwell*, p. 556.

[30] Palmer, *Thornwell*, p. 154.

[31] James Oscar Farmer, Jr., *The Metaphysical Confederacy: James Henley Thornwell and the Synthesis of Southern Values* (Macon, Ga.: Mercer University Press, 1986), p. 62.

[32] Thomas Cary Johnson, *The Life and Letters of Robert Lewis Dabney* (Edinburgh: Banner of Truth, 1977), p. 163.

[33] Robinson, *Columbia Theological Seminary*, p. 121.

South Carolina College student William Boggs described what it was like to listen to Thornwell preach in the First Presbyterian Church of Columbia:

> As I looked up to the pulpit . . . I caught a glimpse of a figure in black that passed somewhat quickly from the side recess . . . up the pulpit steps. I saw more clearly a face thin and rather pallid. Dark hair was closely brushed across the broad forehead and down either side of the face. The spare form stooped at the shoulders . . . Dark eyes rather small and deeply placed in the head glanced swiftly over the congregation.
>
> The preliminary services were conducted very quietly and with reverence . . . The prayers were direct and simple as a child's. No rhetorical sentences, no artificial cadences of voice.
>
> Then came the sermon. The text was always announced simply and quietly . . . The phraseology was briefly explained when occasion required. The context was referred to—that the exact line of thought should be noted. And the main truth was stated as a proposition with transparent clearness and simplicity. Then came the exposition which was an evolution of the main proposition into various heads. Not the traditional 'three heads' by any means. Sometimes four, sometimes five or more were given. This evolution of the main thought was affected by means of lucid statement and reasoning. The truth was unfolded and defended against misconception and cavil. And then as if with the thrust of Achilles' spear the application was made to the hearer's conscience . . . The voice grew in tone and volume. The eye that slumbered in its depths when unmoved seemed to dilate and flash as if it would read the secrets of your sinful heart.
>
> When you had time to think of the speaker at all, you trembled lest the slight soul would burst before your very

> eyes from its frail tenement. 'If,' said a brother in the ministry, 'the roof had been suddenly lifted from the walls and I saw Dr. Thornwell like Elijah mount on a chariot of fire, it, I believe, would have seemed exactly the right thing.'

Boggs, who himself became pastor of First Presbyterian Church, Columbia, in 1866, concluded his description of Thornwell's preaching with these words: 'It is one of the mysteries of God's providence, my brethren in the ministry, that feebler men like us should be called to take up the work that dropped from such hands. But the preacher whom Thornwell most resembled, as I think, comforts us with the saying that God has chosen the weak things of the world to confound the mighty. And to Him be all the glory.'[34]

In a sermon preached in 1986 on the occasion of Columbia's bicentennial, First Presbyterian Church pastor Dr. Glen Knecht described James Henley Thornwell's preaching ministry in Columbia:

> Every time he opened his mouth, it was as if the cross stood between himself and the audience. Each time he spoke, the whole gospel was somehow compressed into a single message. Men said that to hear one sermon of Thornwell's was a life-changing experience, that nothing ever had touched them like that. What a man he was, a genius by nature, a gift of God, but sanctified by grace and made into a powerful instrument of the Holy Spirit. He was sent forth, unleashed upon the world. So, he was a blessing not only to this church, but to the university, to the state, indeed to the nation.

Dr. Thornwell was concerned that his seminary students preach well. He insisted that 'the minister is to be fully furnished for the wants of his age with things new and old—a

[34] 'Centennial Sermon of William E. Boggs.'

copious variety of learning—and the storehouse must be in his mind and not his library, his head and not his shelves.'[35] He urged the students to strive for eloquence in speech, but above all he wanted them to be fervent in their preaching, seeking the Holy Spirit to fill them and their sermons for the good of people and the glory of God.

Thornwell, Benjamin Morgan Palmer wrote, 'commanded the love of young men by the fullness of his sympathy in their struggles with temptations and defeats, in their aspirations, their hopes, their joys.'[36] Thomas Law, a student at the seminary when Thornwell began to teach there, wrote that Thornwell's theology lectures were solemn and reverent, but his 'ordinary recitations were characterized by a freedom and *bonhomie* which relieved them of monotony and tediousness, and always made them bright and interesting.' Thornwell managed to get very close to his students, Law added, and kept in personal touch with them when they went out from the seminary.[37]

The students of the college and the seminary knew that Dr. Thornwell embodied the message that he was preaching. One of Thornwell's colleagues, writing an early history of South Carolina College, ventured to describe Thornwell in a few words and decided on this sentence: 'He is essentially a man of truth.'[38] Among Thornwell's papers was the written prayer: 'May the Lord grant that I may be guided by His Holy Spirit, that I may contend for nothing but the truth, and that in the spirit of the gospel.'[39]

[35] Thornwell, *Collected Writings*, 4:558.

[36] Palmer, *Thornwell*, p. 392.

[37] *Centennial Addresses*, p. 20.

[38] Farmer, *The Metaphysical Confederacy*, p. 63. The writer was Maximilian LaBorde; his history was published in 1859.

[39] LaMotte, *Colored Light*, p. 111.

12

THORNWELL'S LEGACY: CHURCHMAN AND SOUTHERNER

HISTORIAN Philip Schaff wrote in 1846 that 'the great theme of the Present, around which all religious and theological movements revolve, is the Church question.'[1] John Adger maintained that Thornwell's chief work was 'in the field of ecclesiastics.'[2] According to John Leith, 'No one in the history of Presbyterianism has excelled Thornwell in his passionate espousal of Presbyterian polity.'[3] To Thornwell, the doctrines of grace were of more importance than the doctrines of the church, but he believed that the doctrine of the church, including church government, was an essential and inseparable part of the revealed gospel.

Thornwell's central concern was that the Presbyterian Church find not only its doctrine but also its organization and directions for corporate life in the Scriptures. A later Columbia Seminary professor, William M. McPheeters, was eloquent in his praise of Thornwell's doctrine of the church, claiming that God bestowed upon him

> an honor comparable to that granted Athanasius, who in the fourth century was used of God for the formulation of

[1] Philip Schaff, *What is Church History?* (Philadelphia, 1846), p. 9.

[2] *Memorial Volume*, p. 190.

[3] Leith, *Probing the Reformed Tradition,* p. 436.

> the Scripture doctrine of the Godhead; comparable to that granted Augustine, who in the fifth century was used to formulate the doctrines of sin and grace; comparable to that granted Luther and Calvin, who in the sixteenth century were instrumental in formulating the doctrine of salvation by grace through faith.[4]

Thornwell wrote copiously about the Roman Catholic Church, thoroughly discussing 'the principles which discriminate the Romish system as an apostasy from the truth.'[5]

He was concerned to preserve and develop what he saw as biblical Presbyterianism, especially in answer to the Princeton theologian, Charles Hodge. Hodge's *What is Presbyterianism?* was published by the Presbyterian Board of Publication in 1855 and reprinted with a commendation by 'the strictest Presbyterians of Scotland.' Hodge held that the New Testament establishes Presbyterian polity in its major points but does not prescribe in detail the precise organizational form of the church. Hodge believed that within the limits of biblical principles, Christ left his church free to do its work under the guidance of God's providence and the Holy Spirit, in the manner found to be most effective under the changing conditions of time and place.

This issue was met head-on in the 1860 General Assembly—the last before South Carolina seceded and the nation was divided. The May weather in Rochester, New York, was delightful and the fellowship pleasant. Southerners were pleased with their hospitable reception, and even the anti-slavery commissioners praised the Christ-centred and powerful preaching of the ministers from the South. But soon

[4] Thompson, *Presbyterians in the South*, 3:213.
[5] Thornwell, *Collected Writings*, vol. 3.

Charles Hodge and James Henley Thornwell, the greatest theologians in the Old School Presbyterian Church, met in 'titanic conflict' on the specific question of the nature of Presbyterianism. Thornwell—eagle-eyed and small in stature–argued in clear, impassioned language that 'the form of government for the church, and its modes of action, are prescribed in the Word of God, not merely as to its general principles, but in all its details.' Then Hodge presented the position that 'the church is to be governed by principles laid down in the Word of God,' and that beyond those prescribed directions 'the church has a wide discretion in the choice of methods, organs and agencies.' Hodge contended that Thornwell's view—that Christ has ordained a system of church government not only in general principles, but also in its details—was a 'hyper-hyper-hyper-High Church Presbyterianism,' which the church had never held and to which it would not now submit.[6] Thornwell replied that Hodge's principles represented 'no, no, NO Presbyterianism, no, no, NO Churchism!'[7] The General Assembly upheld Hodge's views by a large majority, 234 to 56. The debate was continued and expanded in the pages of the *Biblical Repertory and Princeton Review* and in the *Southern Presbyterian Review*. The Old School Presbyterian Church generally followed Hodge rather than his Southern counterpart, but Thornwell's views were respected by many in the North, and eventually became central to the thinking of the Southern Church.

In his ecclesiology Thornwell elevated the role of ruling elders and deacons, argued for decentralization of the church, and championed the doctrine of the spirituality of the church.

[6] Charles H. Hodge and James Henley Thornwell, 'Debate Touching Church Boards,' in Thornwell, *Collected Writings*, 4:228.

[7] Thornwell, *Collected Writings*, 4, 232.

Thornwell held that the ruling elder is an integral and necessary element of the presbytery, with a right to participate in all strictly Presbyterian acts and to take part in all stages of the process by which ministers of the Word are ordained.[8] He insisted that the ruling elder is the basic office to which teaching and preaching functions are added. Thornwell asserted that the presence of a ruling elder at a session of a church court is necessary if a *quorum* is to be constituted, and that elders should rightfully lay their hands upon a minister when he is being ordained. Deacons constituted a separate and important order of the ministry, Thornwell held, which should be fully utilized in the work of the church.

Thornwell argued against the semi-independent boards of the church, and for committees that were immediately answerable to the General Assembly. 'God gave the Church a work to do in her organized capacity,' he maintained, and the Church cannot delegate that responsibility to another organization.[9] The organization of the ministries of the Southern Presbyterian Church, and later the Presbyterian Church in America, by executive committees of the General Assembly, rather than by boards, is a direct result of Thornwell's teaching.

No issue concerned Thornwell and Southern Presbyterians more than the doctrine of the spirituality of the church. Southern Presbyterians were convinced that the church had a well-defined mandate that prevented it from participating in political and secular matters. Thornwell argued passionately for the church's involvement only in those things that the Bible absolutely commands or permits. 'The Church

[8] James Henley Thornwell, 'The Elder Question,' *Southern Presbyterian Review* (June 1848), pp. 1-67.

[9] Thornwell, *Collected Writings*, 4:221.

is exclusively a spiritual organization and possesses only a spiritual power,' Thornwell said. 'Her business is with the salvation of [people]; and she has no mission to care for the things [of], or to become entangled with, the kingdom and policy of this world.' 'The salt that is to save this country,' Thornwell asserted, 'is the Church of Christ, a church that does not mix up with any political party or any issue aside from her direct mission.'[10]

Princeton's Charles Hodge believed that it was sometimes necessary for the church, as the church, to speak in areas of political concern. In the July 1860 issue of the *Biblical Repertory*, he wrote in protest of the view that 'the action of the state, however inconsistent with the Word of God, could not be testified against.' This 'new doctrine' of the spirituality of the church, asserted Hodge, put 'a muzzle' over the lips of the church and prevented 'her exercising one of the highest and most important prerogatives.' A compromise statement on this issue was adopted by the 1860 General Assembly, which on the one hand 'disclaim[ed] all right to interfere in secular matters' and on the other 'assert[ed] the right and duty of the Church, as God's witness on earth, to bear her testimony in favor of truth and holiness and against all false doctrines and sins.' Hodge never denied that the church was essentially spiritual, but he could not agree that the church should be denied the right of speaking on social and political matters. Thornwell too believed that the church must speak on such issues, but in doing so it should not go beyond the proclamation of the Word of God. While he insisted on the spiritual character of the church, Thornwell did not isolate Christian faith from public life. He felt that the church must limit itself

[10] Thornwell, *Collected Writings*, 4:472-78.

to its spiritual mission and, through the fulfillment of this mission in the lives and work of Christian people, transform society. In his address on 'Dr. Thornwell as an Ecclesiologist,' given at the 1912 centennial of Thornwell's birth, A. M. Fraser explained Thornwell's teaching:

> The object of the Church is to secure the regeneration and sanctification of man—to quicken his conscience, to reinforce his will. Place a man thus restored by divine grace amidst the responsibilities of life, and under all circumstances he will act as a Christian should act. If he has children, he will educate them. If he sees human depravity and suffering, he will reclaim the depraved and relieve the suffering. Give him political power of any sort, whether on the hustings, at the polls, in halls of legislation, under the judicial ermine, or in the executive chair, and he will use that power out of conscience towards God. Thus, while the Church must confine herself to the one work of the salvation of souls, souls cannot be saved without leaving a generic impression upon the face of all society.[11]

Southern Presbyterians agreed that the church was a spiritual institution with a spiritual mission, but found that it was difficult to draw the line between its appropriate work and improper entanglements in social and political issues. In 1860, amid growing Southern sentiment for secession, John Adger wrote: 'There is now a great and solemn question before the people of this State, affecting its very life and being, and that question has, of course, its religious aspects and relations, upon which this body [the Synod of South Carolina] is perfectly competent to speak, and if its deliverance thereupon should have a political bearing, that is a result for which we

[11] *Centennial Addresses*, pp. 45-46.

cannot be held responsible.'[12] Adger, in the July 1861 issue of the *Southern Presbyterian Review,* spoke even more strongly. Concerning the issues leading to the division of the country and the Presbyterian Church, he wrote: 'It seems to us to be the absurdist possible notion of our Church Government, that the Confession of Faith forbids the Church Court from speaking out for justice and right and peace in such a case as this.'[13] An article appeared in thc *Southern Presbyterian Review* for April 1863, by the Rev. James A. Lyon of Columbus, Mississippi, on 'Religion and Politics.' Although Lyon agreed that the church must not in its organized capacity violate its spiritual charter, he stated more forcefully than was usual in the South that when 'the state trenches upon Christian morals, and politics invade the rightful domain of the church, then it is not only the privilege but the duty of the church to lift up her voice on high and, in the name and by the authority of God, to proclaim the divine law on the subject.' Neither did Thomas Smyth fully accept the doctrine of the spirituality of the church. Sometimes he supported the idea of two kingdoms—church and world—but more often he argued that the Christian faith had 'the most vitally important relations' to civil polity and social justice.[14]

Thornwell's insistent championing of the view that the business of the church is spiritual and not political properly concentrated the church's focus on evangelism of the lost and training of Christians; but it was used disastrously in one important area. Since the church cannot legislate where Christ has not, Thornwell tirelessly asserted, slave-holding is not a proper area for church legislation. But Thornwell and

[12] LaMotte, *Colored Light,* p. 144.

[13] LaMotte, *Colored Light,* p. 135.

[14] Holifield, *The Gentlemen Theologians,* p. 154.

the Southern Presbyterians never succeeded, Paul Wooley wrote in his review of William Childs Robinson's history of Columbia Seminary, in answering the assertion that 'slavery is assuredly a subject which deals with moral conduct.'[15] The doctrine of the spirituality of the church did separate the Southern Presbyterian Church from greater influence in affecting American life and Southern culture; it also served, however, as a deterrent against the later trend in the Southern Church to downplay its spiritual mission and substitute other functions and goals.

John Leith further described Thornwell's theology as 'a development of the Reformed tradition . . . in the context . . . of Southern culture.'[16] There were many positive things about nineteenth-century Southern culture. There was a deep sense of family and place, a respect for God and the church, and an appreciation of tradition that led to a basic conservatism—which meant that the South was behind the rest of the nation in things both good and bad. But there were also deep problems with the Southern culture of Thornwell's day, not the least of which was slavery.

Until about 1830 there was considerable openness in the South on the issue of slavery and strong interest in eventually ending it. However, the bitter attacks of the abolitionists, Northern politics, and two slave rebellions created a defensiveness in the South that refused to listen to criticism and advice from even its truest friends. After the 1830s the conservative theologians of the South, including Thornwell, began to develop a biblical defence for slavery. Douglas Kelly writes that these theologians 'did not take into serious

[15] Paul Wooley, 'A Study in Church History,' p. 85.
[16] Leith, *Probing the Reformed Tradition*, p. 442.

consideration the fact that the blacks had been stolen from their homeland and that for Christians to buy stolen property is wrong.'[17]

James Henley Thornwell argued that since the Bible and the Bible alone is the only rule of faith and practice for the Presbyterian Church, and since the Bible nowhere condemns slavery as sinful, the church cannot do so. 'When the Scriptures are silent, she must be silent too,' he insisted.[18] Thornwell saw slavery as part of the curse sin had introduced into the world—like poverty, sickness, disease, and death. Like these things, slavery was not 'absolutely a good' but it was, under the gospel, turned into the means of 'an effective, spiritual discipline.'

Thornwell defended slavery, but in some ways, as Eugene Genovese argues, he was 'no friend to slavery.'[19] Thornwell demanded the legal sanction of slave marriages, the repeal of the laws against slave literacy, and effective measures to punish mistreatment of slaves. He assailed the scientific racism of his day that held that blacks were a separate species. He repudiated the idea that the curse on Ham in Genesis was fulfilled by the infliction of slavery on the Africans. He recognized in black people 'the same humanity in which we glory as the image of God,' and he declared to a white Charleston congregation, 'We are not ashamed to call [the black man] our brother!'[20] 'Upon an earth radiant with the smile of

[17] Kelly, *Preachers With Power,* p. xxiii.

[18] *Southern Presbyterian Review* (January 1852), 61. The Old School Presbyterian Church agreed with this position, stating in 1845 that slave holding was not forbidden in Scripture and that the church had 'no authority to legislate on the subject.' Street, *Southern Presbyterians,* p. 52.

[19] Eugene D. Genovese, *The Southern Front: History and Politics in the Cultural War* (Columbia, Mo.: University of Missouri Press, 1995), p. 39.

[20] *Southern Presbyterian Review* (January 1852), p. 61. Thornwell, *Collected Writings,* 4:403.

heaven, or in the Paradise of God, we can no more picture the figure of a slave,' Thornwell wrote.[21] He strongly opposed the reopening of the slave trade in the United States. In 1856 he wrote to John Adger that his 'judgment and feelings' were 'decidedly opposed to the slave trade.' 'It would change the whole character of the institution, as it now exists amongst us. It is now domestic and patriarchal; the slave has all the family associations, and family pride, and sympathies of the master.' Unfortunately, Thornwell followed these remarks with the assertion that resumption of the slave trade would make 'the institution positively dangerous' by importing 'lawless savages' from Africa.[22] Thornwell criticized the rampant capitalism of the North that claimed a man's labour without providing for his care and comfort. However benign their treatment and however loved as 'part of the family,' slaves were still slaves, chattel property under the law, and regularly passed on to the next generation along with other valuables.

On a trip to Europe in 1860, Thornwell apparently made up his mind to act at once for gradual emancipation of the slaves, because this was 'the only measure that would give peace to the country.' But when he got back home he found it was too late; 'the die was cast.'[23]

James Henley Thornwell held that 'the central principle of all Theology is justification.'[24] He fully appreciated the vertical dimension of justification by faith—that we are justified by God and before God not through our human efforts, but by the grace of God in the work of Christ. However, he did not fully embrace the horizontal dimensions of the doctrine of

[21] Thornwell, *Collected Writings*, 4:419.
[22] Palmer, *Thornwell*, pp. 422-23.
[23] Palmer, *Thornwell*, pp. 482-83.
[24] Robinson, *Columbia Theological Seminary*, p. 213.

justification—that all ethnic and racial barriers in the church of God are done away with, not only in the hereafter but in the here and now. Thornwell and most Southern Christians strongly defended the unity of the human race (against some contemporary scientific thought to the contrary), taught that God loves black people and that Christ died for them, that Christian people must do all they can to promote the evangelization of the slaves and free blacks, and that they belong in the church with whites, sharing together the communion of the Lord's Supper. But in the churches of the South, attended by blacks and whites before the Civil War, there were blatant examples of inequality. The leadership was always in the hands of the whites. Seating was segregated, with the slaves in the gallery or back of the church. All were one in Christ, but not in the church. The full meaning of Scripture, as found in such texts as Romans 3, Ephesians 2, and Galatians 2, is that justification abolishes all ethnic and racial divisions and unites believers in one family of God. Thornwell, and Southern Presbyterians in general, loved their black servants, but they did not see them as equals. 'The middle wall of partition' (*Eph.* 2:14) between Jews and Gentiles, which had been broken down by Christ, still stood between blacks and whites in Southern (and most American) churches.

Thornwell's influence has been diminished by the public support he gave to slavery and Secession, yet—as John Leith writes—'the actual achievements of his life merit for him a significant place in the history of the Reformed tradition in America as well as in the culture of the South.'[25] Marxist historian Eugene Genovese, who later converted to the Catholic Church, writes appreciatively of Thornwell:

[25] Leith, *Probing the Reformed Tradition,* p. 425.

Thornwell rose to become one of the foremost leaders of a state that burst with outstanding men. Calhoun considered him a giant among men, notwithstanding political differences over nullification and much else. He served with distinction as president of South Carolina College, the finest institution of higher learning in the Lower South and one of the finest in the United States. He edited the prestigious and intellectually impressive *Southern Presbyterian Review* and served as pastor of the socially and politically powerful Presbyterian congregation in Columbia. A staunch advocate of *jure divino,* he was widely recognized as a premier ecclesiologist even by his adversaries, northern and southern. His impact upon the most eminent southern divines—Benjamin Palmer, John Adger, John Girardeau, among others—could hardly be exaggerated. Among other accomplishments, his contributions to the theory and practice of education could be read with profit today for the light they throw on current concerns. And by common consent, he emerged as the greatest theologian in the South and among the greatest in the United States.[26]

[26] Eugene D. Genovese, *The Southern Front,* p. 32. John Leith states that 'no faculty member at Columbia Theological Seminary since W. C. Robinson . . . has written as appreciatively of the Columbia theological heritage as has Eugene Genovese.' John H. Leith, *Crisis in the Church: The Plight of Theological Education* (Louisville, Ky.: Westminster John Knox Press, 1997), p. 14.

13

JOHN ADGER AND JAMES WOODROW

BAZILE E. LANNEAU, grandson of Dr. Benjamin Morgan Palmer, was tutor in Hebrew at Columbia Seminary from 1851 to 1856. James Cohen served in the same position from 1856 to 1862. Cohen, born in Algeria of Jewish parents, knew Arabic from childhood. Adolphus Epstein, of Jewish birth in Hungary, studied at the seminary but died in 1856, his senior year.

A native of Selma, Alabama, David H. Porter graduated from Columbia Seminary on June 28, 1855. He preached at First Presbyterian Church in Augusta, Georgia, for five months and then accepted a call to First Presbyterian Church of Savannah. The Augusta session expressed its commendation of 'our beloved young brother' and the wish that 'his future career in Zion be as eminent as his commencement has been promising.'[1] David Porter served the Savannah church until his death in 1873.

* * * * *

Nominated by James Henley Thornwell, John Adger became professor of church history and polity at Columbia

[1] David B. Calhoun, *Cloud of Witnesses: The Story of First Presbyterian Church, Augusta, Georgia, 1804-2004* (2004), p. 53.

Seminary in 1857. Adger's father, an immigrant from Belfast to Charleston, became one of the wealthiest men in South Carolina. He generously used his money in various ways to benefit Charleston, including the support of Second Presbyterian Church's ministry to the slaves.

John Adger attended Princeton Seminary and credited the testimony and piety of the Princeton teachers—Archibald Alexander, Samuel Miller, and Charles Hodge—with his conversion. 'Not only their profound learning,' he wrote, 'but the saintliness of their character, filled me with awe.'[2] Adger graduated from Princeton Seminary and served for twelve years as a missionary to the Armenian people in Constantinople and Smyrna. He translated into Armenian the New Testament, John Bunyan's *Pilgrim's Progress,* the Westminster Shorter Catechism, D'Aubigné's *History of the Reformation,* and C. C. Jones's Catechism for the slaves. A later missionary said that over fifteen hundred people were studying Jones's Catechism in Armenian Sunday schools.

When the American Board of Commissioners for Foreign Missions refused to continue to support Adger as a missionary because his wife had inherited a number of slaves, the Adgers returned to Charleston, where John began a notable work among the black people, slave and free, in the city. There was much opposition to his ministry, since memories of Denmark Vesey's abortive attempt to organize an attack on the white slave owners were still vivid. Adger later recalled: 'The idea of building a church where Negroes were to assemble for worship, separate from the whites, even though the minister was a white man, and the Sunday-school teachers all white gentlemen and ladies, was not only novel, but, to many

[2] Adger, *My Life and Times,* p. 72.

persons, alarming.'[3] On May 9, 1847, to a large congregation at Second Presbyterian Church, Adger preached on Matthew 11:5—'The poor have the gospel preached to them'—and eloquently argued for his innovative experiment:

> [The Negroes] belong to us. We also belong to them. They are divided out among us and mingled up with us, and we with them in a thousand ways. They live with us, eating from the same store-houses, drinking from the same fountains, dwelling in the same enclosures, forming parts of the same families . . . There they are—behold them. See them all around you, in these streets, in all these dwellings: a race distinct from us, yet closely united to us; brought in God's mysterious providence from a foreign land, and placed under our care, and made members of our households . . . They are our poor—our poor brethren; children of our God and Father; dear to our Saviour; to the like of whom he preached; for the like of whom he died, and [to] the least of whom every act of Christian compassion and kindness which we show he will consider as shown also to himself.[4]

Adger held worship services for slaves in the basement of Second Presbyterian Church, and in 1850 a separate church building was completed, a few blocks away on Anson Street. When the church was dedicated, James Henley Thornwell preached to a congregation of white people on Colossians 4:1—'Masters, give unto your servants that which is just and equal, knowing that ye also have a Master in heaven.'

Experiencing serious problems with his eyes, John Adger was forced to leave his work in Charleston. He turned it over to young John Lafayette Girardeau and moved to the Upcountry of South Carolina, where he purchased 'Woodburn' and

[3] Adger, *My Life and Times*, p. 441.

[4] Adger, *My Life and Times*, p. 167.

devoted his time to farming, hoping to improve his failing eyesight. He was soon anxious, however, 'to return to the proper business of a gospel minister.'[5]

When he was elected to the Columbia Seminary faculty, Adger received a letter from Girardeau giving reasons why he ought to accept the call to the seminary. Adger described the letter:

> It was just such an argument as one, then the missionary in Charleston [to the Negroes], might very naturally employ with the former missionary in Charleston [to the Negroes] whom he had succeeded. It was to impress on me what an opportunity I would have to direct the minds of my classes in the Seminary to this great field of negro evangelization, in which we were both so much interested.[6]

Adger, according to E. Brooks Holifield, 'was a man of wide-ranging experience and firm convictions. A twelve-year tenure as a missionary to the Armenians had given him an unusual exposure to cultural and religious diversity.'[7] 'It was his constant aim,' wrote John Leighton Wilson, 'to promote a missionary spirit in the hearts' of the seminary students.[8] The Adgers moved into a fine city home in Columbia but kept a house in the Low Country. John also bought a farm near Columbia and moved the *Southern Presbyterian Weekly,* which he owned and directed, to Columbia.

Adger took a large view of his field of church history. He believed that 'since the church began at the very fall of man, its history should also begin there.'[9] For his course in

[5] Adger, *My Life and Times,* p. 222.
[6] Adger, *My Life and Times,* p. 223.
[7] Holifield, *The Gentlemen Theologians,* p. 177.
[8] *Memorial Volume,* p. 165.
[9] Adger, *My Life and Times,* p. 231.

church polity Adger followed the advice of Thornwell, who told him, 'I should make the fourth book of Calvin's *Institutes* a text book on the subject of church polity and the sacraments.'[10]

On the sacraments, wrote E. Brooks Holifield, Southern Presbyterians 'were not quite "Calvinist" and not quite "Zwinglian",' but somewhere in between.[11] Adger, however, developed a strong Calvinist sacramental doctrine, as set forth in John Nevin's book *The Mystical Presence*. Adger was aware that he was going against the views of his Princeton professor Charles Hodge and his fellow Southern Presbyterian Robert Lewis Dabney. Adger held Hodge to be a 'great theologian,' but believed that he 'never quite comprehended the subtleties of either church government or sacramental doctrine.' Adger had his students read the *Institutes* and study the debate between Nevin of Mercersburg and Hodge of Princeton. He believed that Hodge's analysis of Calvin was 'imperfect, partial, and unsatisfactory.'

Adger, like Nevin, took the incarnation as his starting point, discovering there 'the sublime truth of life for us.' He grounded redemption in the completion and transformation of creation. Salvation, he argued, is not merely the result of forensic imputation; it presupposes the reconstruction of the created self through communion with the incarnate life of Christ. 'There is a legal difficulty which justification removes. But does there not remain a difficulty as to the vital connection?' Adger asked. 'Must there not be some natural tie of life betwixt the Redeemer and his people?'

For some years, students at Columbia Seminary were taught an interpretation of Calvinist theology that came more

[10] Adger, *My Life and Times*, pp. 97-98.
[11] Holifield, *The Gentlemen Theologians*, p. 169.

from Mercersburg than from Princeton and Union, where students were likely to hear of Calvin's excesses. 'Though the sacramental lectures at the two schools [Columbia and Union] did not stimulate any open theological controversy in the South, they do,' writes E. Brooks Holifield, 'suggest something of the diversity in the nineteenth-century southern Reformed theology.'[12]

In his inaugural address in 1858, John Adger stated that the doctrine of the church was the great theological issue of the nineteenth century. He expressed his intention to combat both the tyranny of Rome and the subjectivism of some Protestants. He ably supported the 'high church' movement led by James Henley Thornwell. While not questioning the common distinction between the visible and invisible church, Adger did not allow the idea of the invisible church to weaken the importance of the visible church. The church, he said, is 'our mother, of whom we are born and by whom we are nourished, trained and governed until we are divested of our mortal flesh.'

* * * * *

In 1860 Columbia's population was 8,052, only a fifth of that of Charleston. There were sixty-two students at Columbia Seminary, the largest enrollment in the school's history. At First Presbyterian Church, there were 253 communicant members; thirty-four of them were black people. First Presbyterian continued its work of missions—at home and overseas. A church in the Sand Hills near Columbia had for several

[12] E. Brooks Holifield, 'Mercersburg, Princeton, and the South: The Sacramental Controversy in the Nineteenth Century,' *The Journal of Presbyterian History* (Summer 1976), pp. 238-57.

years been led by the students of the Society of Missionary Inquiry at the seminary. Dr. Howe or Dr. Adger went out for Communion services. Prayer meetings for foreign missions were held in the First Presbyterian Lecture Room every night during the second week of January 1860. During 1860 and 1861, the session investigated the possibility of building another church in the city. First Presbyterian Church's main outreach concern, however, continued to be the African Americans of Columbia. In April 1860, George Whitefield Ladson, a Columbia Seminary student from Midway Church in Liberty County, Georgia, and graduate of Oglethorpe University, was employed by the church for $200 a year to catechize and preach to the slaves and free blacks. His ministry was immediately successful, and a steady stream of black people began to apply for church membership. On June 27, 1860, the session admitted fourteen slaves and four free persons upon profession of faith, as well as two slaves upon letters of dismissal from other churches. On October 9, nineteen slaves and one free person joined the church upon profession of faith and three slaves upon certificate and examination.

On March 27, 1861, the black members of the church met and unanimously passed the following memorial:

> Whereas the Colored members of the Presbyterian Church have during the past two years experienced great benefit from the Religious instructions imparted to them by Mr. G. W. Ladson which has added many members to the Church Roll and which they seriously believe under Providence has been the means of turning many Colored persons from the errors of their way, and building them up in the true faith, they earnestly hope that efforts will be made to retain his services for the future.

Their statement urged the session 'to use every reasonable effort to procure a more commodious place for Mr. Ladson's preaching and, if it be thought advisable, to call him regularly so that his valuable services [might] be continued to them and their children and the whole community.' Mr. Ladson was ordained by the Presbytery of Georgia in April 1862 and continued his ministry to African Americans with First Presbyterian Church until the summer of 1863, when he was granted leave of absence for two months because of ill health.

All Presbyterians, but especially the Negroes, were saddened by the death of George Ladson on July 4, 1864. At his funeral his black friends crowded the place of chief mourners and begged to be allowed to bear all the expenses of his burial and to erect a monument in Elmwood Cemetery to the memory of 'their beloved friend and pastor.'[13]

* * * * *

In 1859, the year in which Darwin's *Origin of Species* was published, Judge John Perkins, who lived at 'The Oaks' near Columbus, Mississippi, endowed a new professorship at Columbia Seminary to teach the students to understand and appreciate true science, to answer objections to religion by some scientists, and to set forth God's revelation in the creation. The idea for this chair, the first of its kind, and the money to found it came from the state of Mississippi. It is by no means true that the Old South was hostile to science. 'Science was alive and well with excellent practitioners at all levels,' according to Robert K. Gustafson. 'Southern Presbyterian ministers wrote astute if not heated articles in the *Southern*

[13] *Memorial Volume*, p. 307.

Presbyterian Review demonstrating both scientific knowledge and theological sensitivity in the Reformed tradition.'[14] In Charleston, South Carolina, the pulpits were filled with distinguished ministers, as Erskine Clarke points out. 'They had been educated at Harvard, Princeton, and Yale, at the Universities of Edinburgh and Berlin. They traveled extensively in this country and abroad, carried on a voluminous correspondence with influential friends in America and Europe, and wrote scholarly books.'[15] One of those ministers was Thomas Smyth, pastor of Charleston's Second Presbyterian Church, and one of those scholarly books was Smyth's *Unity of the Human Races*. Smyth spent three or four years reading and studying at the Medical College of Charleston to produce an answer to the views of the brilliant Swiss-born Harvard professor, paleontologist, and geologist, Louis Agassiz, who had suggested that there were multiple origins for the races. Smyth's book, a defence of the full humanity of the Africans, was favorably reviewed by numerous journals on both sides of the Atlantic.[16]

James Henley Thornwell believed that the study of science would support religion; indeed geology and the Bible 'must kiss and embrace each other, and this youngest daughter of science will be found, like the eastern magi, bringing her votive offerings to the cradle of the Prince of Peace. The earth will never turn traitor to its God,' he wrote; 'its very stones will cry out against any who attempt to extract from it support for infidelity or atheism.'[17]

[14] Robert K. Gustafson, *James Woodrow (1828-1907): Scientist, Theologian, Intellectual Leader* (Lewiston: The Edwin Mellen Press, 1995), p. 29.

[15] Erskine Clarke, *Wrestlin' Jacob*, p. xiii.

[16] Erskine Clarke, *Our Southern Zion*, p. 158.

[17] Thornwell, *Southern Presbyterian Review* (July 1857), pp. 200-10.

Presbytery examination of candidates for the ministry often included questions about science. In 1851 Charleston Presbytery assigned James Dunwoody, graduate of Yale and Columbia Seminary and pastor in the Low Country, to examine in 'natural sciences, including mathematics.'[18]

Not all Southern Presbyterians, however, were happy with the idea of the Perkins chair at Columbia Seminary. Robert Lewis Dabney of Virginia's Union Seminary, despite his interest in chemistry and physics, opposed the addition of science to the seminary curriculum, warning that it could provide a conduit for theological deviation to enter the seminary.[19] T. E. Peck, the protégé of Thornwell who was now a young minister in Baltimore, warned against over-anxious attempts to reconcile Scripture with the latest discoveries of science. 'Before the end of this year,' he wrote, 'the current theory may be as dead as those which have already passed away. Have faith in the Word, and it will take care of itself.'[20]

* * * * *

In 1860 Dr. James Woodrow was elected to the Perkins Professorship of Natural Science in its Relations to Revealed Religion.[21]

James Woodrow was born in 1828 in Carlisle, England, of Scottish Presbyterian parents, Thomas and Marion

[18] Clarke, *Our Southern Zion,* p. 165.

[19] Sean Michael Lucas, *Robert Lewis Dabney: A Southern Presbyterian Life* (Phillipsburg, N.J.: P&R Publishing, 2005), pp. 19, 76.

[20] T. E. Peck, 'The Sufficiency of the Scriptures,' *Southern Presbyterian Review* (October 1853), p. 261.

[21] For the life of James Woodrow, see Marion W. Woodrow, ed., *Dr. James Woodrow as Seen by His Friends* (Columbia: R. L. Bryan, 1909); and Robert K. Gustafson, *James Woodrow (1828-1907): Scientist, Theologian, Intellectual Leader* (Lewiston: The Edwin Mellen Press, 1995).

Woodrow.[22] Thomas Woodrow was pastor of the Lowther Street Church in Carlisle.[23] On November 10, 1835, Thomas and his family set sail from Liverpool to America and arrived sixty-two days later after a nightmarish voyage. Marion never recovered from a violent illness on the ship and died five weeks after they reached New York. Thomas became a missionary in Canada and later a pastor in Ohio. His son James graduated from Jefferson College in Pennsylvania (now Washington and Jefferson College) in 1849, with first honours in a class of sixty. For three years James served as principal of several academies in Alabama. He studied science during the summer of 1853 at Harvard University under the renowned Louis Agassiz and, in 1856, was awarded the PhD degree *summa cum laude* by Heidelberg University, a distinct accomplishment in those days. The Germans offered the brilliant American scientist a full professorship at Heidelberg,[24] but

[22] An ancestor named James Woodrow was a Covenanting preacher and professor of theology at the University of Glasgow. According to family lore, this seventeenth-century Scottish ancestor of James Woodrow was seven years old before he would speak but a few broken words. His father feared a lack of intellect, but at last James overcame his problem. The first time he spoke clearly he repeated the Shorter Catechism, which he had heard his brothers repeating, without missing one word of it, which surprised them all with much pleasure. Evidently the silent small boy had been doing some close listening and thinking. The truth of the Shorter Catechism had stirred his heart and loosed his tongue!

[23] *En route* to the Peace Conference in Paris, Woodrow Wilson, on December 29, 1918, attended services at the Lowther Street Congregational Church in Carlisle. He was unexpectedly called on and gave a few remarks, recorded in his papers as 'At His Grandfather's Church.' Wilson said he remembered his grandfather well but that his feelings were 'too intimate and too deep to permit of public expression.' He paid tribute to his mother, who was born in Carlisle, on December 20, 1826, remarking on her 'quiet character, her sense of duty and dislike of ostentation.' He said that it was appropriate that 'in a place of worship' he should acknowledge his 'indebtedness to her and her remarkable father.' Woodrow Wilson, *Selected Literary & Political Papers and Addresses of Woodrow Wilson* (New York: Grosset & Dunlap, 1925-27), 2:308-309.

[24] According to J. William Flinn, 'Sketch Published in The State of Columbia, and the News and Courier, of Charleston, January 18, 1907,' in Woodrow, *James Woodrow*, p. 10.

Woodrow wanted to return to the southern United States—a land and people he had come to love.

Woodrow became professor of natural science at Oglethorpe University, a Presbyterian college near Milledgeville, then the capital of Georgia. He was the first teacher, it is said, in the history of Georgia to hold a PhD degree. In 1857 James Woodrow married Felie S. Baker. Felie's home was near the campus of Oglethorpe. Her father was professor there and pastor of the town's Presbyterian church. James Woodrow was ordained in 1859 and preached in the mission churches in the area. He often took one of his students, Sidney Lanier, on his preaching trips. During such times 'we were constantly engaged without interruption in our conversation. In these ways, and in listening frequently to [Lanier's] marvelous flute playing, we were much together,' Woodrow wrote. 'We were both young and fond of study. I had just been spending two years or so in studying and wandering in various countries in Europe; so we did not lack for topics.' 'I am more indebted to Dr. Woodrow than to any living man for shaping my mental attitude toward nature and life,' Lanier wrote. 'His spirit and method not only guided and enlarged my scientific knowledge, but they had a formative influence on my thought and fancy in all my literary work.'[25] Lanier became a well-known and loved Southern poet; he died in 1881.

* * * * *

Upon his appointment to the seminary, James Woodrow gave his inaugural address on November 22, 1861, in Marietta, Georgia, before the Board of Trustees of Columbia

[25] Gustafson, *Woodrow,* pp. 24, 25.

Seminary, which was meeting at the same time as the Synod of Georgia.

Woodrow stated that his work at the seminary was 'to scrutinize the nature and force of current and popular objections to the Scriptures; to meet them, and set them aside, by proving that they spring either from science falsely so called, or from incorrect interpretations of the words of the Holy Bible.'[26] His fundamental thesis, he said, was that 'the Bible and nature are both from God. They cannot be contradictory. Apparent conflicts arise from misinterpretations of one, or the other, or both. Remove these conflicts by ascertaining and interpreting correctly the facts of both.'

Woodrow stated that the Bible is not a science textbook, and he warned against a tendency to be overly suspicious of and hostile to science. Because of the imperfections in science, the questions that are faced in the interpretation of some parts of Scripture, and the limitations of language to convey the details of the work or mode of creation, Woodrow believed that 'we may expect to find many unadjusted differences, instead of perfectly established harmony.'

When he took his oath of office, subscribing to the pledge required of all seminary professors that the Confession of Faith contains 'a just summary of the doctrine contained in the Bible,' Woodrow noted his exception to the traditional way of treating the six days of creation as literal days of twenty-four hours.

Woodrow joined Howe, Leland, Thornwell, and Adger at the seminary. John Leith writes that 'in 1860 Columbia Theological Seminary had on its faculty and in its surrounding community as able a group of ministers and teachers as had

[26] Gustafson, *Woodrow*, p. 62.

ever been assembled in American Presbyterianism except around Princeton.'[27]

[27] Leith, *Crisis in the Church*, p. 14.

1. *Above:* Columbia Theological Seminary (1831-1927).

2. *Left:* Historical Marker detailing the history of the old seminary building. The move was carried out over several years. Synod approved the move in 1924. The new seminary president moved to Georgia in 1925 to prepare for the eventual move of the seminary. Students and faculty stayed in Columbia until the 1927 commencement.

3. A postcard showing the buildings of Columbia Theological Seminary

4. First Presbyterian Church, Columbia, S.C.

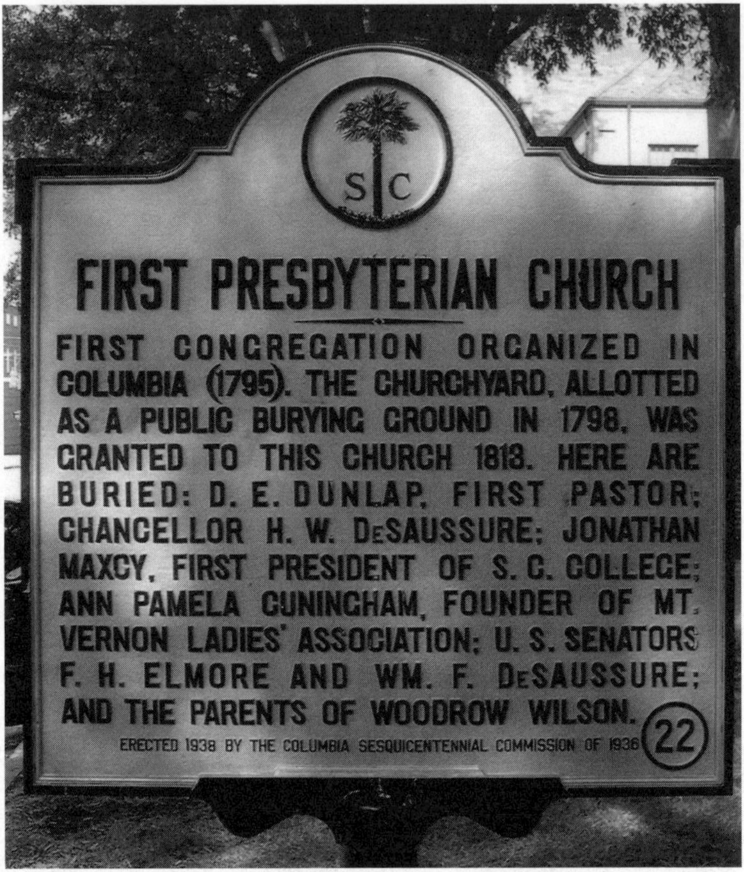

5. Historical marker outside First Presbyterian Church, Columbia, S.C.

6. George Howe

7. John Leighton Wilson

8. James Henley Thornwell

9. John B. Adger

10. James Woodrow

11. Joseph Ruggles Wilson

12. The Wilson home in Columbia, S.C.

13. William S. Plumer

14. John Lafayette Girardeau

15. Girardeau's gravestone

16. Benjamin Morgan Palmer (c. 1872)
17. First Presbyterian Church, New Orleans, La

18. Henry Alexander White

14

THE SOUTHERN PRESBYTERIAN CHURCH

AS early as 1856 Dr. Thornwell had written, 'The prospects of the country fill me with sadness. The future is very dark. The North seems to be mad, and the South blind.'[1] On the night of October 16, 1859, a band of white and black men, under the leadership of John Brown, seized the town of Harper's Ferry, Virginia, hoping to provoke a widespread slave uprising. When Brown was viewed as a hero in the North, many Southerners became convinced that their safety demanded withdrawal from the Union. George Howe, originally from the North but for many years a resident of Columbia, and, through his marriage, the owner of two plantations in Liberty County, Georgia, wrote sadly: 'We have never believed it possible that the Union of these States must come to an end, and never really feared it till now . . . But how can we live together in this perpetual conflict?'[2]

On May 16, 1860, the Republican Party nominated Abraham Lincoln as its candidate for president. The same month the Old School Presbyterian Church held its last united General Assembly. 'The unity of the Spirit in the bond of peace

[1] Palmer, *Thornwell*, p. 405.

[2] George Howe, 'The Raid of John Brown, and the Progress of Abolition,' *Southern Presbyterian Review* (January 1860), p. 812.

. . . was preserved throughout,' J. B. Adger wrote.[3] Benjamin Morgan Palmer, now pastor of the First Presbyterian Church of New Orleans, was nominated by Dr. Gardiner Spring of New York City and elected unanimously to be a professor in Princeton Theological Seminary. Palmer appreciated the honour, but, still committed to the pastorate, he did not accept. The resolutions of Gardiner Spring in the next General Assembly would split the church apart.

Abraham Lincoln was elected president of the United States on November 6, 1860. November 21 was designated a day of fasting, humiliation, and prayer in South Carolina. A large crowd gathered at First Presbyterian Church in Columbia to hear Dr. Thornwell preach 'A Sermon on National Sins.' Thornwell chose as his text Isaiah 37:1: 'And it came to pass, when King Hezekiah heard it, that he rent his clothes, covered himself with sackcloth, and went into the house of the Lord.' 'We are here, not like the Pharisee, to boast of our own righteousness, and to thank God that we are not like other men,' Thornwell told the congregation; 'but we are here like the poor publican, to smite upon our breasts, and to say, God be merciful to us sinners!'[4]

Thornwell explained that he was 'oppressed with a difficulty' in applying his text to the circumstances of the day. 'During the twenty-five years in which I have fulfilled my course as a preacher—all of which I have spent in my native state, and nearly all in this city—I have never introduced secular politics into the instructions of the pulpit.'[5] Thornwell said that his great aim was 'not to expound our complex

[3] John Adger, 'General Assembly of 1860,' *Southern Presbyterian Review* (July 1860), p. 352.

[4] Thornwell, *Collected Writings,* 4:510.

[5] Thornwell, *Collected Writings,* 4:511.

institutions, but to awaken the national conscience to a sense of its responsibility before God. It is not to enlighten your minds, but to touch your hearts; not to plead the cause of States' rights or Federal authority, but to bring you as penitents before the Supreme Judge.'[6] It may be questioned whether the preacher succeeded in his stated purpose, because much of his sermon is taken up with an analysis of the federal nature of the United States government. He deplored the fact that 'the tendency to sink our institutions into a pure democracy has been steadily growing,' so that Congress was becoming a battleground of conflicting wills, and its sole inquiry was reduced to 'What says the voice of the majority? *Vox populi, vox Dei.*'[7] Thornwell blamed the North for the sin of abandoning the idea of federal and representative government. But Southerners also felt the brunt of Thornwell's sermon. He noted Southern sins of profaneness in speech, contempt for the Sabbath Day, and another 'characteristic of our people that they are self-sufficient and vain-glorious.'[8]

Thornwell closed his long sermon with comments on the burning issue of slavery. He defended slavery as 'an organization of labour, an organization by virtue of which labour and capital are made to coincide.' He asked 'on what [other] principle shall labour be organized so as to make it certain that the labourer shall never be without employment, and employment adequate for his support?' In the South, he asserted, 'the master must always find work for his slave, as well as food and raiment.'[9] 'The question now arises,' he continued, 'Have we, as a people and a State, discharged our

[6] Thornwell, *Collected Writings*, 4:514.
[7] Thornwell, *Collected Writings*, 4:536.
[8] Thornwell, *Collected Writings*, 4:538.
[9] Thornwell, *Collected Writings*, 4:540.

duty to our slaves?' He criticized the modern 'scientific' studies that promoted the view of different origins for the races. 'No Christian man,' he said, 'can give any countenance to speculations which trace the negro to any other parent but Adam . . . Let us not repudiate our kindred with the poor brethren whom [God] has scattered among us, and entrusted to our guardianship and care. Let us receive them as bone of our bone, and flesh of our flesh. Let us recognize them as having the same Father, the same Redeemer, and the same everlasting destiny.'[10] Thornwell appealed to his congregation in these words: 'Our slaves are a solemn trust, and while we have a right to use and direct their labour, we are bound to feed, clothe and protect them, to give them the comforts of this life, and to introduce them to the hopes of a blessed immortality.'[11] The long sermon was nearly over. The preacher closed by reminding the South Carolinians that 'our State may suffer; she may suffer grievously; she may suffer long.'[12]

On November 29, 1860, a few days after Thornwell delivered his 'Sermon on National Sins,' his friend Benjamin Morgan Palmer preached a 'Thanksgiving Sermon' in New Orleans. Henry Alexander White describes the scene:

> A great multitude of people came together in Dr. Palmer's church, crowding it from floor to gallery, to hear what counsel he might be prepared to offer to New Orleans and Louisiana . . . A solemn stillness reigned in the vast auditorium, when the speaker arose to face the audience. His discourse was written and, contrary to his usual custom, he read it—read it calmly and slowly, without the use of a gesture during the hour of its delivery.[13]

[10] Thornwell, *Collected Writings*, 4:542-43.
[11] Thornwell, *Collected Writings*, 4:542, 544.
[12] Thornwell, *Collected Writings*, 4:547.
[13] White, *Southern Presbyterian Leaders*, p. 366.

That sermon, it was said, did much to persuade the city of New Orleans and the entire state of Louisiana to the side of Secession and the Confederacy. Thomas Cary Johnson wrote that 'the time came when the wisdom of his course in preaching that sermon seemed less apparent [to Dr. Palmer]; indeed, he is said to have repented preaching the discourse.'[14]

South Carolina seceded from the Union on December 20, 1860, and other Southern states quickly followed. On February 4, 1861, the Constitution of the Confederate States of America was signed and Jefferson Davis chosen as president. In the April 1861 issue of the *Southern Presbyterian Review,* Benjamin Morgan Palmer defended Secession. The idea of withdrawal from the Union was not so novel as many believed, he stated, pointing out that the New England states had threatened Secession in their Hartford Convention. Palmer wrote that while some affirm 'the people to be one, divided into many: we, that they are many, united into one. [They] ascribe sovereignty to the Union: we, to the States. [They] regard the Constitution as creating a government which is over the States: we regard it as a common law established between the States.'

At 4:30 A.M. on April 12, 1861, Confederate guns opened fire on Fort Sumter in Charleston harbor. The Federal fort surrendered the next day. President Lincoln called for 75,000 volunteers to put down the rebellion.

Early in May, with war imminent, Columbia Seminary closed. There were sixty-two students in the seminary—a considerable number from the North, 'highly esteemed by their associates,' according to Dr. Howe. While the Northern students left sadly to return home, most of the Southerners

[14] Wells, *Southern Presbyterian Worthies,* p. 176.

joined the Confederate army, painfully aware that they might soon face their former classmates in a clash of arms. John A. Witherspoon, nephew of Dr. Thornwell and a young man of brilliant promise, fell in the first battle of Manassas. Another Columbia student, Samuel P. Wier, lost his life at Fredericksburg.

* * * * *

In May 1861, the General Assembly of the Presbyterian Church met in Philadelphia. After twelve days and much debate, the Gardiner Spring Resolutions passed with a vote of 156 to 66. The resolutions denounced Secession as an act of treason and called on Presbyterians to do all in their power to 'strengthen, uphold, and encourage the Federal government.' Dr. Charles Hodge of Princeton Seminary (and fifty-seven others) protested the resolutions, arguing that they made a political question a condition of membership in the church—thus violating the constitution of the church and usurping 'the prerogative of its Divine Master.' There was already strong sentiment for a separate Presbyterian church in the South, and the Spring Resolutions caused greater urgency. Delegates appointed by every presbytery in the seceding states convened in Atlanta on August 15. They planned for the meeting of the first Southern General Assembly; it was to be held in Augusta, Georgia—a place 'central, retired,' and 'near to South Carolina,' according to the Proceedings of the convention.

A few days after James Woodrow had given his inaugural address and joined the Columbia Seminary faculty, in December 1861 the first General Assembly of the Southern Presbyterian Church convened at the First Presbyterian Church in Augusta. Fifty-five ministers and thirty-eight ruling elders from all forty-seven presbyteries of the ten Southern synods presented their credentials and were enrolled as commissioners to the General Assembly. Of the ministers, thirteen were alumni of Columbia Seminary.

The assembly was called to order on Wednesday, December 4, and Benjamin Morgan Palmer, pastor of the First Presbyterian Church of New Orleans, preached the opening sermon on 'the supreme dominion to which Christ is exalted as the Head of the Church.' Palmer asked the question 'Do we understand, Fathers and Brethren, the mission of the Church given us here to execute?' He answered: 'It is to lift up throughout the world the testimony for the headship of Christ.' 'This Parliament of the Lord's freemen,' said Palmer, 'solemnly declares that, by the terms of her great charter, none but Jesus may be King in Zion. Once more in this distant age and in these ends of the earth, the Church must declare for the supremacy of her Head, and fling out the consecrated ensign with the old inscription, "for Christ and his crown".'

Dr. Palmer, former professor at Columbia Seminary, was elected moderator; and Dr. Joseph R. Wilson, soon to become a professor there, was chosen as permanent clerk. 'The Assembly began its work,' wrote John Wells, 'with quiet dignity by declaring that the work of preaching the gospel in all the world is the chief work of the Southern Presbyterian Church.'[15]

Columbia Seminary graduate John Leighton Wilson, a pioneer missionary in West Africa, challenged the Southern Church not to forget its missionary responsibility. He urged the church to continue its mission to the Indian tribes, which 'in the providence of God have been thrown upon the care of

[15] Wells, *Southern Presbyterian Worthies*, p. 156.

the Southern church.' Led by Wilson, the General Assembly stated that it desired

> distinctly and deliberately to inscribe on our church's banner as she now unfurls it to the world Christ's last command: 'Go ye into all the world and preach the gospel to every creature'; regarding this as the great end of her organization, and obedience to it as the indispensable condition of her Lord's promised presence.

John Leighton Wilson had gathered a group of ministers and elders in Columbia in the spring of 1861 to direct the church's missionary work until the General Assembly could meet. In October he went to meet the missionaries and native Christians at the Presbyterian mission stations in 'the Indian country, of which there was one among the Cherokees, another among the Creeks, and another among the Choctaws and Chickasaws.'[16] At the General Assembly in December Wilson was elected Secretary of Foreign Missions. On the committee were professors Thornwell, Howe, and Adger of the seminary faculty, two seminary alumni, and a group of Columbia elders most closely connected with the seminary. Wilson chose Columbia for the location of the missions committee, and for many years the work was centred there in the home of James Woodrow, who was elected treasurer. A daughter of Dr. and Mrs. Woodrow remembered fondly that Dr. Wilson was 'one of the first and dearest friends' that she had as a child, 'for he was always so kind to children. We welcomed the time[s] when he came to our home in Columbia to attend the meeting of the Committee of Foreign Missions, for he had a great store of amusing anecdotes that he was always willing to tell us.'[17]

[16] *Memorial Volume,* p. 158.

[17] DuBose, *Wilson,* p. 294.

In 1863 the work of domestic missions was given to Wilson, as well as the task of evangelizing the army. Near the close of the war, Wilson was present with the Confederate troops near Petersburg, Virginia. One windy day in March, according to Robert Lewis Dabney, Wilson preached to a South Carolina regiment in the trenches and even administered the Lord's Supper 'under a dropping picket fire.' The day following, Wilson met with General Robert E. Lee 'concerning the spiritual wants of the army.'[18]

At the first General Assembly, former Columbia Seminary professor Charles Colcock Jones gave an address on the important work of the evangelization of the slaves, the cause to which he had devoted his life. Crippled by 'wasting palsy,' Jones sat on a high stool behind the pulpit and, for an hour and a half, held the large audience spellbound. The Negroes, he said, 'are not enemies, but friends; they are not foreigners, but our nearest neighbors. They are our constant and inseparable associates; whither we go, they go; where we dwell, they dwell; where we die and are buried, there they die and are buried; and more than all, our God is their God.' Jones urged pastors 'as good shepherds,' to follow black people 'into the highways and hedges, into their plantations and into their sick chambers, attend their funerals, and follow them to their graves.' Jones's address, one hearer stated, was 'simple in language, interesting in the facts related, and powerful in its appeal.' The General Assembly was cheered by reports of success in ministry to the blacks. 'In having received so many of the sons and daughters of Africa into our communion,' the 'Narrative on the State of Religion' asserted, 'we have cause of devout thankfulness to our gracious Lord.'

[18] White, *Southern Presbyterian Leaders,* p. 405.

The great moment of the General Assembly came on the eleventh day, December 14, when Columbia Seminary professor of theology, James Henley Thornwell, presented the 'Address by the General Assembly to the Churches of Jesus Christ throughout the Earth,' setting forth the reasons for forming the new Southern Presbyterian denomination. Dressed in a black swallow-tailed coat and high-heeled boots, the gravely ill Thornwell began to read his address. Joseph Ruggles Wilson described the scene:

> The [church] was thronged—galleries and floor. Dr. Thornwell occupied a small space in front of the pulpit, and so near as to gain from its framework a partial support, for even now he felt the approach of fatal disease. Every eye was upon him, and every sound was hushed as by a spell, while for forty historic minutes this Calvin of the modern church poured forth such a stream of elevated utterance as he of Geneva never surpassed.

'We have separated from our brethren of the North,' read Dr. Thornwell, 'as Abraham separated from Lot—because we are persuaded that the interests of true religion will be more effectually subserved by two independent churches, under the circumstances in which the two churches are placed, than by one united body.' He explained: 'To proclaim God's truth as a witness to the nations; to gather His elect from the four corners of the earth, and through the Word, Ministries, and Ordinances to train them for eternal life, is the great business of His people.' Thornwell concluded:

> Brethren, we have done. We have told you who we are, and what we are. We greet you in the ties of Christian brotherhood. We desire to cultivate peace and charity with all our fellow Christians throughout the world. We invite to ecclesiastical communion all who maintain our principles of

faith and order. And now we commend you to God and the Word of His grace.

Benjamin Morgan Palmer, in his *Life of Thornwell,* described the solemn moment when the 'Address' was adopted by the assembly:

> Read, and read again, amid the solemn stillness of an audience whose emotions were hushed with awe, it was finally adopted and laid upon the moderator's table; when, one by one, the members came silently forward and signed their names. We were carried back to those stirring times in Scottish story, when the Solemn League and Covenant was spread upon the gravestone in the Grey Friar's churchyard, and Christian heroes pricked their veins, that with real blood they might sign their allegiance to the kingdom and crown of Jesus Christ, their Lord and Head.

On December 16 the assembly was dismissed. Closing devotional services were held after the reading of the minutes. Joseph Wilson commented that testimony, 'written and oral, bears witness to the fact that the sessions of that Assembly were marked by rare calmness and dignity and by the absence of rancor and bitterness.' C. C. Jones wrote, 'We were laying foundations which, by God's blessing, we hoped would endure for ages, and prove a blessing to our country and to the world.'

* * * * *

A few months later, on March 16, 1862, C. C. Jones died at Arcadia, one of his plantation homes in Georgia. Four days before his death he wrote in his journal, 'My disease seems to be drawing to a conclusion. May the Lord make me to say in that hour, in saving faith and love, "Into thy hands I commit my spirit: thou hast redeemed me, O Lord God of truth."'[19] The night he died Mary wrote in her journal that 'his death, it was not death, it was gently going away, passing into the heavenly light.'[20]

Many years later William Childs Robinson summed up the life and ministry of this 'apostle to the slaves' in a brief article in the *Southern Presbyterian Journal*. Robinson wrote:

> Dr. Charles C. Jones is best known for his great missionary services to the negro slaves of Liberty County, Georgia. Most of his preaching years were given gratuitously to them. For some months he was pastor of the First Presbyterian Church in Savannah, twice he served as professor of Ecclesiastical History and Church Polity in Columbia, once as Secretary of the Board of Home Missions of the undivided church. But none of these positions were able to hold him long away from the chosen preaching to the hundreds of negroes who needed the Gospel. On the day of his death Mrs. Jones spoke to him of the Saviour being present with him. Dr. Jones replied: 'I am nothing but a poor sinner. I renounce myself and all self-justification, trusting only in the free unmerited righteousness of the Lord Jesus Christ.'

* * * * *

A few months later, at noon on August 1, 1862, James Henley Thornwell died of 'typhoid pneumonia' in the home of friends in Charlotte, North Carolina. His wife, a daughter, a son, two friends—John Douglas and John Adger—were there. During his final hours, he seemed to be dreaming that he was in his classroom at the seminary. Once he uttered a

[19] *Memorial Volume*, p. 201.
[20] *Memorial Volume*, p. 188.

statement about the divine attributes. He said, 'Well, you have stated your position, now prove it.' Toward the end he exclaimed, 'Wonderful! wonderful! nothing but space—Expanse! Expanse! Expanse!'[21] Thornwell's body was brought to Columbia. His funeral service was held at First Presbyterian Church, 'where he had so long proclaimed the gospel of his Lord, in the presence of an immense multitude, who had assembled to pay last homage to greatness and to goodness.' Dr. Adger preached, taking as his text Genesis 18:25, 'Shall not the Judge of all the earth do right?' It was, he said, the 'watchword' of Dr. Thornwell.

Dr. Palmer wrote:

> As the long procession moved through the streets of that beautiful town, to the resting-place of the dead, the city bell tolled its solemn and plaintive notes, expressive of the public and the common grief. In the family enclosure in Elmwood cemetery, the precious dust was committed to the earth, by the side of the loved daughter, who, but three years before, was laid to rest. There, in a quiet and beautiful spot, by the banks of a soft murmuring stream, the stranger will find a solid block of pure white Italian marble, upon whose face he will read only this inscription, in bold relief, 'JAMES HENLEY THORNWELL.'[22]

That, to his friends, seemed to be all that needed to be said.

On September 17, Dr. Palmer preached a memorial sermon at First Church for his mentor and friend. 'Our Chrysostom is no more!' he said. 'The "Golden Mouth" is sealed up in silence forever!'[23]

[21] Palmer, *Thornwell*, pp. 523-24.
[22] Palmer, *Thornwell*, pp. 524-25.
[23] Johnson, *Palmer*, p. 266.

The October issue of the *Southern Presbyterian Review* contained an article on the 'Life, Character, and Genius of the Late Rev. James H. Thornwell' by Dr. Palmer. The editors had hoped, they stated in this issue, to include a portrait of Dr. Thornwell, but since it was not finished, it was promised for the January 1863 issue.[24] It was still not ready in January because the federal blockade of Southern ports prevented the engravers' from receiving 'some necessary materials, which they confidently expected from abroad.' Dr. Palmer's substantial volume on *The Life and Letters of James Henley Thornwell* was published in 1875 to the delight of Thornwell's friends and students. William Plumer Jacobs wrote in his diary:

> I am reading with great interest Palmer's life of Thornwell. The name that I have given to this Orphanage [in Clinton, South Carolina] is a sufficient testimony to the esteem of my soul for this great man. I thank God that he was both instructor and friend.[25]

Twenty years after Thornwell's death, John Adger declared:

> How often his name . . . is named in our Church courts and Church papers. What Thornwell held, what Thornwell said, is always felt to be a most potent argument for or against any debatable position. As long as our Church lives, James Henley Thornwell will live in our hearts and his name dwell on our lips.[26]

John Leith writes that Thornwell's 'influence was domi-

[24] B. M. Palmer, 'Life, Character, and Genius of the Late Rev. James Henley Thornwell,' *Southern Presbyterian Review* (October 1862), p. 255.

[25] Thornwell Jacobs, ed., *Diary of William Plumer Jacobs* (Oglethorpe University, Ga.: Oglethorpe University Press, 1937), p. 179.

[26] *Memorial Volume*, p. 188.

nant in the Southern Presbyterian Church for eighty years after his death.'[27] In 1912 the Synod of South Carolina celebrated the centennial of James Henley Thornwell's birth, because of 'his most eminent service to our Church in defining her theological views and in expounding, organizing, and applying her ecclesiastical polity.'[28]

[27] Leith, *Probing the Reformed Tradition*, p. 444.

[28] *Centennial Addresses, Delivered before the Synod of South Carolina in the First Presbyterian Church, Columbia, October 23, 24, 1912, Commemorating the birth of the Reverend James Henley Thornwell* (Spartanburg, S.C.: Synod of South Carolina), p. 3.

15

THE WAR BETWEEN THE STATES

COLUMBIA was mobilized for the Confederate cause. Virtually all of the students at South Carolina College volunteered for military service, and in 1862 the college was closed and the buildings used for a Confederate hospital. When New Orleans fell to Commodore David G. Farragut's fleet toward the end of April 1862, Dr. Palmer—looked upon by Union soldiers as a fomenter of treason—was away from the city. Warned by friends not to return, he met his family in Hazelhurst, Mississippi, and travelled with them to Columbia, where they lived with Mrs. Palmer's mother and stepfather, Dr. and Mrs. George Howe. Dr. Palmer served as a chaplain to Confederate troops. He was with Albert Sidney Johnson before the Battle of Shiloh and later preached to the Army of Tennessee. When in Columbia, he preached at First Presbyterian Church and at a mission church two miles from town, and taught the few students who were left in the seminary.

One of those was William Plumer Jacobs, who entered the seminary in the fall of 1861. The young Charlestonian had prepared himself for seminary studies by translating the Shorter Catechism into Greek, German, and Latin! After an examination on 'personal piety,' Jacobs was admitted to the seminary. His diary for October 26, 1861, describes his seminary work.

> My day's exercises now consist in getting up at six immediately after which I read the Bible in Latin, Greek and German. Read some in Hall's *Meditations*. Prayers at seven, breakfast at seven-thirty. Write this journal—review Hebrew. Recitations at nine, ten and sometimes at eleven. Dinner at one. Recitations and reading until five. Prayers. After supper if not in chapel or visiting I generally sit down to do nothing but think or debate with some of the brethren till bedtime.[1]

Jacobs' first sermon before the faculty was, in his view (and in theirs!), a rather poor attempt at preaching. He promised himself (and them) that he would do better. Later the determined Jacobs preached, he thought, 'fluently and without notes' in the seminary chapel. The faculty, however, still had some criticisms. Jacobs wrote in his diary:

> Dr. Howe criticizes me for too much vim. Dr. Adger for unpleasantly accenting the first word of every sentence and for too much nervousness. Dr. Woodrow for hyperbole. These faults are very grave and I will try to correct them, though I can't but think that my 'hyperbole' as quoted by Dr. Woodrow was literally and exactly true.[2]

Jacobs was invited to preach on November 3, 1861, in a mission church at Tekoa, a little town north of Columbia. By mistake he got on a train in Columbia that was going straight through to Charlotte, forcing the young preacher to jump off, 'flying squirrel fashion,' at the town where he was to preach. He dusted himself off and walked to the little church, where he preached to the congregation of twenty on the verse 'Jesus wept, and the Jews said, Behold how he loved him.'[3]

[1] Jacobs, *Diary of William Plumer Jacobs,* pp. 84-85.

[2] Jacobs, *Diary of William Plumer Jacobs,* p. 104.

[3] Jacobs, *Diary of William Plumer Jacobs,* pp. 85-86. The first sermon Jacobs preached in Clinton was on the same text. Many years later, July 14, 1912, he wrote

William Jacobs, who had worked successfully as a newspaper reporter, was sent by Dr. Adger to the December General Assembly in Augusta to write about the assembly for Adger's *Southern Presbyterian*. Jacobs followed carefully the course of the assembly and assisted Dr. Wilson in his work as clerk. The awe-struck young man wrote in his diary for Sunday, December 15, 'Dr. Palmer is beautiful. Dr. Thornwell is strong. Dr. Palmer is polished. Dr. Thornwell, wonderfully earnest. Dr. Palmer is refined in thought. Dr. Thornwell is broad, deep, clear.'[4] At the end of the fateful year of 1861, Jacobs wrote, 'In this year I have gained rich experience in life—have passed through one of the most eventful periods in the history of the country. I have seen stars fall one by one from the flag of the once glorious United States. A new nation has arisen upon the earth, the Confederate States of America, and I am a citizen of it—proud indeed of the honor.'

When he was sixteen years old, Jacobs, the son of a slaveholder, had written in his diary, 'I have come to the conclusion that slavery at best is a diabolical practice.' Almost a year later he wrote, 'I was awfully a secessionist but now I am a strong unionist. I would not see one quill plucked from the wing of that proud bird which is emblazoned over our Senate hall.' But 'when his state seceded and battle came with the customary stories of horrible atrocities,' Jacobs followed the new flag with 'his heart and prayers.'

On March 12, 1862, Jacobs wrote that the 'whole seminary for the past week has been in a perfect Babel of

in his diary: 'Just fifty years ago this day I preached my first sermon in Clinton. Moreover it was the first sermon I had ever written. I was twenty years old but not licensed. Today I preach it over to a little audience in the Thornwell Memorial. I have never preached it since June 13th, 1862. Jesus wept, and the Jews said, Behold, how he loved him' (pp. 435-36).

[4] Jacobs, *Diary of William Plumer Jacobs,* p. 87.

Confusion—there has been no studying.' While the faculty debated whether or not to close the seminary, the students waited anxiously to know what they should do. Some left to become chaplains or soldiers. Jacobs stayed on, and in looking back over the term, the nineteen-year-old seminary student thought that he had made 'considerable progress.' He wrote:

> I have gained a pretty good knowledge of Hebrew and some of Chaldee and Syriac (though very slight). I have read through the New Testament both in Greek and Latin. I have got a critical knowledge of much of the four gospels and the first epistle to Timothy. I have read many of the Psalms and the book of Joshua (in my private study) in Hebrew. I have written four sermons, have gained much knowledge of our church government and of theology. Have got a more comprehensive view of the plan of salvation. I have read several German books—have written a good deal for the press . . . I trust, too, that I have learned something of practical experimental piety.[5]

At the close of the spring term of 1862, Dr. Thornwell had said to the young seminary student, 'Good-bye, Brother Jacobs. May God bless you and take care of you.'[6] Jacobs always prized those words 'as the blessing of the greatest man' he ever knew. During the summer Jacobs preached in Upcountry churches. He wrote after one sermon, 'I preached with earnestness and I trust that I succeeded in overcoming the feeling of "Is this not great Babylon that I have built", which often afflicts the minister. I lost sight of self and caught sight of Christ. Invariably will the minister find this to be true—first, lose yourself; second, find Christ.'

[5] Jacobs, *Diary of William Plumer Jacobs*, pp. 92-93.
[6] Jacobs, *Diary of William Plumer Jacobs*, p. 98.

When William Jacobs returned to the seminary in the fall he found to his dismay that everything had changed. His friends were gone to join the army—'the lively, merry Cozby and Banks and Otts are gone. Witty brother Cleveland, with his songs and tales, gone. Green, McKinnon, Law gone, gone, all gone. Only one or two left.' But Dr. Adger was there and 'good old Dr. Howe.' It was a sad term, but Jacobs was thankful. 'I have a little fire to sit by,' he wrote, 'and books to read, and I know where my food is coming from for three months. For all this I thank God.'[7]

On September 17, 1862, Benjamin Morgan Palmer gave an address in memory of Dr. Thornwell at First Presbyterian Church. William Plumer Jacobs was present in the 'jammed' church. Palmer's closing words, Jacobs wrote, 'led us up through the shining gates of heaven and showed us . . . Thornwell in immortal converse with Beza and Calvin and Luther, with the thousands of thousands that sit about the throne.'[8]

In 1863 Dr. Palmer was elected to fill the chair of didactic and polemic theology at Columbia Seminary, sadly vacated by Dr. Thornwell's death. For the several sessions he taught theology at the seminary, he followed Thornwell's plan from 'the beginning to the application of the scheme of redemption.' The students read Calvin's *Institutes*, selections from Turretin, Hill, Dick, and A. A. Hodge's *Outline of Theology*. Hodge, said Palmer, was especially helpful 'in mapping out the special topics for investigation.'[9] William Jacobs later wrote: 'Dr. Palmer was my tutor for two years. I say tutor for I was his sole pupil in the Senior class. I loved him truly.'[10]

[7] Thornwell Jacobs, *The Life of William Plumer Jacobs* (New York: Fleming H. Revell Co., 1918), pp. 44-65.

[8] Jacobs, *Diary of William Plumer Jacobs*, p. 102.

[9] Johnson, *Palmer*, p. 272.

[10] Jacobs, *Diary of William Plumer Jacobs*, p. 179.

* * * * *

Many of the Columbia Seminary students joined the Confederate army, including John Leighton Wilson's nephew Leighton B. Wilson, who died from battlefield exposure. Sixteen-year-old Gillespie Thornwell, son of James Henley Thornwell, was wounded by a sabre thrust in Virginia on May 3, 1862. Gillespie returned to duty, and was wounded again, dying a day later.

Harmony Presbytery chose five of its ministers, all Columbia Seminary graduates, to serve as chaplains. Fifteen men from the seminary spent at least some time preaching to the Confederate troops and ministering to them in sickness and death.

Charlton H. Wilson, another nephew of Dr. John Leighton Wilson, graduated from Columbia Seminary in 1855. He ably served for four years as a missionary to Native Americans, pastored two churches in the Pee Dee Valley of South Carolina, and joined the Confederate army as chaplain and infantry soldier. He was wounded and died in Richmond, Virginia, on June 4, 1864. His last sermon was delivered to the Confederate cavalry from the words 'So teach us to number our days that we may apply our hearts unto wisdom.' One of the saddest duties of John Leighton Wilson's life, he said, was preaching Charlton Wilson's memorial service. That sermon, printed on brown Confederate paper because this was the only kind printers in the South could obtain, Hampden DuBose wrote, 'is a precious souvenir' of Charlton Wilson—'the lovely preacher who had held the threefold office of missionary, pastor, and chaplain to the army.'[11]

[11] DuBose, *Wilson,* p. 256. The first missionary sermon that Hampden DuBose heard was preached by Charlton H. Wilson.

Another chaplain from Columbia Seminary was T. R. Markham. He described leading worship and preaching to the troops during the fighting in North Georgia:

> Two or three services were held daily. I did the preaching; and at night, when there was little danger from the firing interchanged between the pickets, ministers who were sent as army missionaries from the different churches conducted the worship. It was a solemn season, a quiet work of grace, the Spirit of God, as 'a still small voice' moving the hearts of men, who, after nightfall, thronged these gatherings. A semi-circle of logs formed our audience room; whose ceiling was a canopy of blue set with night's golden stars. A frame resting in the forks of poles driven in the earth and covered with clay, on which pine knots were piled, was our Astral or Chandelier. Beside this stood the preacher. Our assembling bell was a volume of praise rolling from a half-hundred manly voices.

Seeing Chaplain Markham trudging on foot, an officer requisitioned a horse for him, but Markham refused it, saying, 'I am with my men in the trenches, and I am with the pickets on duty; what do I want with a horse?'[12]

During the war years James Woodrow managed the Medical and Chemical Confederate Laboratory in Columbia. He worked all day in the laboratory, and, with his wife, at night in the seminary chapel, making nitrate of silver for the cauterizing of wounds and peanut oil for food.

John Adger, like many Southerners, was relieved when Emancipation Day, January 1, 1863, came. He told his slaves that they were free (they were glad except for one old man who did not look forward to 'freedom'). James Woodrow

[12] LaMotte, *Colored Light,* pp. 139-40.

wrote to a Northern newspaper that 'we are very glad to have had our responsibilities as Christian slave-holders brought providentially to an end.'[13]

While acknowledging that there were cruel masters, John Adger insisted that Southern slavery helped the Africans by providing them 'the most needful and valuable education for this life, and very many of them for the life to come.' 'The two races were steadily and constantly marching onwards and upwards together,' he maintained. In a prophetic passage for the times, Adger wrote that slavery had helped fit the Africans for the responsibility of voting and given them the ability to become 'statesmen and senators, and, if need be, the presidents of this great republic.'[14]

In 1863 the General Assembly of the Presbyterian Church in the Confederate States of America met in Columbia and received the sad news of Stonewall Jackson's death. The assembly passed an overture that steps be taken 'to bring about a union between the Old and New School Presbyterians in the Confederate States.' Robert Lewis Dabney was appointed chairman of a committee to determine if such a union was possible and desirable. The debate in the next assembly was led by Dabney on the side of union, with Adger and Palmer against union. The assembly voted overwhelmingly to proceed with the union with New School Presbyterians in the South. Union with the Associate Reformed Presbyterian Church was declined by that denomination, but its Alabama and Kentucky presbyteries joined the Southern Presbyterian Church by 1869.

In 1864 the directors of Columbia Seminary moved to transfer control of the seminary to the General Assembly of

[13] Gustafson, *Woodrow,* p. 98.
[14] Adger, *My Life and Times,* p. 163.

the Presbyterian Church in the United States, which in effect would make Columbia the 'national' seminary of the Southern Church, as Princeton was in the North. Union Seminary's Robert Lewis Dabney argued that it was better to continue synodical control, which, he believed, would assist in preserving the church's orthodoxy.[15] The Columbia directors cancelled the usual examinations for graduating students of the class of 1864—only two, J. S. Arbuthnot and William Plumer Jacobs. Jacobs was grieving over the loss of his brother, Pressley, who fell at Gettysburg on July 2, 1863. He was saddened by the condition of the seminary—that 'war-stricken school of the prophets'— and by the desolation of South Carolina and the South. He wrote, 'I will call nothing mine but God, no man master but God, no place home but heaven, remembering that all is momentary that delights us and all is momentary that afflicts. All that is not eternal is nothing.'[16]

On May 27, 1864, Jacobs was ordained and left the seminary for pastoral ministry in Clinton, South Carolina. 'A tear was in Dr. Howe's eye as he bade me farewell,' Jacobs wrote. '"May the divine blessing go with you brother Jacobs", said Dr. Woodrow. "Remember always when you come to Columbia that my house is your home!"'[17]

The *Southern Presbyterian Review* was in desperate need of paper, which had increased in cost more than five times in less than two years. The Bath Paper Mills near Augusta, Georgia, donated some very fine stock worth $1,500. 'This generous and timely liberality,' the editors wrote, 'will go far towards securing the regular publication of the *Review* during the next twelve months; which has been rendered so doubtful

[15] See Lucas, *Dabney*, pp. 79-80.

[16] Jacobs, *William Plumer Jacobs*, pp. 67-68.

[17] Jacobs, *Diary of William Plumer Jacobs*, p. 111.

by the high prices of all things, by the cutting off of many of our subscribers by the advance of the enemy's lines, and especially by the forgetfulness of a majority of our subscribers to pay their dues.' The *Southern Presbyterian Review,* however, continued to have wide appeal throughout the areas of the South to which it could still be mailed. In the April 1863 issue, the editors noted that during the last six months so many new subscribers had been added 'that there are at this time as many subscribers within our reach as before the contraction of our lines by the advance of the enemy in the West.'[18]

Articles related to the war by no means dominated the *Review*. The January 1862 issue carried an essay on 'The Art of Conversation' by Benjamin Morgan Palmer. War or no war, Dr. Palmer wanted to make sure that Southern Presbyterians knew how to talk properly! In the January and April 1863 issues Joseph LeConte, professor of natural science at South Carolina College, presented articles 'On the Nature and Uses of Art.' The April issue also contained an article on 'Geology and its Assailants,' in which the brilliant young Columbia Seminary professor, James Woodrow, defended the new science of geology against a variety of opponents.

The War between the States dragged on, with increasingly alarming results for the South. The year 1865 began with a gigantic bazaar at the State House—a three-day extravaganza for the benefit of Confederate hospitals. Because trade was paralyzed by the Federal blockade at the coast, Columbia's warehouses, basements, and many buildings were bursting with cotton. The city's pre-war population had swollen to more than 25,000—half white, half black. A prisoner-of-war camp inside the city limits held some 1,200 Federal soldiers.

[18] *Southern Presbyterian Review* (April 1863). Inside cover.

During January and early February, General Sherman's army marched from Savannah through South Carolina. The right wing feinted toward Charleston and the left wing toward Augusta, freezing the defenders around those cities. When both wings crossed the Edisto River, it became apparent that the whole army was coming to Columbia. On Thursday, February 16, the Federals reached the west bank of the Congaree River, overlooking the city. Confederate soldiers had burned all the bridges into the city, but Union engineers needed only twenty-four hours to build a pontoon bridge, and Sherman's army of 62,000 poured into Columbia.

The next morning—February 17, 1865—General Wade Hampton, who had been ordered home from Virginia to help with his state's defences, realized that resistance was hopeless and advised Columbia's mayor to surrender. With great sadness, Hampton turned his horse eastward and rode slowly out of his beloved city and away from his beautiful home—soon to be torched by Northern soldiers. By sundown, fires were burning all over Columbia.[19] While some Federal soldiers pitched in to try to put them out, others smashed fire engines and cut the hoses. A large fire near the City Hall lit the sky; a block away flames flew up from the offices of the Southern Express Company. Buildings downwind of burning cotton bales ignited, starting fires everywhere. By midnight, a single fire was burning over an area nine blocks long by four blocks

[19] This description of the fire is from Theodore Rosengarten, 'New Views on the Burning of Columbia,' in *The University of South Caroliniana Society Fifty-seventh Annual Meeting, May 21, 1993*, p. 12. The most recent detailed analysis of the fire is found in a book by Marion Brunson Lucas, *Sherman and the Burning of Columbia* (College Station, Tex.: Texas A&M University Press, 1976). See also Chapter one, 'The Destruction of Columbia,' in Charles Royster, *The Destructive War: William Tecumseh Sherman, Stonewall Jackson, and the Americans* (New York: Alfred A. Knopf, 1991).

wide. Witnesses compared the drone of the wind-driven blaze to the noise of a waterfall. Liquor flowed freely as the fire whipped out of control. One Union soldier wrote, 'It is the biggest drunk and the greatest fire I ever heard of.' A modern historian describes the scene:

> No one knew which way was safe. The crowds in the streets—white women and children, a few older white men, and black people of all ages—milled in different directions, at cross purposes, trying to safeguard possessions. Hundreds of yelling, smoky-faced young soldiers were enjoying themselves. They snatched bundles and blankets, stole or broke valuables, made jokes, and celebrated their revenge on South Carolinians.[20]

Known to the Union soldiers as 'the eloquent and violent divine,' Dr. Palmer was not safe in the city.[21] Urged by his family and friends, he reluctantly departed with the retreating Confederate soldiers. At two o'clock in the morning, Benjamin Morgan Palmer's wife and children were told to leave their house in Columbia because a factory nearby was to be blown up. Carrying bundles of clothes and bedding, Palmer's family made their way among burning buildings and trees to the house of Dr. and Mrs. Howe, Mary Augusta Palmer's mother and stepfather. When fire was set to the Howe's home, the extended family spent the rest of the night in the streets, huddled together around the few possessions they had saved.

As Sherman's army was approaching the city, James Woodrow packed up his laboratory equipment and took it

[20] Royster, *The Destructive War,* p. 22.

[21] *A Columbia Reader,* p. 61. In the fall of 1866, Dr. Palmer preached in Dr. Henry Van Dyke's church in New York City. A veteran of the Union Army asked who the wonderful preacher was. When he learned that he was Benjamin Morgan Palmer of New Orleans, he exclaimed, 'The archrebel of that name! He preaches like an archangel!' Johnson, *Palmer,* p. 295.

away from Columbia. His family stayed behind; Woodrow believed they would be safer in Columbia than with him, if he should be caught transporting the equipment. Woodrow did not think that the Union soldiers would burn private homes, but he was sorely mistaken. Five times Mrs. Woodrow extinguished fires set to her home that night!

Elder Andrew Crawford, whose house was across from First Presbyterian Church, on the northwest corner of Marion and Lady streets, had charge of the church's Communion silver. He and his sister worked for several nights removing one of the flagstones that formed the floor of the basement, dug a hole for a box containing the silver goblets and plates, replaced the stone, and moved a heavy piece of furniture over the spot. Crawford then quickly took the bonds and securities of Columbia Seminary, of which he was treasurer, and departed on the train for Chester. There he turned over the documents to the Rev. John Douglas, who buried them at midnight in his corn field. When Mr Crawford's house was burned in Columbia, the church's Communion silver, though blackened from the heat, was saved.

Seventy-year-old Agnes Law lived near Arsenal Hill in a three-story brick house with a slate roof and large gardens. She was home with her sister and her niece when Sherman took charge of the city. Four guards were assigned to the Law house, apparently well-behaved and sober men. Mrs. Law gave them supper, but when the city began to burn, the soldiers took lighted candles from the mantelpiece and set the curtains in the upstairs rooms on fire. The women fled through the burning city to a friend's house, where they spent the night. A few days later, Mrs. Law 'was found in the corner of her garden under a miserable extemporized shelter.' She was taken to the seminary, where she was cared for during the short time before her death.

Mrs. Aaron Leland was sitting in her dining room with her husband—now an invalid—the night the city was burned.[22] A soldier burst into the house and, rushing to the sideboard, grabbed a glass decanter. Clara Leland attempted to take it from him. As they struggled, they were startled to hear the authoritative voice of a Union officer demanding, 'How dare you attack a lady?' The soldier answered in his own defence, 'But she cussed me, sir, she cussed me!' The officer arrested the soldier and placed a guard at the home. When asked later what exactly it was that she had said to the soldier, Mrs. Leland, a cultured English lady, always replied, 'I will not tell you. I did not know I knew such words.'[23]

By six o'clock in the morning of February 18 the wind had shifted and died, and the fire was at last contained. On that mild, sunny day smoke rose from the rubble; occasionally a wall or chimney crashed. A large part of the city consisted only of brick shells, blackened columns, and smoldering ruins, facing streets lined with bare, blistered trees. Four hundred buildings had burned to the ground, including the State House. 'The ancient homesteads where have gathered sacred associations, the heritages of many generations are swept away,' wrote one of Sherman's aides-de-camp.[24]

Dr. Palmer, with two companions, walked the sixty miles from York to Columbia, following the torn-up railway. The three friends, sustained by cornbread and 'some fine time-cured Madeira wine,' made their way south, stopping to

[22] After the death of his first wife, Dr. Leland married Clara Blight, a native of England, in 1859. He was incapacitated by a stroke in October 1863.

[23] Gist, *Presbyterian Women,* p. 301.

[24] *A Columbia Reader,* p. 63.

spend the Sabbath at Winnsboro, where Palmer preached.[25]

Dr. Palmer took up his ministry to the brokenhearted city, driving wagons into the country to find food for starving people and preaching at First Presbyterian Church. Friends attempted to persuade Palmer to continue as pastor of the church, but he was constrained to return to his people in New Orleans, as he wrote, to 'gather up the fragments of our scattered congregation, and to share with them the poverty to which we will be reduced together.'[26] He went back to New Orleans, where he preached to the people of his church and the city. 'He seemed . . . to be more chastened and subdued than he ever was before,' wrote John Wells. 'With a humbler hope he looked up to the bow of promise which spanned the sky, and with gentler persuasion he called for renewal of the covenant of grace.'[27] For the next thirty-seven years Palmer preached the gospel in New Orleans, cared for the sick and dying during epidemics of yellow fever, and served as the pastor not only of the Presbyterian church but—more and more—of the whole city.

In Columbia, Washington Street Methodist and Ebenezer Lutheran churches were destroyed by the fire. First Baptist Church escaped, as did First Presbyterian Church, although the Presbyterian Sunday school building on Sumter Street was burned.[28] The Communion plate was taken from Trinity Episcopal Church, and its rectory and Sunday school building

[25] Johnson, *Palmer,* p. 287.

[26] Johnson, *Palmer,* p. 279.

[27] Wells, *Southern Presbyterian Worthies,* p. 158.

[28] According to local lore, Sherman's soldiers were determined to destroy the Baptist church because it was the first site of the 'rebel convention.' They were prevented from doing so, however, by the loyalty of the Negro sexton, who deliberately misled them by pointing to the old Baptist frame building on the corner. Other accounts state that the sexton sent the troops to Washington Street Methodist Church, which was soon in flames!

were destroyed. The Columbia Seminary buildings escaped the fire, but the downfall of the Confederacy destroyed the seminary's resources. Thousands of dollars invested in Confederate bonds were lost. People were impoverished and could do little to help.

16

'STREAMS IN THE DESERT'

THE year 1865 was a time of disaster for the South. Her capital had fallen, her armies surrendered, and her land was plundered. The mood of Congress was retaliatory, and nearly all white Southerners were disenfranchised. The region was divided into military districts and subjected to martial law; the 'Reconstruction Era' had begun. Thomas Cary Johnson, in his biography of Benjamin Morgan Palmer, called these years 'the period of military rule and re-destruction.' Government, characterized largely by corruption and misrule, caused much apprehension and confusion.

Many Columbians were homeless and without protection, wandering about the streets. A number of families quartered for days in the Presbyterian church graveyard. There was little food; coffee was made from okra seeds, cottonseed, or sweet potatoes—cut up, dried, and parched. Often there was neither sugar nor milk. William Boggs, who would soon become pastor of the First Presbyterian Church, remembered seeing two of his cousins picking up kernels of corn left in the fence corners by Sherman's horses and using them to make cornbread. But the people shared what they had with each other, and the widows and orphans were cared for. One woman said, 'I never doubt God takes care of me. On one occasion when I lacked, I earnestly prayed; and upon going into a vacant room, I found food: coffee, sugar, flour. An angel brought it.' Someone hearing this story responded, 'Yes, and old Mrs. Howe was the angel!' 'Uncle John,' the emancipated slave who had refused to leave the John Leighton Wilson homestead, brought a load of provisions fifty miles through the High Hills of the Santee and across the Congaree River, to feed those who had gathered with Dr. Howe in the seminary buildings and who had little or nothing to eat. Uncle John liked to say that he had 'gone through the seminary' with Wilson, referring to Dr. Wilson's sharing with him spiritual truths he had learned at Columbia Seminary, and Wilson loved to praise John's skill in managing two four-horse wagons.[1]

Soldiers returned, but many homes were permanently saddened by the loss of a father, a brother, or a son. Hampden DuBose wrote: 'The fathers had fallen asleep, the generation of young men who had escaped the sword had missed a collegiate career, the theological seminaries were closed, the colleges had lost their endowments, few were left to lead in public prayer, and the songs of Zion were sung by mourning women.'[2]

* * * * *

First Presbyterian Church's session, meeting soon after the destruction of Columbia, began with prayer and the examination of a candidate for church membership. When the subject of choosing delegates to the spring meeting of presbytery was discussed, the minutes reported that no one was appointed 'on account of the destruction by the enemy of the railroads leading from Columbia.' Presbytery's 'narrative,' or annual

[1] DuBose, *Wilson,* pp. 104-5.
[2] DuBose, *Wilson,* p. 257.

report, for 1865 stated that the members of the Presbyterian church in Columbia bore their 'terrible afflictions with patience, fortitude and uncomplaining submission. God has not forsaken them to despair nor given them up to rebellion in the midst of their great distress.'

Charleston Presbytery covered a desolate territory, with a scattered and impoverished membership and a disorganized and weary ministry. The devastation in Columbia was so great that the Synod of South Carolina had to move its meeting place to Salem in Black River, a community church in Sumter County. In 1869 Hampden DuBose spent his first Columbia Seminary vacation supplying two small churches. One had had thirty male members at the beginning of the war, of whom only three were left.

'While many were depressed and despondent,' wrote a Presbyterian minister, 'James Woodrow was buoyant with hope and full of resources and enterprise.'[3] In September 1865, amid the scarred rubble of the city, Dr. Woodrow, with professors Howe and Adger, reopened the seminary and welcomed young men who had just recently left camps and battlefields. 'When this beloved seminary seemed to be so near to temporary extinction,' Woodrow later said, 'I have ever thought with infinite satisfaction that, little as it may have been, I could contribute at least something to the restoration of hope and to the resumption of the exercises of that institution absolutely necessary to the well-being of our Church.'[4]

Dr. Woodrow also resurrected the *Southern Presbyterian,* a newspaper operated by Dr. Adger that had been suspended during the war. Woodrow purchased paper and hauled

[3] Gustafson, *Woodrow,* p. 76.
[4] Gustafson, *Woodrow,* p. 169.

printing machinery from Augusta on a mule-pulled cart. He spent over $13,000 of his own money in supporting this newspaper.

The *Southern Presbyterian Review* survived, despite the fact that between five and six hundred subscribers had paid in advance in Confederate money, now no longer of value, during the later years of the war. The editors stated that they would give full credit for the payments but hoped that these subscribers would see fit not to claim credit beyond the close of the war. Costs for publishing the *Review* between March 1866 and July 1867 exceeded income from subscriptions by over $1,800. The editors were determined, however, to continue to publish the *Review* 'as long as they [had] reason to believe it to be useful to the Church, whether it pays its expenses or not.'[5] Dr. Woodrow contributed about $4,000 to keep the *Review* going and opened a bookstore in Columbia to provide people with Christian literature.

No meeting of the Southern Presbyterian General Assembly could be held in May 1865 because of the 'extremely agitated state of the country.' It was not until December, after the war was over and the Confederacy dissolved, that the assembly convened in Macon, Georgia. Dr. George Howe was elected moderator and presided with grace and dignity. The assembly adopted a new name—The Presbyterian Church in the United States—and made plans for its foreign mission work. 'We can scarcely set up a claim to be regarded as a true branch of the Church of Christ, or take an honorable place in the sisterhood of evangelical churches unless we keep this object constantly and distinctly before our minds,' said Dr. John Leighton Wilson, now in his mid-fifties, six feet or

[5] *Southern Presbyterian Review* (July 1867). Inside front and back covers.

more in height, and massive in proportion, 'reminding one of the Doric order of architecture.'[6] The next year a mission to China was approved, and the first missionary sailed in 1867. Within a few years, Southern Presbyterians were serving in Italy, Colombia, Brazil, Mexico, Greece, and Japan. The General Assembly sent out a pastoral letter to its churches, exhorting Presbyterians to 'obey them that have the rule over you' and reminding them of their duty to the Negroes. 'Debtors before to them when bound,' it stated, 'you are still debtors to them free.'[7] And Presbyterians, though poor and afflicted, were challenged to plant churches 'where they are needed.' The letter closed with the promise: 'The Holy Spirit will be poured out from on high. Our desolation shall be repaired, until "streams shall break out in the desert, and the wilderness shall blossom as the rose".'

John Leighton Wilson, in addition to his work in foreign and home missions, directed, at least in part, the ministry of the Confederate chaplains. Looking back over the war, Wilson found some encouragement. He wrote in 1865:

> We should ever be grateful to Almighty God for the repeated and abundant out-pouring of his Holy Spirit upon our armies during the progress of the bloody conflict. That our camps should have been made nurseries of piety is something not only new and unprecedented in warfare, but may be regarded as an encouraging token of God's purpose to favor and bless our future Zion.[8]

[6] Thompson, *Presbyterians in the South*, 2:92.

[7] The Presbytery of South Carolina in 1867 adopted a paper written by Dr. Adger stating their unwillingness to constitute a church purely and solely of colored people because 'the ground of color is a schismatical foundation on which a church may not be built.'

[8] White, *Southern Presbyterian Leaders*, p. 343.

After the war, home missions included the work of 'sustentation'—sustaining congregations that had been weakened by the ravages of war, repairing shattered churches, and sending evangelists throughout the wasted land to plant new churches. Wilson travelled, preached, counselled, encouraged, and exhorted Southern Presbyterians to have hope. He wrote to them:

> A dark cloud hangs upon our horizon, but the great mediatorial King reigns and the church is safe. He who has hitherto defended us from every enemy, upheld us under every trial, and from time to time has bestowed so many precious tokens of his favor upon us as a church, surely will be faithful to the end. Let us then go forward in the path of duty with a firm step and a courageous heart.[9]

William Childs Robinson wrote that Dr. Wilson shone 'with the brightest brilliance' in sustaining and building up 'the torn fragments of the Southern Zion' after the war.[10]

The scars and deep memories caused by the war lasted for years. In the January 1876 issue of the *Southern Presbyterian Review* there was a restrained but painful notice of the *Memoirs of General W. T. Sherman,* especially poignant when the reviewer touched on 'the sack and burning of the city of Columbia.'[11] In 1882, Robert Lewis Dabney wrote to his co-editor, John Adger, sending some copy for the next issue. He included his own critique of Jefferson Davis's *History of the Confederacy,* which Dabney wished to have published anonymously. He believed that the *Review* ought to contain a full notice of such an important work, but he found that

[9] White, *Southern Presbyterian Leaders,* p. 406.

[10] Robinson, *Columbia Theological Seminary,* p. 138.

[11] 'Critical Notices,' *Southern Presbyterian Review* (Jan. 1876), p. 189.

it was almost impossible for him to write it 'candidly and honestly, without expressing a fullness of sympathy with the author, which would communicate to my article a complexion too political, and too partisan for a theological Review.' Dabney had rewritten his review toning it down as much as he could, he wrote, but found that it was 'not much less sharp in spirit.'[12]

* * * * *

Dr. George Howe was the stated supply pastor of First Presbyterian Church during 1865 and the first half of 1866. Gentle and humble, Howe—a large man who now walked with a crutch—moved among the people of the church and the city with words of comfort and preached with love and power. On May 13, 1866, a grateful congregation expressed its appreciation to him and reviewed its own trials of the past year in a resolution adopted at a congregational meeting:

> Since the destruction of Columbia by Gen. Sherman's forces in Feb., 1865, the pulpit of this church has been supplied by the Rev. Dr. Howe. Stricken as we were by the remorseless hand of the enemy, our city burnt, our means of support destroyed, our families scattered, many of us without a shelter of our own, and living under the hospitable roof of some kind friend, the struggle for existence was so great, that any effort on the part of the congregation to obtain a pastor, deprived as we were of resources to supply his wants, would have been futile.
>
> During the whole of this period, with saddened feelings at the termination of the struggle which had elicited the hearty prayers and most earnest aspiration of our people, together

[12] Johnson, *Dabney*, p. 403.

with the crushing weight of our private misfortunes, when the consolations of religion were so much needed; when we needed some faithful man of God to impress upon us the vanity of human affairs, and to entreat us to build our hope of happiness on the only safe foundation—the principles of a true and vital religion—and to point us to the Lamb of God, who alone can take away the sorrows as well as the sins of the world; Dr. Howe, with a sympathetic heart, and ample learning, Sabbath after Sabbath broke to us the bread of life. For more than a year he has continued to serve us unmurmuringly until the present time, when the congregation has been enabled to relieve him, so as to allow him to devote his energies more uninterruptedly in his appointed vocation as Professor of the Theological Seminary.

While we have suffered most grievously by the war which has slain many of our people and desolated our beautiful city, as a congregation we must be devotedly thankful to God that we have been in reach of the droppings of the sanctuary, and should express our obligation to the eminent minister of the Gospel who has served us so acceptably.

Therefore, be it resolved, that the congregation of the First Presbyterian Church of Columbia do hereby return to the Rev. George Howe, D.D., their profound acknowledgment of his services in preaching to them since the burning of Columbia—a service he had to perform under great difficulties, but which we believe has redounded much to the benefit of this church and to the interests of true religion; and that in severing their connection with him as stated supply, they invoke God's choicest blessings upon him, his family, and the institution of which he has been an ornament for so many years.

Dr. and Mrs. Howe were greatly loved by Columbians and by Presbyterians and others throughout the South. At their home on Blanding Street they had taken in many friends and strangers; it was said that they had entertained and housed every missionary of the Southern Presbyterian Church.

* * * * *

Charges were brought against James Woodrow for misuse of mission funds and for participation in too many activities, leading, it was said, to neglect of his duties as a professor in the seminary.[13] Woodrow explained how he had come to have so many irons in the fire. The assembly had elected him to two posts—treasurer of the Foreign Missions Committee in 1861 and treasurer of the Home Missions Committee in 1863. John Leighton Wilson revealed that Dr. Woodrow had personally replaced a loss of $3,000 that the Foreign Missions Committee had suffered through a bank failure in New York, and had also advanced money to meet drafts coming from the foreign mission fields for which the committee itself had no funds. Woodrow took a personal interest in every missionary. On one occasion he accompanied three missionaries to New York as they sailed to China. 'In their stateroom they were committed to the care of Him who holds the seas in the hollow of His hand and were bidden an affectionate farewell.'[14]

In addition to his work at the seminary, Woodrow was professor of chemistry at the University of South Carolina. He was the editor of the *Southern Presbyterian* because 'there was no one else to do it' and was one of the editors of the *Southern Presbyterian Review*. For a time he operated a bookstore and a printing press. He admitted that he had

[13] See Thompson, *Presbyterians in the South*, 2:368.

[14] Samuel Isset Woodbridge, *Fifty Years in China* (Richmond, Va.: Presbyterian Committee of Publication, n.d.), p. 33.

made a good deal of money, but stated that he had financially supported the ministries of the church. The charges against Dr. Woodrow were withdrawn and the General Assembly gave him a unanimous vote of confidence. But Woodrow's teaching at Columbia Seminary would soon become an issue that vexed and divided the seminary and the church for years.

* * * * *

Beginning in May 1866, the Rev. William E. Boggs, pastor of the Presbyterian church in Winnsboro, filled the pulpit of First Church. In October, he became the pastor at a salary of $1,500 a year. In order to raise this amount, pew rents were increased and some five thousand bricks from the ruins of the Sumter Street Lecture Room were sold for sixty-five dollars.

William Boggs was born on May 12, 1838, at Ahmadnagar, India, where his parents were Presbyterian missionaries. He was a young boy when the family was forced to leave India because of sickness. They went to Winnsboro, South Carolina, where young William attended Mount Zion Academy, one of the best schools in the South. He graduated from South Carolina College in 1859 and entered Columbia Seminary, worshipping at First Church where he sat spellbound under the preaching of James Henley Thornwell. In 1861 Boggs joined the troops defending the coast of South Carolina after the fall of Fort Sumter. He was ordained by Harmony Presbytery in April 1862 and served as chaplain of the Sixth South Carolina Regiment. He continued as a chaplain until General Lee's surrender at Appomattox on April 9, 1865. Boggs noted that Lee's eyes flashed as he rode into battle just as James Henley Thornwell's did when he preached! After the war Boggs returned home to Winnsboro and supplied the Presbyterian church there until he was called to Columbia.

A seminarian who for three years heard Boggs preach later described his impressions:

> How almost adoringly the village boy had looked up to the young and gifted Wm. E. Boggs as he stood in that marble pulpit! It seemed to me that I would just die if I had to stand in that elegant old church and that grand pulpit and try to preach! I have since heard Palmer, Girardeau, Hoge, John Hall, and a host of others; but in those three years I got as much from the interesting and eloquent sermons of Wm. E. Boggs as from any Professor in the Seminary. He taught me 'how to do it'—by doing it![15]

* * * * *

In 1866 First Presbyterian Church purchased its first organ from Grace Episcopal Church in Charleston, for $1,400. The organ had been brought to Columbia for protection during the war when it was thought that Charleston, rather than Columbia, would bear the brunt of the enemy's wrath. It escaped damage when Columbia was burned and was installed in the choir loft in the rear balcony of the beautiful church thankfully spared in the great fire. Not everyone was pleased with the organ, however, since some Presbyterians continued to believe that the regulative principle did not allow the use of musical instruments in worship. Some called it 'the great white idol.' John Adger opposed it as 'a sinful addition.'[16]

[15] Woodrow, *James Woodrow*, p. 104.

[16] Willborn, 'Girardeau,' p. 215. Adger's brother-in-law Thomas Smyth of Charleston's Second Presbyterian Church strongly favoured the use of instrumental music in public worship.

* * * * *

William S. Plumer came to Columbia Seminary in 1867 to take the office to which he had been elected in 1862, that of professor of theology, following James Henley Thornwell. He was the fourth professor, with George Howe, John Adger, and James Woodrow.

Plumer, a native of Beaver County, Pennsylvania, studied at Washington College (later Washington and Lee) in Lexington, Virginia, and at Princeton Seminary. An Old School Presbyterian leader, he was elected moderator at the crucial General Assembly of 1838. The same year he received three honorary doctor of divinity degrees—from Washington, Lafayette, and Princeton. In 1857, he was given the doctor of laws from the University of Mississippi. Plumer served churches in the South, including the First Presbyterian Church of Richmond, Virginia, and the Franklin Street Church in Baltimore. He published the *Watchman of the South* to uphold the views of Old School Presbyterianism. In 1854 he was called to Western Theological Seminary in Pittsburgh as professor of didactic and pastoral theology. The 'nearest approach to a pacifist the Presbyterian church produced during the Civil War,' Dr. Plumer was accused of disloyalty to the Union because he refused to pray that God would allow military victories for the Northern army. When his connection with Western Seminary was terminated in 1862, he preached in churches in Pennsylvania until he came to Columbia.

Plumer wrote many books with 'the slow, weary scratching of a cramped infelicitous hand,' including valuable commentaries on the Psalms (more than 1,200 printed pages), Romans, and Hebrews, as well as other works. Some of his books were translated into German, French, and Greek. Hampden DuBose translated Plumer's *The Rock of My Salvation* into Chinese. Dr. Plumer was twice moderator of the Presbyterian Church—of the Old School General Assembly in 1838 and the Southern Assembly in 1871. He served as stated supply at First Presbyterian Church in Columbia from September 1877 to June 1878. During these nine months there were more additions to the congregation than in any previous similar period in the church's history. Richard McIlwaine, who heard Plumer preach in Baltimore, declared that he was the only preacher he knew who could fill a church at night in the summertime and hold his hearers spellbound.[17] According to Moses D. Hoge, one of the best preachers in the Southern Presbyterian Church, Plumer lacked 'logical development of his theme' in his preaching but made up for it by his forceful delivery and 'a wonderfully original power of illustration, drawn chiefly from the experiences and ordinary occurrences of life.'[18] S. L. Morris, who graduated from Columbia Seminary in 1876, wrote: 'Dr. Wm. S. Plumer, our venerable Professor of Theology, with long white beard reaching down to his waist, delivered our diplomas and gave each of us a small Bible, saying, "By this Book you shall live, by this Book you shall preach, and by this Book you shall be judged at the last day."'[19]

[17] Thompson, *Presbyterians in the South*, 2:369.

[18] *Memorial Volume*, p. 213.

[19] LaMotte, *Colored Light*, p. 147.

17

JOSEPH RUGGLES WILSON

THE city of Columbia had risen from the ashes. A Scottish visitor reported:

> Columbia is a city of such magnificent distances that a stranger is never quite sure when he is in it or out of it . . . The town is being built up new by degrees, and many fine brick houses have been erected since the close of the war. But what magnificent outlines of streets, sweeping spaciously for miles over the heights and hollows of that rich landscape, having rows of fine old trees on either side, and, intersected by other wooded avenues equally broad and long, opening up in all directions the most delightful vistas![1]

South Carolina College had reopened as the University of South Carolina. For several years the professors at Columbia Seminary served without a salary, receiving food from time to time and 'some small amounts in current coin.' By the 1870s things looked brighter. Faculty salaries were paid and more students arrived. In 1873 there were fifty-seven students at the seminary, the largest number since the war.

* * * * *

[1] *A Columbia Reader*, pp. 77, 78.

The *Southern Presbyterian Review*—'conducted by an association of ministers in Columbia, South Carolina'—was printed at the Presbyterian Publishing House, opposite the Court House, in Columbia. The enterprising James Woodrow was proprietor, and the *Review* carried an advertisement claiming that the Presbyterian Publishing House was 'fitted up with the best, latest, and most improved machinery.'[2] The January 1876 issue marked a new arrangement in which the present editors invited 'certain brethren in Virginia to a full and equal share with themselves' in the oversight of the *Review*, including Robert Lewis Dabney of Union Seminary. A statement on the inside front cover stated that 'the *Review* will continue to be to a certain extent an open journal, favoring free discussion within limits, but it is the desire of all who have it in charge to make it more representative of our whole Church, as its name imports, and a faithful exponent of the Calvinistic Theology and the Presbyterian Polity.'[3]

Dabney agreed that the *Review* remain a 'free journal' but worried that some articles might be understood in an unorthodox way. He was annoyed with publication delays, especially when his own article on Robertson Smith had been forestalled by William Henry Green's in the *Princeton Review*, which had come out punctually on January 1. 'After so long a time mine will come creeping out and will wear the appearance of a plagiarism of his,' he complained. Dabney was very much opposed to including in the *Review* comments on the International Sunday School Lesson. 'I cannot see, for the life of me, why a Presbyterian pastor should make his Sunday-school study a given passage this Sunday, because

[2] *Southern Presbyterian Review* (Jan. 1870). Front and back cover.

[3] *Southern Presbyterian Review* (Jan. 1876). Inside front cover.

other schools happen to have that passage at Sunday,' he wrote. 'However, this is the fashion of the hour,' he added, 'and I feel that protest is vain. Our people and ministers are determined to be in fashion in the matter.'[4] Dabney's frequent contributions to the *Southern Presbyterian Review* dealt with matters of philosophy, economics, and psychology, as well as treatments of theology, including articles on original sin, 'endless punishment,' the teaching of Alexander Campbell, and Charles Hodge's *Systematic Theology,* and church matters such as preaching and pulpit style, the proper observance of the Sabbath, church government, and church union.[5]

* * * * *

In December 1870 Dr. Boggs received a call from the Second Presbyterian Church of Memphis, Tennessee. To encourage him to stay in Columbia, First Church raised his salary to $2,500 and the Presbytery of Charleston refused to dissolve his relationship with his church; but Boggs 'concluded it was his duty to accept the call' to Memphis. The Columbia congregation regretfully concurred; and on January 7, 1871, he preached his farewell sermons—in the morning at the church, in the afternoon to the Sunday school, and at night to the people of Ladson Presbyterian Church.[6]

[4] Johnson, *Dabney,* pp. 101-4.

[5] Rankin, Index, pp. 13-16 of Author Index. The majority of these titles have been republished in *Discussions of R. L. Dabney,* (Edinburgh: Banner of Truth, 1982), vols. 1-3; and vol. 4 (Harrisonburg, Va: Sprinkle Publications, 1980/1994).

[6] Boggs served the Memphis Church until 1879, when his wife's health—shattered by an attack of yellow fever—required a change of climate. He was called to Central Church in Atlanta. From 1882 to 1885 he was back in Columbia as professor of ecclesiastical history and church government at Columbia Seminary. In 1885 he again became pastor of Second Presbyterian in Memphis. He served for one year (1889) as chancellor of the University of Georgia and in 1900 was called to the First

* * * * *

Joseph Ruggles Wilson, who had served on the Columbia Seminary board since 1863, became professor of pastoral theology and preaching in 1870.

Wilson was born on February 28, 1826, in Steubenville, Ohio, of Scotch-Irish ancestry—the youngest of seven boys in a family of ten children. His father, Judge James Wilson, was a newspaper publisher and state legislator. Joseph graduated from Jefferson College (now Washington and Jefferson). He studied at Western Theological Seminary and, for a year, under Charles Hodge at Princeton Seminary, graduating from Princeton in 1847. He was licensed by the Steubenville (Ohio) Presbytery and ordained and installed in the Presbyterian church of Chartiers, Pennsylvania, in 1849. Soon after his ordination, Wilson married eighteen-year-old Janet (or Jessie, as she was often called) Woodrow, who was born in Carlisle, England. Jessie was James Woodrow's sister.

After two years in the Chartiers church, the Wilsons moved to Hampden-Sydney College in Virginia, where Joseph was professor of chemistry and natural science. He served as stated supply at nearby Walker's Church. Wilson remained at Hampden-Sydney for four years, until he received a call from the First Presbyterian Church in Staunton, Virginia, one of the largest churches in the Presbytery of Lexington. Near midnight on December 28, 1856, Thomas Woodrow Wilson, Janet and Joseph's third child and first son, was born in the Staunton manse. When his uncle, James Woodrow, observed the future president, he predicted a different future. 'That baby is dignified enough to be moderator of the General

---

Presbyterian Church of Jacksonville, Florida.

Assembly,' he said. Thomas Woodrow Wilson 'grew up on family worship, Bible reading, study of the Shorter Catechism, and stories of Scottish Covenanters,' according to his primary biographer.[7]

In the summer of 1857 Joseph Wilson, with Jessie, travelled to Augusta to perform the wedding ceremony for Jessie's brother, James Woodrow, who was teaching at Georgia's Oglethorpe University. While in Augusta Wilson preached at the First Presbyterian Church, and the congregation, impressed with the eloquence and power of his sermon, later called him to be their minister. Early in 1859 Joseph, Jessie, and their three children, Marion Williamson, Annie Josephine, and one-year-old Thomas Woodrow, moved to Augusta.

Dr. Wilson was outgoing and gregarious, with a commanding presence and a gift for conversation. His 'dark eye beams with intelligence, his sunny smile is strongly suggestive of fun and good humor,' a friend commented. He was, someone else said, 'the soul of wit, an inveterate punster, the best company in the world at dinner.' Wilson enjoyed billiards, chess, English novels, and on occasion 'a good nip of Presbyterian Scotch.' He drew the line at cards and dancing, but found it absurd that anyone could describe smoking as a sin.

Joseph Wilson was pastor of First Presbyterian Church in Augusta when the first General Assembly of the Southern Presbyterian Church met there in December 1861. In 1870 the Wilsons moved to Columbia. During their almost four years in Columbia, they lived first in a house at Pickens and Blanding streets and then built a fine house on Hampton

[7] See 'Wilson, (Thomas) Woodrow' in *Encyclopedia of Religion in the South* (Atlanta, Ga.: Mercer University Press, 1984), p. 842.

Street, which they planned to make their permanent home. Jessie planted tea olives, magnolias, and dogwood trees in the garden. The city, the seminary, and the church pleased Dr. Wilson, and the family enjoyed living in Columbia. Years later Tommy, as he was called in his youth, remembered his 'very happy boyhood in Columbia.'[8]

During the winter of 1873-74 Frank J. Brooke lived in the home of Dr. Plumer while he was being tutored by Plumer to enter Davidson College as a ministerial student. Brooke and one of the seminary students conducted devotional services for boys in the seminary chapel. Among those attending was seventeen-year-old Thomas Woodrow Wilson, who made a public profession of faith and, soon after, joined the First Presbyterian Church. The session minutes stated that Wilson and two other boys, 'after a free conversation during which they severally exhibited evidences of a work of grace begun in their hearts,' were admitted unanimously into the fellowship of the church. Years later, as president of the United States, Woodrow Wilson visited Columbia Seminary and commented that he had heard much eloquent speaking in his life but, on the whole, none better than he heard as a boy 'in this little chapel.'[9] In 1874 Frank Brooke entered Davidson College with his friend Woodrow Wilson. Brooke graduated from college and began his seminary studies at Columbia in 1877. When he could not become a foreign missionary because of health problems, he became a pastor in Alexandria, Virginia. Brooke spent time each year in home mission work, planting numerous churches. Louis LaMotte writes: 'Bearing the

[8] John M. Mulder, *Woodrow Wilson: The Years of Preparation* (Princeton, N. J.: Princeton University Press, 1978), p. 37.

[9] LaMotte, *Colored Light*, p. 151. The quote is taken from an article by Thornton Whaling in the *Columbia Record*, June 18, 1924.

burden of care for many churches,' Dr. Brooke 'condemned evil and preached righteousness and redeeming love' until his death in 1924.[10]

From February 1871 to July 1873 Dr. Wilson preached regularly at First Presbyterian Church, while the session, urged on by the congregation, took steps to call a pastor. In October 1872, Wilson resigned as interim, stating that he feared he was 'in the way' of the church's securing a regular pastor. The session accepted his resignation—with praise for his earnest preaching and 'kindly and genial deportment' that had endeared him to the congregation—and asked him to continue to fill the pulpit while they took steps to call a pastor. Several ministers declined calls to First Church. Dr. Wilson resigned again in July 1873, 'to relieve the session of all embarrassment' in the matter. The church then called John H. Bryson as pastor.

* * * * *

When Joseph Wilson and John Adger initiated compulsory Sunday morning chapel services at Columbia Seminary—in obvious conflict with the services at First Presbyterian Church—a battle erupted at the seminary that divided students, faculty, and directors. Howe and Plumer supported voluntary attendance, whereas Adger and Wilson insisted that all students attend the services at the seminary.[11] Thirteen students refused and were dismissed. The matter was taken to the 1874 General Assembly, which debated the issue for several days before finally voting, sixty to fifty-three, to

[10] LaMotte, *Colored Light,* pp. 154-55.

[11] James Woodrow, who was away in Europe at the time, later sided with Wilson (his brother-in-law) and Adger.

recommend that attendance at the seminary worship service be made voluntary. This action was interpreted by some, despite the assembly's disclaimer, as undermining the power of the faculty. Wilson and Adger resigned from the seminary faculty, as did John L. Girardeau from the board of directors.[12] Wilson wrote that he was so divided, in policy and principle, from at least one member of the faculty as to make it impossible to work with him.[13] That faculty member was William Swan Plumer.

* * * * *

From 1872 to 1874 James Woodrow was on leave from the seminary, travelling with his family in Europe. He sent the *Southern Presbyterian* accounts of the highlights of his trip. In Switzerland he attended a meeting of the Swiss Scientific Association. He studied rock formations in England. He was awed at being present for the first general synod of the Huguenots to be held in two centuries, but dismayed when he heard members 'denying the divinity of our Lord Jesus Christ, denying the truth of the Sacred Scriptures.'[14] He found that in Paris there was an almost complete disregard of the Sabbath. At the General Assembly of the Church of Scotland he heard Dr. Alexander Duff preach the moderator's sermon, which went on for some three hours. 'Was I not right in having taken it for granted that brevity is not a Scottish characteristic?' he wrote. He disapproved of a Presbyterian minister in England wearing a black gown with bands but greatly enjoyed the

[12] Wilson soon accepted a call to the First Presbyterian Church of Wilmington, North Carolina. In 1885, he went to the theological school of the Southwestern Presbyterian University in Clarksville, Tennessee.

[13] Thompson, *Presbyterians in the South*, 2:369.

[14] Gustafson, *Woodrow*, p. 92.

enthusiastic singing. Woodrow returned from Europe in 1874 to resume teaching at the seminary—with George Howe and William Plumer. One of Dr. Woodrow's students wrote: 'I can never forget that it was the lectures in Dr. Woodrow's classroom that checked me in a wild, downward career to infidelity and atheism and cheerless blank despair.'[15]

* * * * *

The 1874 General Assembly debated the issue of closer connection with the Northern Presbyterian Church. When the Southern Church came into existence in 1861, Thornwell had written a 'Farewell Letter to the General Assembly of the Presbyterian Church in the United States of America,' giving the reasons why a separate Southern church was necessary but assuring the Northern Church that 'your faith and order are ours. Your noble testimony for the truth, in by-gone days, is still ours. All that is precious in the past is still ours. And we sincerely pray that the two Churches may hereafter have no other rivalry but that of love to the Master, and of holy zeal in His cause. We bid you farewell.'[16] The actions and attitudes of the Northern Presbyterian Church during and after the Civil War, however, had hardened the feelings of those in the South against reunion with the Northern Church. At the 1874 General Assembly Girardeau, who was moderator that year, supported the side that urged the Southern Church to refrain from any correspondence with the Northern Presbyterian Church until that church admitted its past wrongs toward its brethren in the South. Plumer, Girardeau's colleague at Columbia, supported a motion that recommended 'the

[15] J. L. Martin, quoted in Adger, *My Life and Times*, p. 495.
[16] Wells, *Southern Presbyterian Worthies*, p. 32.

appointment of an uninstructed committee to confer . . . on friendly relations and fraternal correspondence'[17] Plumer's view prevailed; the assembly voted for it by more than two to one.

A few years later, Henry Van Dyke, retiring moderator of the General Assembly of the Presbyterian Church in the United States of America, asked the assembly to invite Plumer to address their assembly. Plumer had served as moderator of the Old School General Assembly in 1838; and in 1871, just four years after he came to Columbia Seminary, he was elected moderator of the Southern Assembly. He was the only person to have served as moderator of the two assemblies. As Plumer, 'a patriarch of truly imposing appearance,' made his way down the aisle, the assembly rose and greeted him with applause and cheers.[18] Most Southern Presbyterians, however, were not ready for closer relations with their Northern brethren. In 1882 an open letter in opposition to the restoration of fraternal relations with the Northern church was signed with ninety-one names, including those of Adger, Girardeau, Howe, and Woodrow, all Columbia Seminary faculty.

* * * * *

Some Presbyterians felt that Plumer's gifts did not suit the chair of theology and that he was therefore injuring the seminary. In 1875 Plumer announced that he would leave the chair of theology for that of pastoral theology. Palmer nominated for professor of theology John Lafayette Girardeau, who was elected by a unanimous vote. Several months elapsed

[17] Willborn, 'Girardeau,' p. 284.
[18] Thompson, *Presbyterians in the South*, 2:243.

before Girardeau could bring himself to accept. He was acutely aware of his 'inadequate furniture of scholarship and learning,' as he put it in a letter to the seminary board. Further, he explained, there were 'certain private difficulties,' namely, that as a board member he had supported 'the brethren [Adger and Wilson] who have retired from the Seminary in contending for the principle of obedience to law on the part of theological students. Fidelity alike to principle and to friendship seemed to rise up and dispute my passage to the seminary,' he wrote to the board. He went on to state that both Wilson and Adger strongly favoured his going to the seminary. The action of the General Assembly, with the concurrence of the synods of South Carolina and Georgia, and the desire of the seminary board, led Girardeau, 'somewhat to my own surprise, to take the view that the responsibility is lifted from me and assumed by the Church.'[19]

[19] Blackburn, *Girardeau*, pp. 168-73.

18

JOHN LAFAYETTE GIRARDEAU

JOHN Lafayette Girardeau brought to Columbia Seminary 'a thorough scholarship, the tradition of Thornwell, and a pastor's heart.'[1] From 1876 until his retirement in 1895, he was the greatest influence at the seminary and one of the leaders of the Southern Presbyterian Church.

Lafayette Girardeau was born in 1825 on James Island, South Carolina, to a Presbyterian family of French Huguenot ancestry. He did not like the name 'Lafayette' and, as a young man, added 'John' to his name with his father's approval. He was baptized by Dr. A. W. Leland, then pastor of the Presbyterian church on the island. As a boy he attended church services and Sunday school classes, some of which were taught by Dr. Leland. Girardeau's mother died when he was seven years old. 'Thank God for a mother who was fond and tender,' he later wrote, 'but would not suffer sin in her children . . . She bore the character of an humble, sweet-tempered, useful follower of the Lord Jesus.'[2] When

[1] Willborn, 'Girardeau,' p. 338. For Girardeau's life, see G. A. Blackburn, *Life-work of John Lafayette Girardeau* (Columbia: The State Co., 1916); and C. N. Willborn, 'John L. Girardeau (1825-98)—Pastor to Slaves and Theologian of Causes: A Historical Account of the Life and Contributions of an Often Neglected Southern Presbyterian Minister and Theologian' (Ph.D. dissertation, Westminster Theological Seminary, 2003). Willborn's dissertation has been published. The page notations in this book are from the dissertation.

[2] Blackburn, *Girardeau,* pp. 13, 15.

he was ten years old he was sent to Charleston for further schooling. There Girardeau heard the sermons of Thomas Smyth at Second Presbyterian Church and read extensively in the Reformed theologians. He later wrote at the end of his copy of the *Memoirs of Thomas Halyburton* that Calvin, Owen, Witsius, Halyburton, and Thornwell were 'among the chief of my instructors.' The young man soon came to a saving knowledge of the gospel. It was at the north corner of King Street and Price's Alley in Charleston that Girardeau found Christ 'after a month's conflict with sin and hell! The heavens and the earth seemed to be singing psalms of praise for redeeming love.'[3] A fine student, a splendid athlete, a good musician—and now an eager Christian—Girardeau graduated from the College of Charleston in 1844.

After college Girardeau served as a tutor in the home of a planter near Charleston. He became engaged to the fifteen-year-old daughter of the family, Penelope Sarah Hamlin, whom he married in 1849. During the year between his college graduation and his seminary studies, Girardeau taught school on James Island. He visited slaves on the island plantations on weekday afternoons to catechize and instruct them, and on Sundays held meetings for them in the church, standing on the pulpit steps to address them.[4] Having grown up among the black people of the South Carolina sea islands, Girardeau communicated effectively in the Gullah dialect.

From 1845 to 1848 Girardeau attended Columbia Seminary, where he was united again with his childhood pastor,

[3] Blackburn, *Girardeau,* p. 22.

[4] Girardeau maintained that there was a distinction between 'preaching' and 'exhorting.' He thought that a good way to make such a distinction was for the 'preacher' to occupy the pulpit, and for the 'exhorter' to stand on the floor when speaking.

Dr. A. W. Leland. Benjamin Morgan Palmer was pastor at First Presbyterian Church, and James Henley Thornwell was preaching at the college chapel. Girardeau studied hard, learned much, and conducted mission services in an abandoned warehouse in a poor part of town. When he graduated from Columbia Seminary, he became, at the recommendation of Leland, stated supply at the First Presbyterian Church of Columbus, Georgia, the church served by Thomas Goulding until his death. When interest was expressed in having him as pastor, Girardeau declined. He had a deep burden for the African American people of Low Country South Carolina. 'While at the Theological Seminary,' he wrote, 'I only refrained from going on a foreign mission, because I felt it to be my duty to preach to the mass of slaves on the seaboard of South Carolina.' He rejected a call to the 'large and important church' in Columbus because it had 'very few negroes connected with it.'[5]

When he was twenty-four years old, Girardeau was ordained, preaching his trial sermon on 'Sanctification by Grace' from Romans 6:1, 2. He had already become an able theologian. He told the presbyters:

> Through that faith, which receives a graciously imputed righteousness, we are freed from a guilt-burdened conscience and the fearful apprehensions of a coming wrath, and this is the victory that overcometh the world—even our faith. Not the most untiring expenditure of human effort—not watching, striving, prayers and tears—but simple faith in the free grace of the crucified Savior. Looking unto Jesus, the author and finisher of our faith, is the grand secret, both of freedom from wrath and holiness of life . . . The obedience of Christ

[5] Blackburn, *Girardeau*, p. 76.

> unto death as it has produced remission of guilt and a title to life, has also purchased for the believer the sanctifying influences of the Holy Spirit. It is the meritorious cause of our sanctification.[6]

For six months Girardeau preached at the Wappetaw Congregational Church, near McClellanville, South Carolina, where there was 'a dense body of slaves.' 'The scenes on Sabbath were affecting,' he wrote. 'The negroes came in crowds from two parishes. Often have I seen . . . groups of them "double-quicking" in the roads, in order to reach the church in time—trotting to church!'[7] He was then called to Wilton Presbyterian Church at Adam's Run, near Edisto Island. For four years he laboured among the white membership of the church, which included, Girardeau said, some of the most cultivated gentlemen of the state, and the African Americans. His Sundays were busy. The young pastor preached in the church to the white congregation in the morning, to the black people at noon, in the afternoon to the slaves on the plantations, and again at night to a mixed congregation of blacks and whites.

In 1854 Girardeau was called to Charleston as pastor of the newly formed Anson Street Church—a mission to African Americans begun by Second Presbyterian Church. At his arrival, there were thirty-six members, but in a few years there were over six hundred, with a regular Sunday attendance of 1,500, mostly blacks with a sprinkling of sympathetic whites.[8] White members joined the church 'with the fullest understanding that its primary design and chief purpose is to benefit the coloured and especially the slave population

[6] George A. Blackburn, ed., *Sermons by John L. Girardeau* (Columbia, S.C.: The State Company, 1907), pp. 58, 59.

[7] Blackburn, *Girardeau,* p. 76.

[8] Blackburn, *Girardeau,* p. 32.

of this city.'[9] Against criticism, Girardeau supported his plan of a separate black church (under white leadership) as an accommodation 'to the wants and tastes of the coloured people.' 'Unless they understand the Gospel,' he wrote, 'they cannot embrace it; and unless they embrace it, they cannot be saved.'[10] Girardeau wanted the black members to be the church, rather than spectators of the white services. Black people sat on the main floor of the building, rather than in the gallery or at the back, as was the usual practice in other churches. Girardeau performed weddings for slaves in the church, forcing white owners to recognize the sanctity of marriage among these people. A much larger building was needed and Zion Church, so named by the black congregation, was built for the fast-growing congregation. Girardeau wrote that in April 1859, 'we decamped and went into the immense new building in Calhoun Street.'[11] With a seating capacity of 2,500, it was, in fact, the largest church building in Charleston and possibly in all of South Carolina.

Girardeau wrote *A Catechism for the Oral Instruction of Coloured Persons,* a distinctively Reformed book by which he hoped to produce 'Presbyterian Christians.' Class meetings, or what we might call small group meetings, of about fifty people met regularly 'to promote mutual acquaintance and brotherly love among the members; to apprise them of one another's sickness and need . . . and to further the growth of the members in Christian Knowledge and experimental religion.'[12] Girardeau was concerned not only with the spiritual growth of his black members, but with improving the

[9] Blackburn, *Girardeau,* p. 82.
[10] Blackburn, *Girardeau,* p. 38.
[11] Willborn, 'Girardeau,' p. 121.
[12] Blackburn, *Girardeau,* p. 87.

lives of the African Americans of the city through education and material help.

John Girardeau had worked for twelve years among the slaves of coastal South Carolina when the War between the States broke out. A loyal South Carolinian, he served as chaplain of the Twenty-third Regiment of South Carolina. He saw some of the worst fighting in Virginia and was in Mississippi at the fall of Vicksburg. As Girardeau ministered to the Confederate wounded and dying at the Battle of Jackson, it was said by one who was there: 'I could note the tenderness and faithfulness of his ministrations, as he held up Christ crucified as the only hope of a sinner. All his preaching that I heard in the army, was full of appeal to men to accept Christ and trust him for life and death.'[13] Girardeau was not without flashes of bitterness toward the 'Yankees,' but he was found, on more than one occasion, praying with and helping wounded Northern soldiers. In 1866, after the war had ended, Girardeau said in an address in memory of the Confederate dead at Magnolia Cemetery in Charleston: 'We have repaired to this burial ground to mingle the tears of a common sorrow and to pay . . . tribute of respect to our deceased soldiers . . . The act which we are assembled to perform is suggested not by acrimony toward the living, but by affection for the dead.'[14]

In a letter written from the battlefront at Petersburg, Virginia, on January 10, 1865, Girardeau described his furniture and his portable library:

> There is a table, a chair, and a couple of stools. And there is a little table & a piece of board tacked to the logs on which your humble friend doeth his lucubrations. On it you notice is lying a copy of Edwards on the *Freedom of the Will,* over

[13] Blackburn, *Girardeau,* p. 128.

[14] Blackburn, *Girardeau,* p. 128.

> which he sacks his brains. There in the corner on a little shelf is my library. Shall I tell you what books compose it? Well. Calvin's *Institutes,* Butler's *Analogy,* Whately's *Logic,* Buck's *Theological Dictionary,* A Greek Testament, A copy of the Hebrew Psalms & my Bible.[15]

As the Northern and Southern armies were preparing for the great battle at Petersburg, Robert Lewis Dabney, chaplain to the Army of Northern Virginia, invited Girardeau to preach. The house was crowded to capacity, and just before the service began, General Robert E. Lee and his staff came in and took their seats. An eyewitness wrote: 'Although the siege was in full blast, under the magic of [Girardeau's] eloquence we were forced away from the consideration of this mundane sphere and given a picture of the world where bloodshed is unknown.'[16]

On April 6, 1865, Girardeau was captured at the Battle of Saylor's Creek, while ministering to both Confederate and Federal wounded, and carried to the Federal prison in Ohio. In late June, upon his taking the oath of allegiance to the United States, he was released from the prison camp and came home. As he crossed the border into South Carolina, he jumped from the wagon in which he was riding and threw himself flat on the soil of his 'dear mother state,' as Thornwell was reported to have done on one occasion. Girardeau went to the backwoods of Darlington County, where his family had found refuge during the war, and preached for ten days in the Presbyterian church in Darlington. On a Sunday morning in July he preached to a large congregation on 'The Judgment Day.'[17]

[15] Willborn, 'Girardeau,' p. 303.
[16] Blackburn, *Girardeau,* p. 118.
[17] Blackburn, *Sermons by John L. Girardeau,* pp. 13-38.

Hampden DuBose, a young boy sitting in the gallery, heard Girardeau preach that sermon. In China, half a century later, DuBose was translating Girardeau's sermon to include in a book he was writing on Christian theology. Referring to himself in the third person, DuBose wrote:

> If now and then he paused in his pleasant though difficult task and retired from where he was dictating to his writer to allow the unbidden tear to fall, the thought would arise, 'Why should a man who could preach like this die?' the response would soon be heard in the depths of his soul, 'He is not dead, but speaketh in the tongue of earth's ancient nation for whose evangelization he so earnestly and so frequently pleaded in the pulpits of the Southland.'[18]

Girardeau went home from the war 'to a defeated, depressed, trauma-ridden Charleston, and took pastoral charge again of the remnants of his congregation.'[19] When he disembarked from the train, he was enthusiastically greeted by the black members of Zion Church. They were waiting for his return; indeed they had summoned him in a letter in which they wrote that the relationship between pastor and people was treasured in their hearts, and they urged him to come back to them. To his dismay Girardeau found that Zion Presbyterian was now occupied by a missionary of the Northern Presbyterian Church. It was a year and a half before the Southern Presbyterians recovered the church and Girardeau was restored to his pulpit. He preached his first sermon back at Zion on December 23, 1866, from 2 Corinthians 4:5—'For we preach not ourselves, but Christ Jesus the Lord; and ourselves your servants for Jesus' sake.'

[18] Blackburn, *Girardeau*, pp.123-24.
[19] Kelly, *Preachers With Power*, p. 135.

For some years Girardeau preached each Sunday in two churches, to his white congregation on Glebe Street and to his black flock at Zion. One who attended Glebe Street described the services led by Girardeau in both churches:

> Neither was there any reading in concert, or repeating of creeds and prayers; but only the simple, old-time Presbyterian worship, handed down to us by our fathers, consisting of solemn, earnest prayers led by the minister, plain congregational singing, the impressive reading of the Scriptures, and the zealous, faithful exposition and application of the Word, followed by an offering for the service of the Lord.[20]

J. B. Mack, pastor in Sumter County, was called to assist Girardeau in the work of the two churches and was installed as co-pastor on December 29, 1867.

On August 15, 1869, Zion ordained and installed ruling elders, becoming 'the first Southern church governed by African-American elders.'[21] Girardeau preached on Acts 14:23—'And when they had appointed for them elders in every church, and had prayed with fasting, they commended them to the Lord.' Girardeau had insisted on white leadership for his Charleston church before Emancipation, and he continued to believe that African Americans would be dependent, at least for some time, upon white Christian leadership. He favoured a plan in which the black members of a congregation would elect their own elders and deacons. White members would also elect their officers, and both groups would serve their respective congregations under one name and one pastor. Black officers, however, would have no standing in presbytery or synod. Girardeau compromised his ecclesiology, C. N. Willborn writes, 'in hopes of keeping the

[20] Blackburn, *Girardeau,* p. 42. The quotation is from Thomas Law.

[21] Willborn, 'Girardeau,' p. 203.

church together—black and white—and raising up a generation of qualified African-American leaders for the church.'[22]

Girardeau wrote in a letter of resignation to his Zion congregation on June 5, 1871, 'I can scarcely bear the thought of parting with you—no more to preach to you the precious gospel of Christ, no more to mingle my prayers and praises with yours on earth, no more to minister to you in times of affliction and distress. There is not one of you whom I am not conscious of tenderly loving in Christ Jesus.' He went on to write: 'It will cost me a bitter pang not only to part with you, but to leave Charleston. Her very dust is dear to me. And I pray God that if it is His blessed will, I may not be sent out of South Carolina, but be permitted to suffer with her in her present trials, and to contribute what labor I am capable of for the interests of her beloved and afflicted people.'[23] The congregation pled with him to continue after taking some vacation time, and he consented and remained their pastor for another four years.

Harmony Presbytery was encouraged that there was among the African Americans 'some disposition to return to our communion.' We can never forget, continued the presbytery report,

> the time when they crowded to our sanctuaries, when they listened to the Gospel as preached to their owners, and then to the additional discourse designed especially for them. We can never forget the communion table spread for master and servant; the bread and the wine administered to each by the same hand and from the same vessels and at the same table.[24]

[22] Willborn, 'Girardeau,' p. 196.
[23] Blackburn, *Girardeau*, p. 151-52.
[24] LaMotte, *Colored Light*, p. 169.

In 1867 the Presbytery of South Carolina adopted a paper written by John Adger stating their unwillingness to constitute a church 'purely and solely of colored people,' because 'the ground of color is a schismatical foundation on which a church may not be built. We are all one in Christ Jesus, and there is neither Jew nor Greek in Him.' The idea of two churches, one for blacks and one for whites, Adger continued, would permit 'the organization of a church of poor men, or of rich men, or that of a church composed of farmers, or lawyers, or of mariners exclusively. We greatly desire that the colored people should continue to hold a fellowship of ordinances with us as of old, and that our churches in this Southern country should continue to be composed as hitherto of men of both colors.' Adger concluded that if the African Americans were resolved 'to separate themselves from us, whilst we cannot approve the step, they shall still have our best wishes, both for this world and for that which is to come.'[25]

The cause of an integrated Presbyterian church in the South, however, was soon lost. In 1874 the General Assembly, under the urging of Benjamin Morgan Palmer, approved the formation of fully organized Negro churches under Negro ministers and sessions. Columbia Seminary professor James Woodrow concurred with the opinion of the assembly. He believed that 'colored people, as a mass, prefer to have their own churches. This is natural and reasonable, and we add inevitable.'[26] Girardeau's was the single voice against the assembly's decision. He sadly commended the black Christians 'as immortal beings to the powerful and merciful care of the

[25] LaMotte, *Colored Light*, pp. 169-70.

[26] Gustafson, *Woodrow*, p. 104.

Shepherd and Bishop of souls.'[27] South Carolinian Thomas Peck also opposed the separation of white and black Presbyterian churches. Peck argued that as Christ welcomed the poor and needy, so should the Southern Presbyterian Church welcome the African Americans. To refuse to do so means that the church lacks 'one mark of a Christian church.'[28]

The decision of the 1874 General Assembly ended Girardeau's pastoral relation 'to the Zion Coloured Church and, probably, to the coloured people,' he wrote with a heavy heart on July 29, 1874. Zion Church leaders for some years, Girardeau wrote, 'declined to separate themselves from the Southern Presbyterian Church, and even after its Assembly had, in 1874, recommended an organic separation of the whites and blacks, they continued to maintain an independent position. Only at a late date did they resolve to connect themselves with the Northern Presbyterian Church.'[29]

Girardeau continued as pastor of the Glebe Street Church. On several occasions he declined calls to the prestigious Second Presbyterian Church of Charleston, the mother church of the Zion Church. When Girardeau became convinced that God was leading him to accept a position as professor of theology at Columbia Seminary, he reluctantly departed from his beloved Charleston, preaching one last time at the church on Calhoun Street 'to an immense congregation of coloured people.'[30] Leaving the Low Country for Columbia was hard for Girardeau and his wife. He described the move to a friend as 'leaving "duck sauce & rice" for plain corn hominy.'[31]

[27] Willborn, 'Girardeau,' p. 204.

[28] Willborn, 'Girardeau,' p. 205.

[29] Blackburn, *Girardeau*, pp. 80, 81. In 1879 Zion united with the Atlantic Presbytery of the Northern Presbyterian Church.

[30] Willborn, 'Girardeau,' p. 218.

[31] Willborn, 'Girardeau,' p. 280.

Girardeau began his duties at Columbia Seminary on January 18, 1876. At his first lecture, he was 'anxious almost to sickness,' he wrote, 'but the Lord helped me.' Girardeau prayed: 'I commit myself and this work to which I did not call myself, to the Almighty, faithful hands of the Lord Jesus, Glorious Savior! I adore, I admire, I love Thee! Use me to show forth Thy matchless beauty, loveliness and glory! Enrich me with all knowledge and utterance, for Thy name's sake.'[32] In his first meeting with the senior class he announced that their theology text would be the recently published three volumes by the Princetonian Charles Hodge. He added, 'Get Calvin and get him as well in the original as in the translation.' He also required his students to read Thornwell's second volume on election and reprobation, atonement, the priesthood of Christ, the gospel, the personality of the Holy Spirit, and Christian ethics. Additional reading was required in the works of George Hill and Francis Turretin. In his classes students gave reports or summaries from their reading. Girardeau asked them questions and gave daily lectures.[33] He required his students to produce 'written analyses of each day's exercise.'[34]

The students appreciated their new teacher. Thomas P. Hay wrote:

> I entered the junior class in the Seminary about a month before Dr. Girardeau entered the institution as Professor of Theology. And it was my privilege to be his scholar during the period of his transition from the eloquent pulpit orator

[32] Blackburn, *Girardeau*, pp. 173-74.

[33] The written lectures were published as *Discussions of Philosophical Questions and Discussions of Theological Questions* (Richmond, Va.: The Presbyterian Committee of Publication, 1900 and 1905).

[34] Blackburn, *Girardeau*, pp. 174-75.

> to the professor and teacher. He impressed and greatly helped me by his gift of analysis and of clarifying things by making distinctions, and of the logical development of his thought; and by the happy faculty of fixing thought and truth, thus elucidated by the illustrations of his imagination and the charms of his eloquence.

Another student, B. P. Reid, wrote: 'Wonderful as was Dr. Girardeau's mental power, there was something in him far beyond this, because, under him, we got an impression of a man which lingers with us as an inspiration in life.'[35]

* * * * *

A later Columbia Seminary professor, William M. McPheeters, wrote, 'Our Church has not done her duty to the colored people. But if she has failed, it has been for no lack of shining examples of genuine devotion to the spiritual interest of that people.'[36] C. C. Jones, John Adger, and John L. Girardeau were called directly from a ministry to the African Americans to professorships at Columbia Seminary. William Childs Robinson wrote: 'Almost a tradition to this effect was established; and Columbia may unabashedly compare this tradition with that of other Presbyterian institutions: the road to her professorial chairs was an apprenticeship of spiritual service for the slave brother.'[37] These men loved and served the black people of the South. But they were slave owners, who did not reject the institution of slavery, however much they may have disliked it. And their ministry to the slaves, as

[35] Blackburn, *Girardeau*, pp. 203-205.
[36] Robinson, *Columbia Theological Seminary*, p. 122.
[37] Robinson, *Columbia Theological Seminary*, p. 128.

Douglas Kelly writes about Girardeau, 'was not purged from a definitely paternalistic attitude.'[38] R. C. Reed, who later became professor of church history at Columbia Seminary, deplored the failure of the Southern Presbyterian Church to fully include the African Americans in its church life. During the days of slavery, the negroes sat in the gallery of the white churches and fed upon 'the crumbs of the children's bread.'[39]

* * * * *

Benedict College was founded in Columbia in 1870 by the American Baptists for the education of African Americans. In 1880 Payne Institute of the African Methodist Episcopal Church moved to Columbia and was incorporated by the state legislature on Christmas Eve that year as Allen University. It was named in honour of Richard Allen, the founder of the A.M.E. Church.

* * * * *

After a short ministry of two and a half years at First Presbyterian Church, Joseph B. Mack, who had been Girardeau's associate in the ministry to blacks in Charleston after the War between the States, resigned in January 1881 to raise funds for Columbia Seminary. He explained to the congregation that he was accepting the post because the seminary, as a training school for ministers of the gospel, was of vital importance

[38] Kelly, *Preachers With Power,* p. 129.

[39] R. C. Reed, 'The Southern Presbyterian Church and the Freedmen,' *Southern Presbyterian Review* (January 1885), p. 84.

to the whole Southern Presbyterian Church. Many church members, however, had been unhappy with Mack's preaching, including James Woodrow, who stayed away while Mack served as pastor.

In March the session invited John Girardeau to serve as supply pastor. He accepted the call with the understanding that in assuming the position, he was formally disclaiming 'before God and men any participation in the responsibility growing out of the use of instrumental music in the public worship of the church.'[40] In his sermon on 'The Discretionary Power of the Church' before the General Assembly in St. Louis in 1875, Girardeau defended the regulative principle in doctrine, polity, and worship. Preaching from Matthew 28:20—'Teaching them to observe all that I have commanded you'—Girardeau told his fellow Presbyterians that in these last words that Christ spoke to his church,

> we have the principle tinctured with the blood of our Puritan, Covenanter and Huguenot forefathers—that what is not commanded, either explicitly or implicitly in the Scriptures, is prohibited to the church. She can utter no new doctrine, make no new laws, ordain no new forms of government, and invent no new modes of worship. This is but a statement of a fundamental principle of Protestantism, contra-distinguishing it from Rationalism on the one hand and Romanism on the other—that the Scriptures, as the Word of Christ, are the complete and ultimate rule of faith and duty.[41]

It is not surprising that the Columbia church was eager to get Girardeau for their pulpit. Joseph Mack's first meeting with Girardeau had been in John Adger's home in 1860, when

[40] Willborn, 'Girardeau,' p. 315.
[41] Willborn, 'Girardeau,' p. 289.

Mack was a student at Columbia Seminary. Pointing to Girardeau, who was on the other side of the room, Adger said emphatically to Mack and several others, 'There is the Spurgeon of America, the grandest preacher in all our Southland.' 'This statement,' wrote Mack, 'then seemed to me a very extravagant one, and provoked the criticism, "See how these South Carolinians love one another." But afterwards I often realized that it was strictly and entirely true.'[42]

Girardeau's preaching was characterized as 'vivacious conversational address.'[43] Trained by his years of preaching to the slaves, he used simple, plain language. It was said that in his preaching Girardeau stood between Palmer and Thornwell, wielding 'the logic on fire of Thornwell, with much of the graceful oratory of Palmer.'[44] 'His pulpit eloquence,' wrote R. A. Webb, 'was not like the gradual ascent of the Rocky Mountains, by one long, splendid, continuous climb; there were a succession of climatic flights in each sermon, like the undulating beauty of the picturesque Blue Ridge.'[45]

Thomas Law long remembered a series of five sermons Girardeau preached to his African American congregation in Charleston. They were all based on a single short text—'And ye will not come to me, that ye might have life' (*John* 5:40). Each sermon stressed one word from this text. (1) 'And ye *will* not come to me'; (2) 'And ye will not *come* to me'; (3) 'And ye will not come to *me'*; (4) 'And ye will not come to me that ye might have *life'*; and (5) '*Not* coming to me ye cannot have life.'[46]

[42] Blackburn, *Girardeau,* p. 52. Adger's love for Girardeau was strained and their relationship broken during the evolution controversy.

[43] Blackburn, *Girardeau,* p. 126.

[44] Blackburn, *Girardeau,* pp. 139, 140.

[45] Blackburn, *Girardeau,* p. 208.

[46] Blackburn, *Girardeau,* pp. 138, 139.

On one occasion Girardeau was called to preach before the legislature of South Carolina, with the specific request that he preach his sermon 'The Last Judgment'—a sermon reminiscent of Jonathan Edwards' 'Sinners in the Hands of an Angry God.' He did so in First Presbyterian Church. R. A. Webb wrote:

> A great congregation was present, crowding both the floor and galleries, which were then on three sides of the building. The preacher was fully up to himself, in voice, gesture and spirit. Contrary to his general custom, he delivered [the sermon] from the manuscript. It was an hour and a half long. Attention was tense from the first. But when the flute-like voice rose to its best, reinforced by the silent language of gesture and face, many of the hearers stretched themselves forward as far as they could reach. Tears poured down cheeks . . . When the preacher's voice hushed, the multitude fell back into position with an audible heave, which sounded as if it had come simultaneously from every breast.[47]

For over a year, the congregation of First Presbyterian listened to the great preacher. Mary Jane Macfie McMaster wrote to her son John: 'We are enjoying the most delightful preaching now. Dr. Girardeau is our stated supply and will preach for us until next September. Our church is packed on Sunday mornings and our prayer meetings are well attended. Oh! how often do I wish you were here to hear him.'[48]

One Sunday night Girardeau preached on 'The Office of the Works of Charity in the Last Judgment,' from Matthew 25:40, at the request of the Ladies' Benevolent Society of the

[47] Blackburn, *Girardeau*, pp. 208, 209.
[48] *A Columbia Reader*, p. 84.

church. He carefully distinguished works as a means of salvation from works as the evidence of salvation.

> There has been but one doer of the law . . . Christ, as the divinely appointed substitute of sinners, has completely obeyed it both as to its precept and its penalty; and his vicarious righteousness, received by faith, constitutes the only ground of acceptance with God, either in this world or at the judgment-bar. When, therefore, the Bible asserts that men shall be judged according to their works the meaning is, not that they will be pronounced in the great day to be justified and acquitted on the ground of, or on account of, their works. The meaning is, that the works of the righteous will furnish the evidence that they are justified on the ground of, or on account of, Christ's merits; and that they possess a character which makes them meet for the enjoyment of God's presence and the fellowship of heaven.

The preacher then stressed the 'singularly conspicuous place' that will be assigned to charity, or love, in 'the last, great day':

> Turning to those on his right hand, the King will utter the thrilling words, 'Come ye blessed!' But why? What title have they to such a welcome? Does the King say, Ye were just, ye were true, ye were faithful, ye were temperate, ye were orthodox, ye adhered to my church in life, and ye died in its communion? No. All that may be involved in the character of those whom He will approve and receive amidst the solemnities of that day. But He does not say that He will signalize those traits. What will the King say to the righteous? Ye fed the hungry, ye gave drink to the thirsty, ye entertained the stranger, ye clothed the naked, ye visited the sick and those who were in prison.[49]

[49] Blackburn, *Sermons by John L. Girardeau*, pp. 71-72.

Some of the younger members of the church asked Girardeau to teach a Bible class on Sunday nights explaining the distinctive doctrines of Calvinism. At first Girardeau taught the class informally, with questions and discussions. Later, when outsiders began asking questions 'to start difficulties rather than to seek light,' he wrote out and read his lectures. Attendance grew—a fact, Girardeau wrote, 'which seemed to militate against the common opinion that doctrinal discussions would prove dry and unacceptable to a popular audience.' In these lectures, published in 1890 as *Calvinism and Evangelical Arminianism,* Girardeau answered the taunt that 'Calvinism is dying.' His profound conviction was that Calvinism expresses 'the faith of martyrs, confessors and reformers, the faith in which the majority of Christ's true people have lived and died; that it is the truth of God; and that, instead of dying, it is as immortal as that Inspired Word which liveth and abideth forever.'[50]

[50] John L. Girardeau, *Calvinism and Evangelical Arminianism: compared as to Election, Reprobation, Justification, and Related Doctrines* (Columbia: W. J. Duffie, 1890). When the book appeared Girardeau wrote that he would be grateful if God 'would be pleased to use it for arresting, at least in some degree, the tendency now manifested on the part of some professed Calvinists seriously to modify the doctrines of the Calvinistic Symbols' (p. viii).

19

'THE DEAR SEMINARY'

IN 1876 Columbia's General Wade Hampton III, the state's popular hero of the Confederacy, became governor. He endorsed justice, education, and greater educational opportunity for all, and appointed some African Americans to minor public offices. On April 7, 1877, President Rutherford B. Hayes ordered the removal of federal troops from the South Carolina State House, ending the long years of Reconstruction.

That same year, Columbia Seminary's William Plumer was one of fourteen delegates from the Southern Presbyterian Church who crossed the Atlantic to attend the Presbyterian Council in Edinburgh, Scotland. Moses D. Hoge, another delegate to the meeting, wrote that Plumer 'commanded the most marked attention' in Edinburgh, 'and left an impression upon the thousands who saw and heard him, which will not be forgotten in this generation.'[1] In 1880 Plumer retired from the seminary and was made professor emeritus by the board of directors. He preached at various churches in Maryland until his death on October 22, 1880. The pulpit of Columbia's First Presbyterian Church was 'draped in mourning for the period of thirty days' as a testimony to the people's love for him. At the funeral service, Moses Drury Hoge, who had

[1] White, *Southern Presbyterian Leaders*, p. 292.

served as Plumer's assistant at the First Presbyterian Church of Richmond, Virginia, spoke of Plumer's kindness, consideration, and encouragement to him as a young minister. Hoge, who became one of the best-known preachers in the Southern Presbyterian Church, characterized Plumer's ministry by saying, 'If he was a son of thunder on the platform and in the pulpit, he was a son of consolation in the sick room and among the bereaved of his people.'[2]

Finally adopted by the General Assembly in 1879, the revised *Book of Church Order of the Southern Presbyterian Church* derived mainly from the principles advocated by Thomas Cartwright in England and the *Second Book of Discipline of the Church of Scotland*. The 'new book,' a victory for Thornwellian principles, would rule the Southern Church for many years. Before the final vote in 1879, probably a hundred or more ministers had been involved in one way or another with the revision. Much of the work, however, had been done by John Adger, assisted by James Woodrow, in the Columbia Seminary chapel—originally the carriage house of the mansion that was the seminary's main building. William Childs Robinson wrote in his history of Columbia Seminary: 'Perhaps the license will be allowed, of recalling, in this connection, that the Book of Church Order for a Church which glories to acclaim Christ alone as King who was cradled in a manger, was composed in a house built for a carriage-stable.'[3]

The 1880 General Assembly met in Charleston. R. A. Webb, a student at Columbia Seminary, 'went down to the old city by the sea, to gaze upon this great gathering of the

[2] *Memorial Volume,* p. 213. Moses D. Hoge also said of Dr. Plumer, 'The longer he lived, the more to him did life seem worth living' (p. 216).

[3] Robinson, *Columbia Theological Seminary,* p. 94.

distinguished fathers of the Church.' The issue facing the assembly was whether the *in thesi* statements of the General Assembly should be understood as judicial, and so binding, or as advisory only. Columbia Seminary professors Woodrow and Girardeau debated the issue for two days. Finally, John Adger offered a motion accepted by both Girardeau and Woodrow that both judicial and *in thesi* declarations 'are alike interpretations of the Word by a church court' and both 'must be submitted to, unless contrary to the Constitution and the Word.'[4]

* * * * *

Columbia Seminary had faced a serious financial crisis for several years and managed to continue only by the self-sacrifice of the faculty. Two of the most important chairs, theology and church history, were vacant. The school was forced to close in 1879. Six of the students transferred to Union Seminary in Virginia, and fifteen went to Princeton.

Even though Columbia Seminary was closed, friends and former students met at First Presbyterian Church from November 4 through November 7, 1881, to organize an alumni association, and to celebrate the semi-centennial of the seminary and Dr. George Howe's fifty years of service as professor. The celebration began with the singing of a hymn and prayer by the Rev. James Beattie, one of the original five students of Dr. Goulding at Lexington, Georgia, before the seminary moved to Columbia. In his opening address Benjamin Morgan Palmer explained 'the double character' of the celebration—commemorating 'the founding of an institution

[4] Willborn, 'Girardeau,' p. 225.

that has been a blessing to the Church of God, and the life-long labors of this revered father in our Israel, beginning almost with its birth and running through its history to the present hour.' Palmer said that indeed the celebration took place 'under the shadow of a cloud.' All of us, he said, 'feel the depression of the hour,' but 'faith does not know the meaning of the word despair . . . It may know disaster, as we know it today, but it knows not defeat.'[5]

Girardeau described the scene:

> The Presbyterian church edifice was crowded with an intelligent and distinguished assembly. The music was inspiring. An eloquent opening speech, which thrilled all hearts, was pronounced by the Rev. Dr. B. M. Palmer. That veteran preacher of the gospel, the Rev. J. H. Saye, a member of the graduating class of 1837, delivered to [Dr. Howe] a congratulatory address, while he courteously stood to receive it. It was a picture for the brush of a painter. The light fell upon a grand and massive head which had grown white in the service of his Master and the Church. Saintly and venerable was his appearance. The dense auditory was hushed into profound silence, and many an eye was dimmed with tears, as with unaffected humility and grace, in rich and melting tones, and in a manner simple, but sublime, [Dr. Howe] acknowledged the kindness of his brethren, and dwelt upon the wisdom and the goodness of that holy providence which first led him to cast in his lot with theirs, and had conducted him through all the vicissitudes of so protracted a term of labor to that auspicious hour.[6]

Letters were read from a number of theological seminaries: Union in Virginia, Princeton, Western, Northwest,

[5] *Memorial Volume*, pp. 3, 4.
[6] *Memorial Volume*, pp. 393-94.

Danville, Auburn, and San Francisco. South Carolina native Thomas Peck, from Union Seminary, expressed his joy for the 'grand rally for the revival of a Seminary which has done a noble work in times past for the Church by the training of her ministers.'[7] Alexander T. McGill, who had taught at Columbia Seminary during the 1852-53 school year, had been chosen by the Princeton Seminary faculty to represent them at the Columbia semi-centennial but was sadly prevented from attending by 'the advance of age' and 'the grating of railway travel.' 'We [at Princeton] rejoice to know,' he wrote, 'that the sunny and fertile South is rapidly recovering her own resources, which were once liberally sent here to help this mother Seminary in its infancy and long struggle to secure an adequate foundation. Beloved brethren of the South, be of good cheer. God will not forget your work of faith and labor of love and patience of hope in ministering to the wants of Princeton more than half a century since.'[8]

Dr. Howe, in his address on the 'History of Columbia Seminary' for the semi-centennial celebration, listed by name the professors at the seminary during his fifty years on the faculty, and added:

> It has been a privilege, never, never to be forgotten, to have been associated with such men; to have been enlightened by their wisdom and stimulated daily by their example, and to emulate their achievements, it may be, whenever that was practicable; for neither by nature nor education are we made wholly alike, as is doubtless wisely ordained in the government of God.[9]

[7] *Memorial Volume*, p. 37.
[8] *Memorial Volume*, pp. xx, xxii.
[9] *Memorial Volume*, p. 155.

Four lectures followed. T. E. Peck, professor at Union Seminary in Virginia, spoke on 'The Spirit of Presbyterianism.' Henry M. Smith, pastor of the Third Presbyterian Church in New Orleans, lectured on 'The Old Testament in History.' John Girardeau's topic was 'The Federal Theology: Its Import and Regulative Influence.' C. A. Stillman, pastor of the Presbyterian church in Tuscaloosa, Alabama, spoke on 'The Pulpit and the Pastorate.' Stillman told how the seminary strove to put 'theology in all its depth and grandeur' into the hands of 'loving, sympathizing, considerate' pastors who would labor for 'the spiritual good of all classes' of people. Preachers, he said, must not be 'mere sign boards.' They are guides who go along with their people to show them the way they must travel. Stillman concluded:

> It is a matter for profound thankfulness that this beloved Seminary, in the fifty years of its noble history, has never been conducted as a mere school of learning, rhetoric, or philosophy, or even as a mere theological institute, but has ever given the conspicuous place to the spiritual and practical aspects of the ministerial work; and it is our devout prayer that it may, in the long years of the future, be pre-eminently God's chosen instrument for giving to his Church many 'pastors according to his heart, who shall feed his people with knowledge and understanding' . . . It is not merely to an institution of learning that we . . . dedicate our efforts on this occasion, but to the cause of divine truth, to the salvation of souls, the interests of holiness, the upbuilding and comfort of the Church, and above and through all these, to the glory of Christ.[10]

* * * * *

[10] *Memorial Volume*, pp. 88, 94-95.

Columbia Seminary reopened on September 20, 1882, with twenty-two students from nine states. The seminary had been controlled by the General Assembly since 1863, but in 1881 it was returned to the synods of South Carolina, Georgia, Alabama, and South Georgia/Florida, with the General Assembly retaining the right of review. Provision was made by the seminary's directors for the regular study of the English Bible, as well as instruction in the history and needs of foreign missions.

Columbia graduates continued to go out as pastors to churches in many states. Charles S. Vedder graduated in 1862 and became the minister of the famous French Huguenot Church in Charleston for over fifty years. Samuel Fisher Tenney of the class of 1868 became pastor at Crockett, Texas, in 1870 and served there for fifty-four years, the longest pastorate in the history of the Synod of Texas. He travelled in the North and in Canada to raise money to build a church and school in Texas for African Americans. During his long ministry he organized some fifteen new churches. He promoted missions among the Native Americans who had moved into Texas. C. W. Grafton, a graduate of 1873, was pastor at Union Church, Mississippi, for over sixty years and became known as 'the grand old man of Mississippi.'

John Thompson Plunkett graduated in 1880. John was the ninth of ten children born to Scotch-Irish parents in Franklin, Tennessee. His family moved to nearby Nashville, and John joined the First Presbyterian Church when he was fifteen. Six years later he became a deacon. The young man engaged in business for a few years before he returned to school, studying literature and history at the University of Nashville. He graduated from the Southwestern Presbyterian University in Clarksville, Tennessee, and entered Columbia Seminary.

During the spring of 1880 Plunkett was licensed to preach by the Presbytery of Nashville and was called to the historic Steel Creek Church near Charlotte, North Carolina. He was ordained by the Presbytery of Mecklenburg. Plunkett later served churches in Covington, Kentucky, and Detroit, Michigan, before coming to the First Presbyterian Church of Augusta, Georgia, in 1890.

A church member noted that although Plunkett's predecessors at First Presbyterian had been 'noted pulpit orators,' the church had declined because 'internal discord had done its inevitable work in sapping to some extent the spiritual vitality of the church.' Plunkett brought to First Presbyterian Church 'Christian zeal, generous sympathy, practical wisdom, fine common sense, and almost infinite tact'; and 'in a short time the voices of dissension were silenced, harmony was restored, and the whole church membership was reunited in the bonds of Christian fellowship.' An outstanding preacher and dedicated churchman, Plunkett soon became known as one of the vital leaders of the Southern Presbyterian Church. In 1896 he was a commissioner to the Pan-Presbyterian Council that met in Glasgow, Scotland. He was a commissioner to the same gathering in Liverpool, England, in 1904. Plunkett declined invitations to become pastor of First Presbyterian Church of Dallas, Texas, and president of Columbia Theological Seminary.

On June 27, 1909, Plunkett accepted the call to the South Highlands Presbyterian Church in Birmingham, Alabama. He told his people in Augusta, 'I feel that I have fulfilled my mission here. My work now is elsewhere.' A little over a year after he moved to Birmingham, Plunkett died. The Augusta newspaper called him 'one of the most beloved men of the Presbyterian Church of the whole South.' A resolution passed by the congregation of Augusta's First Presbyterian Church stated that 'all of us have felt the influence of his gentle courtesy and almost divine sympathy.' The centennial history of First Presbyterian Church stated that Plunkett was 'revered and greatly beloved by every man, woman, and child composing his own congregation, and indeed it may be truthfully added, no less so by all the people of the city of Augusta entire, without regard to creed, sex, or color.' At a memorial service at First Presbyterian in Augusta on November 17, Dr. McPheeters of Columbia Seminary paid tribute to the graduate of the seminary who was for many years one of its directors.

W. E. Boggs returned to Columbia in 1882 as professor of church history and polity at the seminary. Boggs had served the Second Presbyterian Church in Memphis from 1871 to 1879. During this time a terrible epidemic of yellow fever struck the city, and Boggs and his wife, Marion, gave themselves to the task of caring for the sick and dying. They were both stricken with the disease and almost died themselves. In 1879 Boggs accepted a call to the Central Presbyterian Church in Atlanta and served there until he became a professor at Columbia Seminary.

C. R. Hemphill came as professor of biblical literature in 1883. After graduating from Columbia Seminary in 1874 he taught Hebrew at the school, then held a Greek fellowship at Johns Hopkins University. He taught at Southwestern Presbyterian University for a few years. For his inaugural address at Columbia Seminary, Hemphill addressed the higher criticism that was influencing many Christian churches and seminaries, choosing for his topic 'the stirring question of the authorship of the Pentateuch.' His conclusion was,

> that Christ must be held responsible, not only for the historic character and inspiration and Divine Authority of the Pentateuch, but also for the Mosaic authorship of the book. If this be a just exposition, it must be acknowledged that the question which more than any single question absorbs the attention of Old Testament scholars today, is not left to be decided by purely scientific inquiry, but has been settled for the loyal believer in Christ by the great Teacher himself.[11]

* * * * *

John Lafayette Girardeau ended his preaching at First Presbyterian Church in October 1882. He had written to the session declining an invitation to continue and added, 'I have received unbounded kindness from you, my brethren. May the Master supply [you] with a tenderer and everyway better shepherd than I have been.' Girardeau was followed in the pulpit by former minister William Boggs and Charles Hemphill, both professors at the seminary, who served jointly as supply pastors for a year.

Girardeau now devoted much of his time to a new Columbia congregation that had begun as a mission Sunday school in 1883, when a few members of First Presbyterian Church met in a building on the old fairgrounds. Methodist minister Dr. J. M. Buckley and a pastor friend stopped over one Sunday in Columbia. Buckley wrote:

> We arrived in Columbia on Saturday evening. After being settled at the hotel we walked through the city and were charmed with it. After a walk of two or three miles we went into a book store to make a few purchases. I said, 'Sir, whose

[11] Thompson, *Presbyterians in the South,* 2:452.

church would you advise a stranger, who wished to hear the best preacher, to visit tomorrow?' Without a moment's hesitation he answered, 'Dr. Girardeau's Mission,' and a gentleman standing by looked acquiescence.

Never was there a more beautiful day than [that] Sunday ... in Columbia. There have been days as fine; none finer; the perfection of a spring day ... Every window was open; the trees were full of birds, the streets of children; the peach and other fruit trees in blossom and many flowers in bloom.

On reaching 'Dr. Girardeau's Mission' we found every seat occupied and some of the congregation standing. Perceiving that we were strangers, an usher procured chairs and placed us very near the pulpit. As we were about to enter, one of us said to the other, 'We don't get the chance to hear others preach often. I would like to hear something that would move my soul.'

The first thing noticed was the character of the congregation. It was the most refined and intelligent congregation of its number that I had ever seen in the South—and I do not remember to have seen it surpassed in the North—more solid-looking gentlemen and ladies of striking appearance. And the young people were of the best sort. Never did I see an assembly that looked so little like a 'mission.'

Buckley continued his account with praise of Girardeau's preaching:

I have now to say that, having heard Thomas Guthrie of Edinburgh, James Hamilton of London, and Mr Spurgeon six or eight times, it has never fallen to my lot to hear a more absorbing, spiritual, eloquent and moving sermon on an ordinary occasion . . . It made all the preaching I have ever done, and nearly all I have ever heard seem like mere sermonizing. Looking around to catch the eye of my friend, I saw that two thirds of all men in the audience were in tears.

> It was no rant or artificial excitement or mere pathos, but thought burning and glowing. None but a man of equal intellect, learning, piety and eloquence could preach such a discourse without notes.[12]

* * * * *

On the first Lord's Day in April 1883, Dr. Howe received Communion at First Church. On his way home, his carriage broke down at the corner of Bull and Taylor streets, and Howe fell and suffered a broken leg. Two weeks later he died. He had asked his wife to read to him the last two chapters of the book of Romans. Taking the Bible, he read those same chapters to her. He then prayed, ending with petitions for 'the dear seminary.' This was his last audible prayer, a fitting close to a long life of faithful service to Columbia Seminary. His body was carried to the First Presbyterian Church, where a large congregation had assembled. The funeral service was conducted by the members of the seminary faculty—professors Woodrow, Hemphill, Boggs, and Girardeau. Howe was buried in the churchyard near the tombs of his first wife and his children who had died, and not far from the grave of his colleague Dr. A. W. Leland.

For over a half century 'this northern-born saint,' wrote William Childs Robinson, 'kindled a flame of like consecration in the hearts of his Southern pupils' and endeared himself to the people of his adopted city.[13] Howe's love for South

[12] Blackburn, *Girardeau,* pp. 56-57. Thomas Guthrie (1803-73) was a minister of the Church of Scotland and, after the Disruption in 1843, of the Free Church of Scotland; his preaching attracted rich and poor in great numbers. Charles Spurgeon (1834-92), Baptist minister of London, is recognized as one of the greatest preachers of all time.

[13] Robinson, *Columbia Theological Seminary,* p. 162.

Carolina expressed itself in various ways—not the least his monumental *History of the Presbyterian Church in South Carolina,* the last pages of the second volume sent to the printers only a few days before his death.

Columbians long remembered Dr. Howe as a large and gentle man with a large and gentle heart. They marked his grave in the Presbyterian churchyard with a monument inscribed in English, Greek, Hebrew, and Latin. Howe was the one member of Charleston Presbytery, it was said, who could converse fluently in Latin!

At the meeting of the Columbia Seminary Alumni Association on May 9, 1883, Girardeau delivered a long eulogy to Howe. Howe, Girardeau said, was not inclined to be, 'strictly speaking, an ecclesiastic' nor 'addicted in practice to the discussion of questions pertaining to church order,' but took a great interest in the spread of the gospel throughout the world. Girardeau stated that the seminary's long-time professor never gave 'any uncertain sound in reference to the great and vital doctrine of the plenary inspiration of the Sacred Writings.' 'Truth was his end,' Girardeau explained, 'and truth his road to reach it.' He added, 'May the day never come when that fundamental truth shall be shaken in this institution! Better would it be that its invested funds should be withered up, its doors be bolted, and that the youthful seekers of truth should repair for instruction to the pastors of Christ's flock who remain faithful to his word.'[14]

[14] *Memorial Volume,* p. 408.

20

'THE LORD'S ORDERING'

THE presentation of Reformed doctrine continued to be the central purpose of the *Southern Presbyterian Review*. In July 1878 Thomas E. Peck, professor at Virginia's Union Theological Seminary, presented a substantive review of 'Thornwell's Writings.' The four 'elegant and portly volumes,' Peck stated, were full of 'the deepest and most inspiring thought of one of the greatest thinkers of the age.'[1] Peck wrote that Thornwell regretted that he did not write more. In a letter to Peck in 1853, Thornwell said that it had been the mistake of his life that he had written so little. 'Learn from my experience,' he counselled the young man.[2]

Comment on contemporary events also appeared regularly in the *Review*. In 1876 James Woodrow wrote an indignant editorial about the mistreatment of the American Indians. Woodrow was dismayed by the cry for vengeance following the massacre of Custer's forces. He stated that the United States government had broken treaty obligations with the Indians and urged fairness and honesty in the place of the hatred being shown toward Native Americans.[3]

[1] T. E. Peck, 'Review of Collected Writings of James Henley Thornwell,' *Southern Presbyterian Review* (July 1878), p. 413.

[2] Palmer, *Thornwell*, p. 374.

[3] Gustafson, *Woodrow*, p. 110.

In the April 1883 issue of the *Southern Presbyterian Review,* Benjamin Morgan Palmer summarized the history of the attempt to establish 'official correspondence' between the Northern and Southern Presbyterian Churches, a matter with which, he wrote, he had been connected 'from the start.'[4] Palmer opposed attempts to bring the two churches back together. There were bitter memories of past grievances in Palmer's mind, but his chief concern was that the two denominations were not in doctrinal accord and could not be expected to walk together in harmony. For all his intransigence on this issue, however, Palmer was known to be an open-hearted and generous man. The Jews of New Orleans held him in high regard. 'They loved him,' Thomas Cary Johnson wrote, 'because he loved them.' Speaking out on the suffering of the Jews in Russia, Palmer exclaimed, 'When a Hebrew suffers I suffer with him.' After Palmer's death, a rabbi said: 'Only great men have the capacity of harboring strong convictions, and at the same time of allowing others to differ; only good men will take an opponent by the hand and say, "Be my friend."'[5]

James Woodrow also resisted any suggestion for union of the Northern and Southern Churches. He objected to the political nature of the Northern Church and to the different ideas about confessional subscription. The church in the North adopts 'the most liberal and loosest rules of construction,' he wrote in 1871, 'while in our church . . . the rules of strictest construction prevail.'[6] In 1887 Woodrow, though still opposing organic union, penned some kind words about the

[4] B. M. Palmer, 'Fraternal Relations,' *Southern Presbyterian Review* (April 1883), p. 306.

[5] Wells, *Southern Presbyterian Worthies*, pp. 169-70.

[6] Gustafson, *Woodrow*, p. 96.

Northern Presbyterian Church:

> Honestly, we desire real spiritual unity with our Northern brethren. We honor them as intelligent Christian people; we love them as brethren. In the true sense of the word we are now one with them in Christ, for we regard Christ the head and king of all his subjects as the true bond of Christian union. We wish to live on terms of charity and affection for them.[7]

The 1882 General Assembly voted almost unanimously for fraternal relations with the Northern Church. So in 1883 Southern delegates travelled north for the General Assembly of the Presbyterian Church in the United States of America and were welcomed and seated with their Northern brothers for the first time since 1860. In 1885 R. C. Reed, who later became professor of church history at Columbia Seminary, wrote: 'We believe, and the belief awakens no feeling of sadness, that the conviction is gaining ground among us that we can well afford to cherish a much more fraternal spirit towards our brethren of the Northern Church.'[8]

Girardeau, Woodrow, and Palmer, however, continued to warn the Southern Church not to move toward organic union with the Northern Presbyterian Church. At the same time these 'Old Columbians' were ecumenical in their embracing of all evangelical denominations as sister churches, and promoting 'correspondence' and 'fraternal relations' between the various churches of the Reformed world. While maintaining that the Presbyterian Church most closely approaches the biblical model, Woodrow held that 'we must recognize as

[7] Gustafson, *Woodrow,* pp. 101-02.

[8] R. C. Reed, 'The Southern Presbyterian Church and the Freedmen,' *Southern Presbyterian Review* (January 1885), p. 107.

genuine parts of Christ's church all bodies which believe in the crucified and risen Lord Jesus Christ, the eternal Son of God, and man, in two natures and one person forever.'[9] At the celebration of George Howe's fifty years of teaching at Columbia Seminary, Girardeau spoke of Howe's generous spirit. 'All God's people, of whatever name, he owned as his Father's children,' he said; 'every servant of Jesus he recognized as a brother beloved.' R. A. Webb tells this story about Girardeau: Dr. Gadsden, an Episcopal clergyman, said to him, 'Girardeau, the older I get the less denominational I become.' Girardeau replied, 'Gadsden, the older I get the more denominational I become.' Gadsden answered, 'Your statement is surprising; I thought you were growing in grace.' Girardeau replied, 'My denominational creed teaches me that there are other sheep not of the Presbyterian fold; and the older I get the more heartily do I believe it; hence, as I grow in grace I am growing in denominationalism.' Girardeau was making the point that the Westminster Confession requires that Presbyterians view the church in its larger form and see their own church as one denomination among others.[10]

* * * * *

On July 13, 1886, John Leighton Wilson died. From 1875 to 1884 Dr. and Mrs. Wilson had lived in Baltimore, where Wilson's office as secretary of foreign missions was located. In 1884 the Wilsons moved to Salem in the Black River community, in South Carolina. Wilson was happy to be back home. He planted a fine garden and experimented with seeds

[9] Gustafson, *Woodrow*, p. 232.
[10] Blackburn, *Girardeau*, p. 213.

that missionaries from many countries sent him. He did not preach to the white congregation at Mount Zion, but was always ready for service at Mount Sinai, where the black people worshipped, a church that he helped to build. His last sermon—from the words 'Let this mind be in you which was also in Christ Jesus'—was to his friends of African descent at Mount Sinai. In July 1885 Mrs. Wilson died, followed almost exactly a year later by her husband. A large crowd, black and white, followed him to his last resting place. His lifelong friend, James Woodrow, preached the funeral sermon. Before the casket was closed, Woodrow kissed the forehead of Wilson—'the man he had loved so long and so well.'[11] 'Side by side,' Dr. and Mrs. Wilson 'are sleeping today near the door of the house of God in which his fathers offered worship, the sanctuary among the pine trees known as Mount Zion,' wrote Henry Alexander White.[12] At the opening of the Synod of South Carolina in 1890, a memorial sermon was preached on the life and character of Dr. Wilson, from the appropriate text 'King of Salem, priest of the most high God' (*Heb.* 7:1).

Following his own outstanding mission work in Africa, Wilson helped develop missions in the Presbyterian Church in the United States and, after 1861, in the Southern Presbyterian Church. He had played an important role in the beginning of the Brazil mission of the PCUSA, when he supported Ashbel Green Symington's desire to be sent to that country although most of the mission board was opposed. He pled with the board to allow Symington to go to Brazil, because 'his mind and heart were so strongly drawn to its evangelization, that it should be regarded as the guiding hand of Providence.'[13]

[11] DuBose, *Wilson*, p. 319.
[12] White, *Southern Presbyterian Leaders*, p. 408.
[13] DuBose, *Wilson*, p. 238.

Wilson led the work of missions in the Southern Presbyterian Church for twenty-five years, supporting and continuing the earlier mission to the Native Americans in the South, and adding overseas missions to China, Italy, Colombia, Mexico, Greece, Japan, and Brazil. Two men from the Columbia Seminary class of 1869, influenced by the words of Wilson and following the example of Symington, began the Southern Presbyterian mission in Brazil. But the longing of Wilson's heart to see a Southern Presbyterian mission to Africa was not to be realized in his lifetime. In 1890, four years after Wilson's death, Samuel Lapsley and William Sheppard began mission work in the Congo. John Leighton Wilson loved missions because 'it is the Lord's ordering' and he loves missions 'more than any of us can do,' he wrote to Hampden DuBose. Wilson was often encouraged but sometimes found it a hard thing 'to have to stand between a dying world and an indifferent, hesitating church.'[14]

'The church to this day,' wrote Robert Lewis Dabney, 'is feeling the sacred influence of Dr. John Leighton Wilson in her foreign missionary work. Its wonderful power and progress are largely the result of his teachings, his sustained energy and statesmanlike plans.'[15] In 1936, John Miller Wells wrote to a number of Southern Presbyterian missionaries and mission leaders to ask what principles they followed in their work. They responded with five: Christ is the head of the church; the pre-eminent duty of the church in its foreign missions work is the preaching of the gospel; the leadership of the Holy Spirit must be sought and followed; the importance of placing upon the native Christians and church the task of

[14] DuBose, *Wilson*, p. 278.

[15] Wells, *Southern Presbyterian Worthies*, pp. 72-76.

saving their own people and land should be recognized; obedience to Christ's command in foreign missions is the hope for the church itself here at home. Every one of these principles, Wells wrote, was 'held, taught, and used by our first great secretary'—John Leighton Wilson.

* * * * *

Hampden Coit DuBose, who could never forget the sermon he had heard John Girardeau preach in his home church in South Carolina in 1865, went to China as a missionary in 1873. Of Huguenot ancestry, Hampden DuBose was born in 1845 in Darlington, South Carolina, not many miles from the birthplace of John Leighton Wilson.[16] DuBose's father died when he was seven years old. The cause dearest to the heart of his mother, Margaret Thompson DuBose, was foreign missions; she prayed daily for the conversion of the world. Hampden DuBose studied at the Citadel Military Academy in Charleston and served for three years in the Confederate army. He graduated from the University of South Carolina in 1868 and from Columbia Seminary in 1871. At DuBose's ordination William Plumer preached the sermon, and John Leighton Wilson, whose biography DuBose would write, delivered the charge. DuBose always remembered Wilson's words about the abiding presence of Christ with his disciples. Wilson said, 'Once on a journey under the equatorial suns of Africa, sick, weary and exhausted, I threw myself down in the shade of a tree, feeling that this might be the place where I would breathe my last, when suddenly a bright light

[16] See the book *For the Glory of God: Memoirs of Dr. and Mrs. H. C. DuBose of Soochow, China,* compiled by Mrs. Nettie DuBose Junkin, and printed privately.

seemed to shine around me, and lit up the tree under which I was lying. I arose refreshed and invigorated, and pursued my journey.'[17]

Hampden DuBose and Pauline McAlpine were married on April 3, 1872. His first glimpse of her was while she was teaching a Sunday school class. The same thing had happened to John Leighton Wilson when he first saw his wife-to-be teaching a class in the African Sunday school in Savannah. In 1873 Hampden and Pauline went to Soochow (Suzhou), China, a city of gardens and canals, but sometimes a place of dangerous riots. There were very few preachers in the interior of China and only a handful of churches. The Chinese described DuBose as 'the man with a long black beard' who says 'he is only twenty-six years old.' On asking a Chinese person where he had heard the gospel, later missionaries often received the reply, 'From the man with the long beard.' The Chinese did not always remember his name, but they remembered his striking appearance and his fluent speech and gracious manner.

In January 1896, twenty-four years after he had landed in China, Hampden DuBose was able to organize the Anti-Opium League of China. Success came to his efforts in 1906 when the British Parliament declared the opium trade 'morally indefensible.' Just as John Leighton Wilson had fought the slave trade in West Africa, so DuBose fought the opium trade in China. DuBose served in China for thirty-eight years, until his death in 1910. Two days before his death he preached his final sermon. On his last afternoon he worked on the theology book he was writing for the Chinese and played a happy game with his little grandson. That night he dictated letters. He said to his wife, 'I am going to do as the catechism says

[17] DuBose, *Wilson,* p. 116.

we must do, I shall glorify God as long as I live and then go Home to enjoy Him forever.' He led in prayer, praying earnestly for the Chinese Christians and for his family, and ended with his childhood prayer:

> Now I lay me down to sleep,
> I pray the Lord my soul to keep.
> If I should die before I wake,
> I pray the Lord my soul to take.

He died that night. The Chinese Christians placed a memorial tablet at the entrance of the Yang Yoh Hang Chapel in Soochow. Inscribed was a long summary of his life, ending with the words 'Noble Teacher! China and America together unite in paying respects to your memory.' Pauline DuBose courageously carried on their mission work until her death four years later. She was buried next to her husband in the Shanghai cemetery, beside the graves of two of their children and two grandchildren.

It was fitting that Hampden DuBose write the life of John Leighton Wilson. The two men came from the same section of South Carolina, both studied at Columbia Seminary, and both became missionaries—one to Africa, the other to China. Most of the work on the *Memoirs of Dr. Wilson* was done while DuBose—the 'editor,' he called himself—was in China. In his preface, DuBose wrote that 'a kind Providence watched over the pages that were sent to a distant land, especially over the old letters from Africa, yellow with age. When on the passage to China, during a storm, the baggage was immersed in lubricating oil, and one trunk broken to pieces and the contents well soaked. The letters were in the other trunk, else they would have been illegible.'[18]

[18] DuBose, *Wilson*, p. 5.

Following Hampden DuBose in China was Samuel Isset Woodbridge, an alumnus of Rutgers, who graduated from Columbia Seminary in 1882. He married Jeanie Wilson Woodrow, daughter of James Woodrow, and they went to China, where Woodbridge served for many years preaching, teaching, and editing the *Chinese Christian Intelligencer*.[19]

[19] A son, Charles Woodbridge, was born in China in 1902. He served as pastor of the Independent Presbyterian Church in Savannah, Georgia, from 1945 to 1950, and later as professor at Fuller Theological Seminary. For an account of Charles Woodbridge's life, see Calhoun, *The Spendor of Grace,* pp. 378-403.

21

THE EVOLUTION CONTROVERSY

THE evolution controversy, 'the longest and most disturbing in the history of the Southern Church,' began unfolding in earnest in 1882 and continued for at least ten years.[1]

In the 1860s James Woodrow, the Perkins Professor of Natural Science in Connection with Revelation at Columbia Seminary, and Robert Lewis Dabney clashed in the pages of the *Southern Presbyterian Review,* with articles concerning the Christian attitude to physical science. Dabney's anonymous essay, 'Geology and the Bible,' published in the *Review* in 1863, insisted that the biblical accounts 'must be absolutely authoritative in all their parts, without waiting on or deferring to any conclusion of human science whatsoever.' Science, in a subordinate position, may illustrate the Bible, he held, but it may not substitute for or stand above biblical truth.[2]

Woodrow agreed that 'the results of science . . . could illuminate but not dictate to Scripture,' and went on to argue that Scripture provides the necessary religious understanding not permitted within the defined sphere of science. One of his concerns, however, was to retain the integrity of geology as a valid scientific discipline. Furthermore, Woodrow thought

[1] Willborn, 'Girardeau,' p. 212.
[2] Gustafson, *Woodrow,* p. 121.

that the Bible was silent on the mode of creation. The Bible does not say whether God created 'a finished world of sea and land,' or whether God used 'nebulous matter which he endowed with properties such that it would pass through successive changes until it reached the condition in which we now see it.' Dabney believed that the Bible did state how God had created, whereas Woodrow believed that the apparent silence of the Bible on matters of science made many scientific theories possible.

The public debate died down for a few years—during the Civil War and Reconstruction—but concerns about Woodrow's teaching continued. In an 1883 meeting of the Board of Directors of Columbia Seminary, J. B. Mack, who was the financial agent for the seminary, proposed that Dr. Woodrow be requested to give an address about evolution and to publish it in the *Southern Presbyterian Review*. On May 7, 1884, directors, alumni, and students of Columbia Seminary, and citizens of Columbia assembled at the First Presbyterian Church to hear Woodrow's address.

Woodrow stated that he had come to the conclusion that the content and aims of the Bible and science were so different that it was better to establish the principle of 'non-contradiction' rather than that of 'harmony.' He insisted that the Bible was not intended to teach science such as astronomy, quoting John Calvin, who wrote that to learn astronomy and 'other recondite arts,' one must 'go elsewhere.'[3] Woodrow stated

[3] Gustafson, *Woodrow*, p. 137. Calvin wrote in his commentary on Genesis 1:6: 'Moses describes the special use of this expanse "to divide the waters from the waters", from which words arises a great difficulty. For it appears opposed to common sense, and quite incredible, that there should be waters above the heaven. Hence some resort to allegory, and philosophize concerning angels; but quite beside the purpose. For, to my mind, this is a certain principle, that nothing is here treated of but the visible form of the world. He who would learn astronomy, and other

that his belief in the divine inspiration of every word of the Bible was not shaken. 'I have found nothing in my study of the Holy Bible and of natural science,' he said, 'that shakes my firm belief in the divine inspiration of every word of that Bible, and in the consequent absolute truth, the absolute inerrancy, of every expression which it contains from beginning to end.'[4] Woodrow's study of the Bible, however, had led him to believe that it was clear that God created all things but so far as he could see there was nothing to indicate how he created. He insisted that 'neither the idea of design or purpose were eliminated in evolution; rather they were incorporated in the Divine mind behind the creative process.'[5] Furthermore, Woodrow argued that the issue of how God made Adam from the dust of the ground was scientific, not theological, and that just as the church had no business making political deliverances, it had no right to make scientific declarations. Woodrow now believed that when the Bible says that the first man was made of dust, it could refer to either 'organic dust' or 'inorganic dust.' If organic dust, then it would be possible to accept the view that the body of man had evolved from earlier forms of creation. The soul of man, however, differs in degree and kind from anything in the animal world, and was immediately created by God. Woodrow added that the first woman was created immediately by God from Adam, as clearly stated in the Bible. He ended his address with the

recondite arts, let him go elsewhere. Here the Spirit of God would teach all men without exception; and therefore what Gregory would teach all men without exception; and therefore what Gregory declares falsely and in vain respecting statues and pictures is truly applicable to the history of the creation, namely, that it is the book of the unlearned.' John Calvin, *A Commentary on Genesis* (London: Banner of Truth, 1965), pp. 79-80.

[4] Robinson, *Columbia Theological Seminary*, p. 175-76.

[5] Gustafson, *Woodrow*, p. 143.

statement that evolution, as he had presented it, may well be true. It could be, he believed, God's plan of creation, and

> instead of being tempted to put away thoughts of him as I contemplate this wondrous series of events, caused and controlled by the power and wisdom of the Lord God Almighty, I am led with profound reverence and admiration to give glory and honor to him that sits on the throne, who lives for ever and ever; and with fuller heart and a truer appreciation of what it is to create, to join in saying, Thou art worthy, O Lord, to receive glory and honor and power; for thou hast created all things, and for thy pleasure they are and were created.[6]

William Childs Robinson summed up Woodrow's position: he held 'that creation and evolution are not contradictory; but that evolution within the limits of natural science necessarily deals only with the mode in which the effect is produced, while creation deals with the power which produces the effect.'[7]

James Woodrow's address was published in the July 1884 issue of the *Southern Presbyterian Review*. A period of difficult and intense debate followed, dividing the church and the seminary and setting friend against friend. When the *Review* published a number of articles in defence of Woodrow's views, including John Adger's 'Calm and Candid Review of Evolution,' most of the editors resigned, including Dabney and Girardeau. This proved to be a fatal blow, and the *Southern Presbyterian Review* suspended publication the next year with its October 1885 issue.

Several weeks after Woodrow's address, J. B. Mack wrote a letter in which he asserted that some in the church were refusing to support Columbia Seminary as long as Woodrow

[6] Gustafson, *Woodrow*, p. 152.

[7] Robinson, *Columbia Theological Seminary*, p. 175.

remained a professor there. He also charged Woodrow with 'neglect of the sanctuary.' Evidently, Woodrow did not attend services regularly during Mack's ministry at First Presbyterian Church, finding, with many others, according to Woodrow's nephew Woodrow Wilson that Mack's preaching was 'exceedingly uninstructive.' So he, 'very unwisely, but with no want of love for Christ and his gospel,' decided, wrote Woodrow Wilson, 'to content himself on Sabbath with private worship at home.'[8] Neander Woods, then pastor of First Presbyterian Church, answered Mack's charge, declaring that Woodrow regularly attended services, 'and though his family was not large enough to fill one whole pew, he always paid for two of full size.' 'In all my ministry I have never known a more devout and attentive listener than was Dr. Woodrow,' Woods stated.

The seminary directors met in September and passed, by a vote of 8 to 3, a statement in support of Woodrow: 'This board is in fullest sympathy with the godly jealousy of the church for the infallible truth and absolute inerrancy of the Scriptures of the Old and New Testaments as God's word to man, and we rejoice in the full confirmation by Dr. Woodrow that he stands immovably with us in the same position.'[9]

Each of the four synods that controlled the seminary (South Carolina, Georgia, Alabama, and South Georgia/Florida) responded to the board's decision. The Synod of South Carolina debated the matter for five days, with James Woodrow and John Adger on one side and John Girardeau and J. B. Mack on the other. A member of Congress who heard the debate said that 'for ability, dignity and force, he had never

[8] Gustafson, *Woodrow,* p. 278.

[9] Willborn, 'Girardeau,' p. 250.

heard its equal in the Senate of the United States.'[10] Presbyter William Plumer Jacobs was not so impressed. He deplored the spirit in which Girardeau and Mack attacked Woodrow and his supporters.[11] Finally the synod expressed its willingness to allow evolution to be taught in the seminary in a 'purely expository manner, with no intention of inculcating its truth.' The other synods, however, made no such concessions and ruled that evolution not be taught at all in the seminary. The board of directors (recently reconstituted with new members sympathetic to the views of the three synods opposing Woodrow) voted on December 10, 1884, by a vote of 8 to 4, to ask Woodrow to resign. Woodrow refused because he believed that he had not taught anything contrary to Scripture and the Confession of Faith. The board then voted to remove him from his professorship. William Boggs and Charles Hemphill resigned in protest, leaving Girardeau alone on the faculty.

James Woodrow called for a trial by his Augusta Presbytery, which declined, stating that they had found nothing to warrant a trial for heresy. Woodrow appealed to the Synod of Georgia, which ruled that the presbytery should reopen the case and either declare that there were no grounds for judicial process or, if there were such grounds, to proceed to trial. The synods controlling Columbia Seminary split evenly on Woodrow's appeal. The Synod of South Carolina and the Synod of South Georgia and Florida disapproved his removal from his professorship, whereas the Synod of Georgia and the Synod of Alabama approved the board's decision to remove Woodrow from his position at the seminary.

By a vote of 8 to 5, the seminary's directors again requested Woodrow's resignation 'in order to stop the agitation, and

[10] Blackburn, *Girardeau,* p. 234.

[11] Jacobs, *Diary of William Plumer Jacobs,* p. 264.

promote the highest interests of the seminary.' Again Woodrow refused. The board then took a vote to remove him, which lost, 7 to 6! Girardeau resigned in protest over the board's failure to vote for Woodrow's removal.

The Augusta Presbytery, following the instructions of the Synod of Georgia, reopened the Woodrow case. A member of presbytery drew up an indictment against Woodrow with charges and specifications. Before the trial could take place, however, the 1886 General Assembly met in Augusta. A committee was appointed to consider the overtures from several presbyteries concerning the evolution issue. The committee presented a report that included the statement that 'Adam's body was directly fashioned by Almighty God of the dust of the ground, without any natural parentage of any kind, out of matter previously created from nothing,' and that any teaching 'at variance therewith is a dangerous error' and will lead to 'the denial of doctrines fundamental to the faith.'[12] The General Assembly adopted this report by an overwhelming vote of 137 to 13.

The Augusta Presbytery met on August 14, 1886, to try Woodrow. Contrary to custom, the minister facing the heresy trial, in this case Woodrow, was invited to preach the opening sermon, rather than the moderator. Though 'feeble and already overwhelmed with work,' Woodrow accepted, preaching on 'The Presbyterian View of the Bible.' He affirmed that the Bible is the true Word of God: 'It is absolutely true in every part in the sense in which it was the design of its real author, the Holy Spirit, that it should be understood.'[13] While Woodrow embraced the view of the church as to the inerrancy of Scripture, he differed from many on some key points:

[12] Gustafson, *Woodrow*, p. 210.

[13] Gustafson, *Woodrow*, pp. 213-14.

'his understanding of the essential as opposed to the incidental purpose of the Bible, his grasp of the inability of language to convey certain types of meaning, his belief that the Scriptures do not teach science.'[14] In Girardeau's testimony before the presbytery, he insisted that Woodrow's position on the antiquity of the earth was out of accord with the 'traditional interpretation of Scripture and the Standards of the Church.'[15] Woodrow maintained that none of his teachings contradicted the Scriptures or the Confession of Faith, although he had on several occasions taken exception to the statement that God made all things 'in the space of six days,' assuming that the Westminster Confession meant six twenty-four-hour days.

The presbytery found Woodrow not guilty. The verdict was appealed to the Synod of Georgia. The Synod of Georgia sustained the appeal and annulled the decision of the Augusta Presbytery. Woodrow gave notice that he would complain to the General Assembly. A newspaper reporting these events noted whimsically that 'whenever things get dull with the Presbyterians of the South, they turn to and try Professor Woodrow for heresy. The trial usually comes earlier in the season, but this has been an exceptional year for early crops and things are a little mixed. The Augusta Presbytery has just finished the heresy drama for this year.'[16] In a letter to his fiancée, Woodrow's son James comments that his father was 'not a bit cast down, but as brave as ever, knowing that time will bring all things right.'[17]

Finally, the four synods concurred in the dismissal of Woodrow. The seminary's board of directors, at its December

[14] Gustafson, *Woodrow,* p. 216.
[15] Willborn, 'Girardeau,' p. 277.
[16] Gustafson, *Woodrow,* p. 217.
[17] Gustafson, *Woodrow,* p. 221.

10, 1886 meeting, removed him as a professor and suspended the operations of the seminary until September 1887, because of the 'serious complications arising out of the evolution controversy.'[18]

The 1888 General Assembly, meeting in Baltimore, voted 109 to 34 not to sustain Woodrow's appeal and repeated its statement against evolution adopted in 1886. The assembly also declared, in apparent agreement with Woodrow, that

> the wisdom of God prompted Him to reveal the fact, while the inscrutable mode of His action therein He has not revealed. Therefore the Church does not propose to touch, handle or conclude any question of science which belongs to God's kingdom of nature. She must, by her divine constitution, see that these questions are not thrust upon her to break the silence of Scripture and supplement it by any scientific hypothesis concerning the mode of God's being or acts in creation which are inscrutable to us.

Thornton Whaling, who would in a few years become president of Columbia Seminary, presented a protest for himself and others, asserting that 'the Westminster Standards simply reproduce without interpretation the statements of the Scripture in reference to the creation of Adam's body; and, as the views of the complainant are not in conflict with the statements of the Scriptures, so neither can they be with the teachings of the standards.'[19]

Many—probably most, maybe all—Southern Presbyterians were dismayed by the long controversy. Columbia Seminary was damaged, First Presbyterian Church in Columbia was divided, and friendships were broken. Robert A. Webb

[18] Gustafson, *Woodrow,* p. 221.
[19] Gustafson, *Woodrow,* p. 225.

expressed the feeling of many when he wrote that the 'eight weary years' of debate 'satisfied my appetite for controversy for life.'[20] William Plumer Jacobs came to the decision not to vote on either side during the many attempts to settle 'the Woodrow case.' He wrote in his diary after one such debate in synod, 'I, as usual, would not cast a vote. I am determined to have nothing to do with the case in which grievous wrong is being done on both sides and there is no disposition to right that wrong.'[21]

At the 1886 General Assembly in Augusta, Benjamin Morgan Palmer gave an address commemorating the founding of the Southern Presbyterian Church in that city twenty-five years earlier. No doubt reflecting the great issue that had troubled the church for a decade or more, the eloquent Palmer stated his reluctance to speak on that occasion and ended with these words:

> There was but one recourse to me, to utter with unhesitating frankness the convictions of my own mind, and to ask you to accept them as the confession of one who painfully recognizes that he belongs to the generation which is past. It is at least a testimony to principles which he has labored throughout his lifetime to establish, and to which, in his judgment, the Church must ever return for her protection and repose. If, however, there be no escape from the clash of steel in forensic debate, there is comfort in the hope that the disputants will sit down together at last upon the mount of God and heal their wounds with the leaves from the tree of life.[22]

[20] Willborn, 'Girardeau,' pp. 4, 292.

[21] Jacobs, *Diary of William Plumer Jacobs*, p. 289.

[22] Benjamin Morgan Palmer, 'The Church A Spiritual Kingdom,' *Memorial Addresses Delivered Before the General Assembly of 1886* (Richmond: Presbyterian Committee of Publication, 1886), p. 63.

R. A. Webb concluded his chapter on 'The Evolution Controversy' in the 1916 volume, *The Life Work of John L. Girardeau,* with the words:

> The primary object of Dr. Girardeau . . . was to prevent the Church from committing itself to the doctrine of evolution, and inculcating it as the truth, in one of its Theological Schools . . . Today it [evolution] is the regnant philosophy. It has overpassed all the limits affixed by Dr. Woodrow . . . And now . . . the question that trembles upon the lip of the world and challenges the Christian apologist is, 'Can the old faith live by the side of the new science?'[23]

In his history of Columbia Seminary, William Childs Robinson comments: 'Dr. Woodrow is the proof that a minister of unswerving faith in Scripture—even his opponents being witness that his views are not heresy—can hold "as probably true" a theory which he designates as evolution.' Robinson attempted to find value in the views of both Woodrow and Girardeau. 'Truly the labors of neither have been in vain in the mysterious providences of God,' he wrote. Woodrow showed how a limited view of theistic evolution could be compatible with 'faith in the Lord Jesus Christ' as 'supernatural Saviour.' Girardeau warned the Southern Church of the 'danger that the pupils would not stop where their teacher stopped, that "mediate evolution" would soon become real evolution, that naturalism would pare down the grand particularities of the historic Christian religion.'[24]

Louis LaMotte, in his history of Columbia Seminary, states that there were many factors in the long controversy. 'Temperamental differences . . . should be considered,' he wrote.

[23] Blackburn, *Girardeau,* pp. 283-84.

[24] Robinson, *Columbia Theological Seminary,* pp. 190-91.

> Dr. John L. Girardeau was a man of sweeping intellect and strong emotional drive. He was an orator who carried his hearers along, entranced. Dr. James Woodrow was a man of exact and detailed thinking, with emotions disciplined and always subjected to intellect. He was accustomed to careful planning and efficient practical procedure. He moved men by calm reasoning and intellectual depth and clarity. Dr. Girardeau's avocation was poetry. Dr. Woodrow's was chemistry. With the passing of Dr. Howe, these two men came into leadership of the affairs of the Seminary. They might have proved a wonderful balance each to the other, but instead of being drawn closer together, they were pulled apart.[25]

* * * * *

Augusta Presbytery assured Woodrow that he remained a minister in good standing, and at the October 1888 meeting he was elected moderator. In 1901 he was elected moderator of the Synod of South Carolina. Woodrow continued to teach geology, mineralogy, botany, and zoology at South Carolina College. The seminary faculty decided to prohibit their students from attending his lectures at the college. The controlling synods split on this issue, so that the board, in 1890, directed the faculty that requests from seminary students to attend Woodrow's lectures at the college be referred to each student's presbytery. In 1891 Woodrow became president of the University of South Carolina. Thornwell had moved from the presidency of the college to the faculty of the seminary; Woodrow left the seminary to become president of the college. The students at the college appreciated his friendliness

[25] LaMotte, *Colored Light*, p. 206.

and kindly interest in them. He always seemed pleased to have students visit with him, concerning the content of his class or for any other reason. One Jewish student remembered how, during an after-lecture chat, Woodrow enthusiastically 'spoke of my religion, and how he impressed upon me the proud history of Judaism.'[26] Woodrow retired in 1897, after serving as the college's president for six years, described by Daniel Hollis as 'The Lean Years.' Woodrow felt that he had been 'steadfast in his duty' during these 'dark days.'[27] He continued as adjunct professor until his death in 1915.

* * * * *

Dr. Woodrow's time at the seminary ended, but his chair continued, more broadly defined as the chair of apologetics. Perkins professors following Woodrow were Francis R. Beattie (1888-93), graduate of Knox Theological College and pastor in Canada; Samuel Spahr Laws (1893-98), graduate of Princeton Theological Seminary; and Thornton Whaling (1911-21), who became Columbia Seminary's first president.

Samuel Laws was born in Virginia in 1824. After graduating from Miami College in Ohio and Princeton Seminary, he served a short pastorate in St. Louis and then became the first president of Westminster College in Fulton, Missouri, in 1855. With the outbreak of the Civil War, the college closed in 1861. During the turmoil of that year Laws was charged with disloyalty to the Federal government, arrested, and imprisoned in St. Louis, where he spent three months in a damp cell. He was released on the condition that he would leave

[26] Gustafson, *Woodrow*, p. 242.

[27] Daniel Walker Hollis, *University of South Carolina: College to University* (Columbia, S.C.: University of South Carolina Press, 1956), 2:177.

the country. Laws spent part of the war period in Europe, then returned to New York City, where he engaged in further studies and earned degrees in law and medicine. He became interested in the financial life of the city, accumulated a modest fortune, and was elected vice-president of the New York Exchange. Laws invented the Laws Gold Indicator, a predecessor of the ticker tape machine. In June 1869, he hired a penniless would-be inventor named Thomas A. Edison as his mechanical supervisor. Laws became the president of the University of Missouri in 1876. Frank F. Stephens writes in his *History of the University of Missouri* that 'Laws was such a dominating personality that it is scarcely possible to think of the institution apart from him during his connection with it.'[28] Laws lived in Columbia, Missouri, and in Kansas City after his retirement in 1889. In 1892 he moved to Cincinnati and then to Columbia, South Carolina, when he received an invitation to teach at Columbia Seminary.

* * * * *

One of the issues coming out of the evolution controversy was that of the nature and purpose of a theological seminary. The long debate did not focus on whether or not Dr. Woodrow was guilty of heresy. Most of those who opposed him agreed that he was not, as did his Augusta Presbytery. It had to do with what a professor could and could not teach in a theological seminary of the Southern Presbyterian Church. Once again two old friends differed. John Girardeau maintained that the issue was not whether Woodrow's view

[28] Frank F. Stephens, *History of the University of Missouri* (Columbia, Mo.: University of Missouri Press, 1962), p. 317.

contradicted the Bible in its 'absolute and infallible sense as intended by God' (which we cannot know), but whether his hypothesis contradicted the Bible as understood by the Southern Presbyterian Church. The purpose of a theological seminary, Girardeau believed, was to teach the doctrine of its church. The church had every right, he maintained, to demand conformity to her confessional standards as the church understood them, and to demand silence on points of difference by professors in its theological schools. John Adger took the other side. He wrote, 'They tell us the genius of the Theological seminary is dogmatic. I maintain that its genius is that of inquiry into all truth.'[29]

As the evolution debate dragged on, Columbia Seminary suffered loss of financial support and a decline in students. The seminary was forced to close again in 1886. Although it opened a year later, there were only fourteen students. Suggestions were made that the seminary move to Atlanta or combine with Union Seminary in Virginia. South Carolina Presbyterians fought any attempt to move their beloved seminary, and it remained in Columbia. In the 1890s the Synod of Georgia revived the idea of a Presbyterian university for the South. It was suggested that Southwestern University in Clarksville, Tennessee, and Columbia Seminary could be combined to provide the beginning for a major Presbyterian university in Atlanta. Nothing came of this suggestion. In 1890 the Presbyterian Institute for Women moved into the Hampton-Preston mansion across the street from Columbia Seminary, and by 1902 had an enrollment of three hundred.[30]

[29] Adger, *My Life and Times*, p. 646ff.

[30] The school later came under the control of the Synod of South Carolina, merged with Chicora College of Greenville, South Carolina, and in 1930 moved to Charlotte, North Carolina, and combined with Queens College.

Two former professors who had resigned from the seminary during the Woodrow controversy returned in 1882. They each stayed at the seminary for only three years. W. E. Boggs, a graduate of Columbia Seminary and pastor of First Presbyterian Church in Columbia from 1866 to 1871, left the seminary in 1885 for the pulpit of Second Presbyterian Church in Memphis, and four years later became chancellor of the University of Georgia.[31] Charles Hemphill also left in 1885, when he was called to the Second Presbyterian Church in Louisville, Kentucky, where he became the chief founder of Louisville Presbyterian Theological Seminary.

James Doak Tadlock, 'a veritable saint' according to one history, joined the Columbia faculty in 1885 to teach church history.[32] A graduate of Princeton Seminary, Tadlock was chosen as the founding president of King College in Bristol, Tennessee, in 1867. During the eighteen years of his presidency, there were only sixty-three graduates, but these men made their mark. Forty became ministers (seven of whom were foreign missionaries), ten were lawyers, and another ten college professors (five of whom became college presidents). During his first year in Columbia Tadlock supplied the First Presbyterian Church.

[31] Boggs remained at the University of Georgia for ten years, then returned to the pastorate in St. Joseph, Missouri, and Jacksonville, Florida. In 1909 the General Assembly named him Secretary for Schools and Colleges. He died in 1920 and was buried in the little cemetery in Waynesville, North Carolina, where he had a summer home.

[32] Jones and Mills, *The Presbyterian Church in South Carolina*, p. 426.

22

GIRARDEAU'S LEGACY

ON May 8, 1894, Dr. John L. Girardeau presented a letter of resignation to the Board of Directors of Columbia Seminary. Dr. and Mrs. Girardeau then travelled to Mount Pleasant on the South Carolina coast, as they had for many summers. Knowing that it would probably be his last summer in his beloved Low Country, he said, 'I must open my eyes and mouth wide.'[1] In February 1895, Girardeau suffered a stroke that left him partially paralyzed on one side.

Girardeau's retirement was keenly felt. He was known throughout the church as a great preacher and theologian and attracted many students to Columbia. James H. Taylor, who became Woodrow Wilson's pastor in Washington, graduated from Yale University in 1894. Many of his Yale classmates urged him to go to Princeton, but he wanted to attend a seminary in the South and meet the men with whom he would be associated in the Southern Presbyterian Church. He entered Columbia Seminary in the fall of 1894. One important reason for his going to Columbia was that Girardeau, 'one of the great men of the Church,' was there. Girardeau had been the pastor of Taylor's family at Glebe Street Presbyterian Church

[1] Willborn, 'Girardeau,' p. 342.

in Charleston. When Girardeau retired, Taylor transferred to the new seminary in Louisville, Kentucky.

For twenty years John L. Girardeau had been the theologian of Columbia Seminary. Thornton Whaling described him as 'the most philosophic of theologians,' 'one of the most biblical of theologians,' and 'a loyal and consistent Confessional theologian.'[2] He was through and through a Calvinist. In the opinion of Whaling, 'No theologian of our day has studied Calvin more . . . or understood him better' than Girardeau.[3] Girardeau maintained independence of thought, however, taking positions when necessary against such theological giants as Jonathan Edwards and his own beloved Thornwell.

Benjamin Morgan Palmer and the Alumni Association of Columbia Seminary, meeting in 1881, 'respectfully and earnestly' suggested 'to their beloved brother, the Rev. J. L. Girardeau,' that he could not render any service to the Southern Church more important than 'to take up and complete the system of theology begun by the late and lamented Dr. Thornwell . . . giving to the world a complete work issuing from this Seminary, and the lasting testimony borne by it to the immutable truth of God'—as Charles Hodge did for Princeton, and Robert Lewis Dabney for Union.[4] It was not to be. George A. Blackburn stated that the course Girardeau marked out for himself was 'only to write on such subjects as in his judgment had not been satisfactorily treated by any other author whose writings were accessible to the church.'[5] He was, as C. N. Willborn puts it, 'not an innovator but a refiner.'[6]

[2] Blackburn, *Girardeau,* pp. 304-6.
[3] Blackburn, *Girardeau,* p. 307.
[4] *Memorial Volume,* p. xvii
[5] Girardeau, *Discussions of Theological Questions,* Editor's Preface, p. v.
[6] Willborn, 'Girardeau,' p. 306.

Girardeau's writings are not only clearly argued but also strongly polemical. Whaling admits that Girardeau 'could not keep the peace with opposing systems because of their unscriptural and irrational character.' 'A Calvinism which smiles indiscriminately upon all its historical opponents has lost its vitality and is in danger of burial,' comments Whaling. 'Dr. Girardeau was professor of Didactic and Polemic Theology, and he must be both in order to be either. While having the largest charity for all of God's people, he did not construe this to be a reason for failing in loyalty to God's truth or for failing to expose false doctrine in any of its forms.'[7]

* * * * *

Girardeau championed federal, or covenant, theology. His address on the occasion of the semi-centennial of Columbia Seminary was 'The Federal Theology: Its Import and Its Regulative Influence.' Federal theology had received 'massive . . . if not an exhaustive' treatment by Dutch theologians and had been taught by 'some of the most illustrious divines of England and Scotland.' Nevertheless, Girardeau said,

> while Cunningham, Hodge, and our own Thornwell have trodden in their footsteps, and evinced in their discussions their sense of the importance of the federal system—a fact for which the present generations of Calvinists should be devoutly thankful—it is to be feared that indications are beginning to manifest themselves of a growing tendency towards a departure from this type of theology.[8]

Girardeau feared that with the weakening of federal theology, the pulpit would 'more and more cast its instructions in

[7] Blackburn, *Girardeau,* pp. 338-39.

[8] Willborn, 'Girardeau,' p. 322.

the mould of a wretched legalism . . . or sink its high didactic office into that of a vapid and sensational haranguer.'[9]

In the preface to his *Freedom of the Will in its Theological Relations,* Girardeau explained his long interest in the topic of the human will. In 1849 he had read a sermon by Thornwell in which he found the sentence: 'The only efficient cause which exists in the universe is the fiat of the deity.' If this is true, Girardeau thought, then the will of God is the sole efficient cause of sin. He arranged to meet Thornwell at his study on the campus of South Carolina College, explained his problem, and asked, 'Doctor, what do you do with this difficulty?' 'I cannot do anything with it,' Thornwell replied. He explained that there was even more of a problem in taking the opposite view—that God is not the only efficient cause of everything.

Unable to concur with Dr. Thornwell, Girardeau wrote:

> I reached upon painful reflection, the conclusion that as God, by creation, imparted to the Intellect the power to think, to the Feelings the power to perceive beauty and deformity, pleasure and pain, to the Conscience the power to pass moral judgments, so he imparted to the Will the power efficiently to cause acts, and held man responsible to him for the exercise of this power, bounding, ordering and controlling it for the ends of his government.

'During the War between the States Jonathan Edwards' work on the Will was one of my companions,' Girardeau wrote, 'and was carefully studied whenever active operations gave way to the quiet of camp life.' Girardeau found Edwards' 'theory of necessity' problematic in that it tended 'to the implication of the divine efficiency in the production

[9] Willborn, 'Girardeau,' p. 322.

of sin.'[10] After the war Girardeau continued to study assiduously the doctrine of the will, translating Calvin's treatise on the will and the related work of Calvin's adversary Pighius.

In 1871, when the first two volumes of Thornwell's *Collected Writings* appeared in print, Girardeau at once turned to Thornwell's discussion of sin and its origin and discovered that Thornwell had come to believe that 'moderate Calvinists . . . have been compelled to admit that there is a sphere in which God leaves personal agents to themselves, and in which they are permitted to act as real, efficient causes.' 'We should give God the glory of his supremacy,' Thornwell wrote; 'we should not deny to the creature the properties that God has bestowed.' Girardeau was delighted when he discovered that Charles Hodge in his *Systematic Theology* took substantially the same position as Thornwell, 'though not so clearly.' Girardeau wrote:

> The Necessitarianism of Edwards was obviously not the norm of recent Calvinistic thought. It had been grafted by his powerful hand into the Theology of the Reformed Church, and for a time, in this country, almost dominated it; but it became evident that the Calvinistic Theology is extricating itself from the iron embrace of the Necessitarian Philosophy as one of universal application.

Girardeau acknowledged the 'polemical character' of his own book on the will but offered no apology. 'The great work of Edwards was avowedly polemic,' he wrote. 'Truth is always most clearly presented in its contrast to error.'[11]

[10] Willborn, 'Girardeau,' p. 324.

[11] John Lafayette Girardeau, *The Will in Its Theological Relations* (Columbia, S.C.: W. J. Duffie, 1891), pp. 11-16. This book collects the various articles first printed in the *Southern Presbyterian Review* into a single volume with an added introduction. For the original publication dates in the *Review* see Rankin's Index.

In the view of George A. Blackburn,

> The book on *The Will in Its Theological Relations* is [Girardeau's] master-piece. This book will live because it illuminates a problem that will always live—Free Agency and Divine Sovereignty. It places one hand on the throat of Arminianism and the other on the throat of necessitarianism and says to them, 'You are equally wrong—the truth lies between you.'

Blackburn, Girardeau's son-in-law, adds, in a perhaps pardonable exaggeration, 'Dr. Girardeau's book on the will has probably given the final answer of the human intellect to the questions, "How can sin exist and God be Sovereign?" And "How could a holy being become a sinner?"'[12]

* * * * *

Although given a separate chapter in the Westminster Confession of Faith, the doctrine of adoption received scant attention in Reformed theologies. In *First Things* for May 2, 1993, Dr. Glen Knecht, pastor of First Presbyterian Church in Columbia, wrote:

> There have been moments in the history of the Christian church when Columbia, South Carolina, and specifically the church we love, was the only place that lifted up certain aspects of Christian doctrine. Not that doctrine was developed in our church, but that it was rediscovered and reapplied from our pulpits and classrooms. Much of this revived teaching centered around the truth of our 'adoption' into the family of God.[13]

[12] Blackburn, *Girardeau,* p. 365.

[13] The present senior pastor of First Presbyterian Church, Sinclair Ferguson, has written on the doctrine of adoption in his *Children of the Living God* (Edinburgh: Banner of Truth, 1990).

Dr. Girardeau played an important role in recovering and preaching the wonderful message that when God extends his grace to us in Jesus Christ, he not only releases us from our guilt but also receives us into his family.[14]

The main point of Girardeau's treatise on adoption was to show that adoption has 'a distinctive and peculiar value of its own' alongside the doctrines of regeneration and justification. He defined adoption in words indebted to John Owen: 'Adoption is an act of God's free grace, whereby, for the sake of Christ, he formally translates the regenerate from the family of Satan into his own, and legally confirms them in all the rights, immunities and privileges of his children.'[15] Girardeau beautifully captured the heart of the doctrine in a few words when he wrote: 'The servant, with hat in hand, stands at a respectable distance awaiting the orders of his master; the child of God, as Luther has graphically suggested, rushes into the presence of his Father, leaps into his lap, and nestles in his bosom.'[16] In 'a very modest ninety-three pages,' according to C. N. Willborn, Girardeau established 'the proper biblical grounds, the rights, the privileges, the duties, and the evidences of adoption.'[17] Willborn suggests that while Girardeau's motivation in writing on adoption was biblical and theological, it also grew out of pastoral experience in Charleston when he served the African Americans who were slaves but, more important, sons and daughters of God.

[14] Nineteenth-century American Presbyterians—Breckinridge, Thornwell, and Girardeau—and Baptists—Boyce and Dagg—wrote on this topic. All resided in the South of the United States (Breckinridge in Kentucky) and three were native South Carolinians.

[15] Willborn, 'Girardeau,' pp. 332-33.

[16] C. N. Willborn, 'Adoption: A Historical Perspective with Evangelical Implications,' in *Sanctification: Growing in Grace,* eds. Joseph A. Pipa, Jr. and J. Andrew Wortman (Taylors, S.C.: Southern Presbyterian Press, 2001), pp. 69-70.

[17] Willborn, 'Adoption,' pp. 56-57.

* * * * *

Not only did Girardeau present theology in books and sermons, he also wrote it in poems, such as in these lines on the doctrine of justification by grace alone:

Nothing to pay? No, nothing, to win
Salvation by merit from law and from sin;
But all things, to buy, without money and price,
The wine and the milk of a free Paradise.

Nothing to do? No, not to procure
A heaven, by infinite blood made secure;
But all things, with labour and sweat of the face,
To honor my Saviour and magnify grace.

What of the law? Its thunders were stilled
Against my poor soul, by the blood that was spilled;
But the hands which were nailed to the wood of the Tree
Now wield its commands to be honored by me.

Nothing of guilt? No, not to my God,
As Judge and Condemner, uplifting His rod;
But, ah, I am guilty of breaking His Word
In the house of my Father—the Church of my Lord.

What am I waiting for? Spare me a while
To tell of Thy love to a sinner so vile!
Then take me to Heaven, which is not my due,
And give me the crown of Fidelity, too![18]

* * * * *

Girardeau followed and developed Thornwell's ecclesiology. He held Thornwell's view that the office of elder was

[18] Blackburn, *Girardeau*, p. 350.

a single office, with preaching added to the responsibilities of those who were ministers, or, better, teaching elders. Girardeau was disappointed when the 1879 *Book of Church Order* presented the office of elder under two headings—'The Minister of the Word' and 'The Ruling Elder'—rather than one, as Thornwell and Girardeau would have it.

The revised *Book of Church Order* of 1879 included a fuller section on the office of deacon—reflecting much of Girardeau's view on the diaconate—'a Thornwellian principle elaborated,' according to William Childs Robinson.[19] The revised book stated that the duty of deacons included ministry 'to those who are in need, to the friendless, and to any who may be in distress.' Girardeau declared that 'no body of Christians can grow in the divine life who habitually neglect the cultivation of the grace of love.' Neglect of the poor, he insisted, checks the growth of the church. The world looks on and expects to see the church care for its own; when it does not, there is left 'an unhappy impression that thwarts the kingdom harvest.'[20]

* * * * *

Thornton Whaling maintained that Girardeau was the Southern Presbyterian Church's 'greatest philosopher.'[21] Girardeau's large *Discussions of Philosophical Questions* presents in detail his approach to the great metaphysical issues and debates of his time. Girardeau, like Thornwell and so many nineteenth-century theologians, embraced Scottish Common Sense Realism. This philosophical system, so

[19] Robinson, *Columbia Theological Seminary*, pp. 85-88.
[20] Willborn, 'Girardeau,' p. 302.
[21] Willborn, 'Girardeau,' p. 313.

popular during the first half of the century, had fallen out of favour with many; but even after the Civil War, Reid and Stewart were honoured names in the Old South and elsewhere in America. James McCosh of Princeton did not publish his major work on the Scottish philosophy until 1875. R. A. Webb wrote that Girardeau's mind 'roamed, with intoxicating delight, the raised fields of loftiest speculation, but always settled down at the footstool of . . . Common Sense.'[22] Girardeau believed that the Scottish philosophy 'provided a superior foundation for sound thinking and systematization of the doctrines of Holy Scripture.'[23] But he did not accept this system uncritically. Neither did his philosophical commitments control his theology. His Calvinism was not based upon his philosophy; rather his philosophy supported his Calvinism. For Girardeau, as Thornton Whaling writes, theology and philosophy 'are united in the Revealed Word, for there is a biblical philosophy as there is a biblical theology; and we can not really accept the Revealed theology if we refuse the Revealed philosophy—they are so builded together as to be one and inseparable.'[24]

* * * * *

During his last year at the seminary, Girardeau completed an article on 'Natural Religion and the Gospel' for the *Presbyterian Quarterly*. It is fitting, writes C. N. Willborn, that Girardeau's last published article was 'a sweeping survey of redemptive history wrapped up in the great theme of federal

[22] Blackburn, *Girardeau*, p. 209.
[23] Willborn, 'Girardeau,' p. 3.
[24] Blackburn, *Girardeau*, p. 304.

theology.'[25] Girardeau finished with the words—perhaps his last for publication:

> This then is the distinctive peculiarity of the gospel—redemption from sin, death and hell. Jesus incarnate, Jesus living and dying, Jesus rising, ascending to heaven and sitting upon the throne, Jesus interceding and sending the Spirit of all grace, Jesus coming again to raise the dead and dispense the final measures of mediatorial rule—this is the burden of the gospel, this its glory and its crown.[26]

[25] Willborn, 'Girardeau,' p. 342.

[26] John L. Girardeau, 'Natural Religion and the Gospel,' *Presbyterian Quarterly* (July 1893), p. 352.

23

'NO UNCERTAIN SOUND'

ALTHOUGH there was no force like James Henley Thornwell, no one who served so long and with such influence as George Howe, no theologian-preacher of the calibre of John L. Girardeau, the Columbia Seminary professors of the late nineteenth and early twentieth centuries were men of integrity and ability who faithfully taught the Bible and the doctrines of the Reformed faith to several generations of Southern Presbyterian ministers. In their history of the Presbyterian Church in South Carolina, Jones and Mills write: 'Due honor may be ascribed to those worthy Christians and instructors by the pen of some later writer, but no question of invidiousness may occur in the mention of Dr. Tadlock and Dr. Hall for their saintliness; of Dr. Reed for his scholarliness and humanity of spirit; of Dr. Brimm for his remarkable skill as a teacher; of Dr. McPheeters for his keenness of mind and many qualities as a scholar and gentleman.'[1]

When the seminary reopened in 1887, there were fourteen students and three teachers. One of the students was R. M. Latimer, a lineal descendant of Francis Makemie, 'the father of American Presbyterianism.'[2] The three professors were

[1] Jones and Mills, *The Presbyterian Church in South Carolina,* p. 431.

[2] Latimer graduated in the class of 1889 and served pastorates in North Carolina, Tennessee, South Carolina, and Virginia.

Girardeau, Tadlock, and Hersman. Charles C. Hersman, a graduate of Princeton Seminary, served as professor and then president of Westminster College in Missouri, before coming to Columbia Seminary in 1887 as professor of Greek and Hebrew exegesis. After a year at Columbia, he went to Southwestern Presbyterian University as chancellor, and in 1891 to Union Seminary in Virginia, where he taught until his death in 1924.

In 1888 Francis R. Beattie, born of Scottish parents in Guelph, Ontario, Canada, joined the Columbia faculty as professor of apologetics, James Woodrow's old chair. Beattie was a graduate of Toronto University and Knox Theological College. During pastorates comprising eight years in Canada before he came to Columbia Seminary, Beattie saw fourteen young men become ministers from the churches he served.

Beattie described for Canadian Presbyterians the denomination into which he had thrown his lot. He wrote:

> The first feature of the Southern Presbyterian Church which has marked it from the outset is its close adherence to the doctrinal system of its standards. Its type of doctrine is distinctly Old School. In its seminaries this has always been the type of doctrine taught without any toning down or explaining away. In other words, it adheres strongly to the Calvinism of its doctrinal symbols. The great majority of her pulpits are manned by men who preach the Gospel with doctrines after the manner of Calvin, of Knox, of Augustine, of Paul . . . In regard to the inspiration of the scriptures, the sovereignty of God, the lost estate of man in sin, the atonement of Christ, the necessity of grace to recover him, the security of the believer and similar doctrines of the Calvinistic system, there is almost no uncertain sound.[3]

[3] Thompson, *Presbyterians in the South*, 3:302.

R. A. Webb, who studied at Columbia Seminary, characterized Beattie as 'clear and conservative in his exposition of evangelical truth.' 'He is a Calvinist,' continued Webb, 'of the school of the Hodges. He stands with our own matchless Thornwell.'[4]

Also in 1888, William McPheeters joined the faculty of Columbia Seminary as professor of biblical literature. He was born in St. Louis, Missouri, in 1854, the son of a Presbyterian pastor, Samuel Brown McPheeters, and his wife, Eliza Shanks McPheeters. William graduated from Washington and Lee University in 1874 and from Union Seminary in 1878. He married Emma Gold Morrison of Rockbridge Baths, Virginia.

William Childs Robinson recalled a story McPheeters enjoyed telling on himself. When he was a young professor in the seminary, at a faculty gathering someone raised the question, 'What would you be, if you were not a Christian?' McPheeters ventured to suggest, 'If I were not a Christian, I think that I would be a pantheist.' 'If you were not a Christian, my young brother,' answered Dr. Girardeau, 'you would be a lost sinner.'[5]

* * * * *

Samuel Macon Smith came as pastor to First Presbyterian Church in Columbia in September 1889. He would not only serve First Presbyterian with distinction, but also Columbia Seminary, and become an important and revered presence in the city.

[4] Thompson, *Presbyterians in the South*, 3:211.

[5] William Childs Robinson, *Our Lord: An Affirmation of the Deity of Christ* (Grand Rapids: Wm. B. Eerdmans Publishing Company, 1949), p. 179.

Samuel Smith descended from Virginia families that traced their roots back to the German Calvinists of the Palatinate, to the Huguenots of France, and to Scotch-Irish Presbyterians. His father, Jacob Henry Smith, was born in Lexington, Virginia, in 1820. He studied at Washington College (now Washington and Lee University), where he became great friends with a fellow student called 'Jack'—later to become famous as 'Stonewall' Jackson. Jacob Smith studied law for several years, but upon hearing a sermon preached by his fellow Virginian and founding professor of Princeton Theological Seminary, Archibald Alexander, he resolved to become a minister. In the fall of 1843 Jacob entered Union Seminary at Hampden-Sydney and received his certificate three years later. He was ordained on July 31, 1847, and installed as minister of the Presbyterian church at Pittsylvania Courthouse, Virginia. The next year Jacob married Catherine Malvina Miller of Powhatan County. From 1850 to 1854 Jacob Smith worked at the Samuel Davies Institute in Halifax County, as principal and professor of Latin and Greek.

Samuel was born to the Smiths in 1851. His mother, Catherine, died in 1854, and his father moved to Charlottesville to become pastor of the Presbyterian church there. In 1857 Jacob was married to Mary Kelly Watson by Dr. William H. McGuffy, professor at the University of Virginia and author of the famous *McGuffy Readers*. In 1859 Mary and Jacob Smith, eight-year-old Sam, baby Mary Lynn, a family slave named Pocahontas—called 'Poky'—and Poky's brother, Jim Henry, moved to Greensboro, North Carolina, where Jacob Smith took up his duties at the First Presbyterian Church. He would serve that church—as eloquent preacher and beloved pastor—for over thirty-seven years.

Samuel Macon Smith was educated at the University of Virginia and studied for the ministry at Union Seminary. In 1879 he married Ella Friend Daniel. The Smiths lived in Washington, North Carolina, where Samuel was pastor of the Presbyterian church, until the call to Columbia came in 1889.

'If inquiry be pressed whether the pulpit in these later days is declining in power and efficiency,' wrote Henry Alexander White, 'let the answer be found in the life and work of Dr. Samuel Macon Smith.'[6] In Samuel Smith, the pulpit of First Presbyterian Church had a worthy successor to its great preachers of the past. 'His Hebrew Bible and his Greek Testament were his constant companions,' said a professor at the seminary, 'and he knew how to use them in his pulpit work as very few preachers have ever been able to use them.' His sermons appealed especially to men—and occasionally there were more men than women in the church. Seminary and college students flocked to hear him. Dr. Smith was an important figure at the University of South Carolina—the chosen counsellor of both faculty and students. In 1898 he began to serve as lecturer in pastoral theology and preaching at Columbia Seminary. He was later called to a professorship at the seminary but died before he could give his answer.

Smith was recognized as the leading preacher of the Synod of South Carolina, and those who heard him often declared that he had few equals in the Southern Presbyterian Church. When the General Assembly of 1897 met in Charlotte, North Carolina, leading Southern Presbyterian preachers and scholars, including Robert Lewis Dabney, gave addresses to commemorate the 250th anniversary of the adoption of the Westminster Confession of Faith. Smith

[6] White, *Southern Presbyterian Leaders,* p. 460.

spoke on 'The Westminster Symbols Considered in Relation to Current Popular Theology and the Needs of the Future.' He described 'modern' theology as 'a sort of theological cave of Adullam into which every man that hath any quarrel with his creed doth resort with great gladness and not seldom with some noise.' The new theology professes great reverence for the spirit of Scripture, Dr. Smith said, but makes scant appeal to its letter. It opposes all systematic theology in general and Calvinism in particular. It abhors exact definition and minimizes the miraculous. It holds to a progressive theology that amends, corrects, and improves the Scripture. Against these ideas Smith set the Westminster theology. Westminster theology's coherence of thought, compactness of logical structure, definiteness and clearness of statement, unswerving loyalty to God's Word, constant resort to that Word as its ultimate appeal and final and infallible authority, exaltation of God as sovereign, humbling influence on the pride and prejudice of man, emphasis on the doctrines of divine grace—all fit it to serve both as a test of truth and as a bulwark against error, at once the safe guide and the safeguard of pure, scriptural doctrine.[7]

* * * * *

In 1892 Columbia Seminary tried to bring back Benjamin Morgan Palmer to teach pastoral theology, sacred rhetoric, and English Bible. A long letter signed by the entire faculty—Tadlock, Girardeau, Beattie, McPheeters, and Brimm—made its case. By returning to his native state and to his alma mater, the faculty argued, Dr. Palmer could crown his 'long and

[7] *Memorial Volume of the Westminster Assembly*, pp. 222-23, 253.

useful life' with 'a fine opportunity to form and fix the views of many of our future ministers in an age of unrest, and of departure, in some quarters, from "the old paths".'[8] Palmer declined the call, but he never lost the deep affection he had for Columbia—seminary, church, and city. Columbia was dear to him as the place of his early ministry, where old friends who 'bore with me in the greenness of my youth,' he wrote, were, one by one, 'passing through the gates into the city' of heaven, and where his first two children had lived and died. He wrote to a friend that he had 'almost a passionate wish to be [in Columbia] . . . with a longing something like that of a pilgrim for some holy shrine.'[9]

Columbia Seminary graduate Daniel Johnson Brimm taught Hebrew and Greek and then New Testament at the seminary from 1893 until 1900. Brimm presented to the presbytery a paper expressing his belief that miracles of healing continued to the present day. To avoid criticism of the seminary, he resigned and became professor of Bible at Presbyterian College in Clinton, South Carolina.

During the year 1898-99 Patterson Wardlaw, professor at the University of South Carolina, gave a series of lectures at the seminary on Sunday school methods; and Dr. Samuel Macon Smith, pastor at First Presbyterian Church, taught homiletics and pastoral theology.

John Wright Davis was professor of New Testament literature and exegesis from 1900 to 1902. Davis was a graduate of Davidson College and Union Seminary in Virginia. He went to Soochow, China, in 1873 and served there as a missionary until 1899. After two years of teaching at Columbia Seminary

[8] Johnson, *Palmer*, pp. 539-43.
[9] Johnson, *Palmer*, pp. 598, 607.

he returned to China. In 1905 he became professor in the Presbyterian Theological Seminary in Nanking. In 1911 Davis went back to Soochow, where he worked as an evangelist until he died in 1917.

Samuel Craig Byrd, an 1892 graduate of Columbia Seminary, was adjunct professor of English Bible and of pastoral theology and homiletics from 1898 to 1902. While a student at the seminary, Samuel met Wilhelmina Cozby, who was professor of Latin at the College for Women in Columbia. Cozby grew up in Sumter County, where her father, a native of Liberty County, Georgia, was pastor of Mount Zion Presbyterian Church. Wilhelmina and Samuel married and moved to New Orleans, where he served for a time as assistant pastor with Benjamin Morgan Palmer at First Presbyterian Church. After his time as teacher at Columbia Seminary, Samuel was pastor of the old Sion Presbyterian Church in Winnsboro. He became president of Chicora College, then in Greenville, and Wilhelmina served as the college dean and professor of Bible. When in 1930 Chicora combined with Queen's College in Charlotte, North Carolina, Dr. Byrd became president emeritus.

The seminarians studied Greek and Hebrew, Old Testament and New Testament exegesis, church history and church polity, homiletics and pastoral theology. They worshipped in the city's churches, particularly at First Presbyterian, where they heard with delight the sermons of Samuel Smith. They found places of service in and around the city, teaching Sunday school classes, preaching in country churches, and participating in Columbia's civic life. They also found time for exercise and relaxation. Columbia Seminary students are credited with introducing tennis to Columbia during the 1890s.[10]

[10] Moore, *Columbia and Richland County*, p. 358.

In a visit to Columbia in 1906, William Plumer Jacobs recalled the Columbia he knew as a seminary student forty-two years earlier. He wrote in his diary: 'Memory is busy with the Columbia of '64. What a contrast. Now it is an electric city. Its growth like that of all our Piedmont country is upward and onward. One sky scraper. The State house and that sky scraper dominate the city.'[11]

Bell Telephone Company had opened an office in the city in 1880, with sixty-two subscribers. In 1882 the Columbia Street Railway Company was incorporated, building a street railway system that began with four miles of tracks, six passenger trolleys, and thirty horses to pull them. By 1900 Columbia was the hub of nine railroads, with 144 arrivals and departures every day.

Columbia saw its first automobile on June 4, 1900. It came to the city to promote the sale of Octagon soap. In a short article on the bottom of an inside page, the State newspaper reported that 'the first horseless carriage, a light automobile, made its appearance in Columbia yesterday. It was manipulated by two young men who had no difficulty in doing so. Many watched the machine with great interest.'

It was reported in the city directory that in 1902 Columbia had five banks, twenty-eight policemen, six colleges, twenty-eight barbers, twenty-three blacksmiths, seventy-one boarding houses, five liquor dispensaries, ten dentists, thirty-nine physicians, thirteen dressmakers, twenty drug stores, twenty-two fruit stands, six hotels, three steam and four Chinese laundries, thirty-one Negro lunch rooms, eighteen restaurants, twenty-one shoemakers, nine stables, forty-four secret societies—and one theological seminary! There were twenty-four white churches—six Methodist, five Presbyterian,

[11] Jacobs, *Diary of William Plumer Jacobs,* p. 378.

four Baptist, four Episcopal, three Lutheran, one Catholic, one Christian—and one Jewish synagogue. There were twenty black churches—eight Baptist, five Methodist, five Episcopal, one Presbyterian, and one Congregational.

Controversial Benjamin Ryan Tillman was governor of South Carolina from 1890 to 1894. His administration was marked by growing racism, and the number of lynchings of African Americans increased. The new state constitution of 1895 made racial desegregation illegal and, for a time, eliminated African Americans from a meaningful political role in South Carolina.

24

COLUMBIA AND LOUISVILLE

IN 1893 a new Presbyterian seminary that would have many connections with Columbia was founded in Louisville, Kentucky. In 1901 this seminary joined the Danville Theological Seminary, creating an institution sponsored by both the Northern (Danville) and the Southern (Louisville) Presbyterians. Robert Jefferson Breckinridge, a friend of Thornwell, was the main force in the founding of Danville; and several prominent Columbians would serve at Louisville. The control of the seminary by the two denominations had no effect on its conservative theology, since both schools were strongly Old School before the merger, and this stance continued.

* * * * *

Dr. C. R. Hemphill, who taught at Columbia Seminary from 1882 to 1885, was the chief founder of Louisville Presbyterian Theological Seminary. He served as professor and chair of the faculty, president, and then dean. James Taylor, who spent one year at Columbia Seminary, transferred to Louisville to study under Hemphill. Taylor described Hemphill as 'a man of charming personality and a loyal friend. He taught the Greek New Testament and knew how to make it most interesting. I do not recall that his classes were ever dull or ever seemed too long. He was a splendid preacher, and many of us attended the services at Second Presbyterian Church of which he was the beloved pastor.' Taylor recalled that Hemphill occasionally read to the students the *Uncle Remus* stories and, 'being a South Carolinian, could give the right pronunciation and emphasis.'[1] Another student of Hemphill at Louisville was Henry Woods McLaughlin, who became a pastor in Virginia. A few weeks before McLaughlin's death in 1950, he spoke about his teacher:

> Dr. Hemphill was one of the truly great men of the church. He had the ability to make men enthusiastic about his classes. In speaking of Dr. Hemphill, I am reminded of what one of my elders said to me one day. This elder, when a young man, furnished General Robert E. Lee with beef in Lexington, Virginia. I said to him, 'What impression did General Lee make upon you?' He answered, 'I never saw General Lee that he didn't make me want to straighten up and be a man.' That is the kind of impression Dr. Hemphill always made upon me, even down to the time of his last illness when I visited him in his room.[2]

Dr. J. Gray McAllister, who became a professor at Louisville in 1909, said of Hemphill that he was 'courteous, considerate, chivalrous, generous in his appreciation of the work of others, scholarly, practical, [and] held the esteem and love of the great host who knew him down the years.' Hemphill disliked writing, McAllister said, 'and yet was one of the most forceful and effective of the letter writers of his day,' showing 'breadth of vision and ecclesiastical statesmanship

[1] Robert Stuart Sanders, *History of Louisville Presbyterian Theological Seminary, 1853-1953* (Louisville, Ky.: Presbyterian Theological Seminary, 1953), pp. 39-40.

[2] Sanders, *Louisville Seminary,* p. 40.

of the first order.' McAllister remembered Hemphill's early morning New Year's services at Second Presbyterian Church, especially the time he spoke feelingly on Isaiah 40:26: 'Lift up your eyes on high, and behold who hath created these things, that bringeth out their host by number: he calleth them all by names by the greatness of his might, for that he is strong in power; not one faileth.' 'He made us see,' wrote McAllister, 'God leading the procession of the stars as a shepherd leads his sheep.'[3]

* * * * *

In 1893 Francis Beattie, after serving at Columbia Seminary for five years, went to Louisville Presbyterian Seminary as professor of systematic theology and apologetics. He was also treasurer for the new school, where his Scottish thrift was tested to the utmost to keep the seminary alive during its early years. James Taylor, who had come to Columbia Seminary to study under Girardeau, followed Beattie to Louisville. Beattie had preached in Charleston, Taylor's hometown, for several summers and, as a close friend of the family, was a constant guest in the Taylor home. In Louisville, Taylor lived in Beattie's home. Taylor wrote about Dr. Beattie:

> He had the art of imparting knowledge. He was far ahead of his time as he furnished the class with what seemed to be a mimeographed outline of every lesson. He called this outline a 'syllabus.' The course in Theology was three years, and at the end of that time the 'syllabi' would be a complete resumé of Theology. One day Doctor Beattie asked me if I thought the students were really getting an understanding of Theology. I said to him, 'Doctor, you can teach theology to

[3] Sanders, *Louisville Seminary*, pp. 54-55.

> a curbstone and it will get it.' I recall how he just lay back in his chair and chuckled over it.[4]

Francis Beattie used the Westminster Standards to organize and guide his theology course. In his book *The Presbyterian Standards: An Exposition of the Westminster Confession of Faith and Catechisms,* Beattie followed closely the order of the topics found in the Shorter Catechism. He incorporated the contents of the Larger Catechism and the Confession of Faith, to give in a single exposition the contents of the three documents. He sent forth this substantial volume 'with the earnest prayer that it may be of some service to those who are seeking to advance Christ's kingdom on the earth.'[5] In his 'Summary and Conclusions,' Beattie characterized the Westminster Standards as 'a definite creed with a catholic spirit . . . They give lofty views of God; they present honest descriptions of sin; they unfold a full, free gospel; they outline a high ideal of life and destiny; they exhibit a very exalted conception of the church of Christ; and yet all through, there breathes the spirit of true freedom and a large liberty.' Beattie described the Westminster theology as 'generic, consistent, well-balanced Calvinism.' In his view, the Confession of Faith and Larger and Shorter Catechisms contained 'the most complete and scriptural outline of Christian doctrine to be found in any of the great creeds.' He was inclined to think that 'none of our modern theologians have made any notable or valuable additions to the system of the Standards.' At the same time one must not dogmatically take the documents, he wrote, as a 'finality.' They express 'for the time being, the general outline

[4] Sanders, *Louisville Seminary,* pp. 38-39.

[5] Francis R. Beattie, *The Presbyterian Standards: An Exposition of the Westminster Confession and Catechisms* (Richmond: The Presbyterian Committee of Publication, 1896), p. 6.

of divine truth, which the church, taught by the Holy Ghost, finds in the Scriptures. The Spirit may lead into new views of the truths of God's word and of their relations and connections, and he may enable the church more fully to understand the mind of the Lord as revealed in the Scriptures.' Beattie concludes:

> Generic Calvinism is not dying out, nor shall it be allowed to die. Its noble history, often bathed in tears and baptized with blood; its deep philosophy of the facts of nature, of providence, and of grace; and its absolute submission to the will of God as made known in the Scriptures, guarantee its vitality and efficiency till time shall be no more, and grace be fully crowned in glory.[6]

Dr. Beattie taught apologetics at Louisville, as he had in Columbia. He defined apologetics as 'a reasoned defense and vindication of the essential truth, supernatural origin, divine authority, and inherent sufficiency of the Christian system of doctrine, worship, ethics, and redemption, together with systematic refutation of all opposing theories.' He charged that higher criticism was unscientific, because it ruled out the Bible as inspired without taking seriously the Bible's own evidence, and as dangerous because it questioned the Bible's authority. His articles, collected in a book, defended the traditional view of the Scriptures against attacks of higher criticism. A review of Beattie's book in the *Union Seminary Magazine* stated that 'no work from the pen of any southern Presbyterian writer since the [Civil] war has been received more cordially or referred to more respectfully by all kinds of literary and religious journals inside and outside our bounds.'[7]

[6] Beattie, *The Presbyterian Standards,* pp. 407, 409, 415-16, 420.
[7] Thompson, *Presbyterians in the South,* 3:215.

Beattie held that there could be no contradiction between natural science and Christianity because all truth comes from God. Speaking specifically of evolution, Beattie rejected the view that organic or living matter arose out of inorganic matter. Life could only come from life, actually from pre-existent life, that is, from God. The only real question, Beattie maintained, was whether some kind of first genus or germ was created from which all life developed—organic evolution—or whether there was a creation of each separate species—special creation. Organic evolution, he thought, remained unproven, but he added that he 'would not close the case, but leave it open for future discovery and more light.'[8]

Beattie's *Apologetics* was published in 1903 with an introduction by B. B. Warfield. Warfield praised the comprehensiveness of Beattie's book, which, Warfield wrote, 'develops with serenity and sanity' the entire contents of apologetics. Warfield added: 'We have had many apologies; perhaps no branch of scientific theology has been more fruitful during the past two centuries. But we have had comparatively few surveys of the whole field of Apologetics. Perhaps Dr. Beattie's is the first to be produced by an American Presbyterian.'[9]

* * * * *

Also taking part in the founding of Louisville Seminary was Timothy Dwight Witherspoon, graduate of the Columbia

[8] Rick Nutt, *Many Lamps, One Light: Louisville Presbyterian Theological Seminary. A 150th Anniversary History* (Grand Rapids: William B. Eerdmans Publishing Company, 2002), pp. 36-38.

[9] Francis R. Beattie, *Apologetics: or the Rational Vindication of Christianity*, 3 vols. (Richmond, Va.: Presbyterian Committee of Publication, 1903), pp. 19-32.

Seminary class of 1859. Witherspoon was engaged to Dr. and Mrs. Thornwell's daughter, Nannie, who died a few days before their wedding. He later married Charlotte Vernon Ingram; they had eight children. Witherspoon was born in Greensboro, Alabama, on January 17, 1836. He graduated from the University of Mississippi in 1856 and did his theological studies at Columbia Seminary. His first pastorate was in Oxford, Mississippi. During the War between the States, he enlisted as a private soldier and later was a chaplain, serving the Mississippi infantry regiments and the Army of Northern Virginia. A fellow chaplain wrote that Witherspoon was 'one of the most devoted, untiring, self-sacrificing, and efficient chaplains that we had in the army.'[10] Suffering from wounds he received in battle, Witherspoon returned to Oxford, where he was pastor of the Presbyterian church, until he was called to Second Presbyterian Church in Memphis. He was chaplain at the University of Virginia for three years, and minister at Tabb Street Presbyterian Church in Petersburg, Virginia, until 1882, when he was called to First Presbyterian Church in Louisville. He was tireless in promoting evangelism and church planting in the Synod of Kentucky, including in the destitute mountain regions of the southeastern part of the state. Witherspoon worked with Hemphill in establishing the Presbyterian Theological Seminary in Louisville, where he was professor of homiletics and pastoral theology until his death in 1898. Because of his teaching and Christian life he was called the 'Saint John of Southern Presbyterians.'

* * * * *

[10] J. William Jones, *The Confederate Veteran*, vol. 7 (1899), p. 178.

Robert A. Webb succeeded Beattie as professor of apologetics and systematic theology at Louisville Seminary in 1908. Webb was born in Oxford, Mississippi, on September 20, 1856. When he was fifteen, his family moved to Nashville, Tennessee, where his mother died and Robert was stricken with cholera. He recovered and believed that through this experience God was calling him into the ministry. He graduated from the Southwestern Presbyterian University at Clarksville, Tennessee, in 1877. Hearing John L. Girardeau preach Southwestern's baccalaureate sermon, Webb was drawn to Columbia Seminary to learn from Girardeau. The young student spent many hours in conversation with Girardeau, who became not only his esteemed teacher but also his father-in-law.[11] Webb graduated in 1880 and, on the advice of Girardeau, took a country church in York County, South Carolina. Girardeau believed that it was better for young men to serve first in country churches for a few years so as to have time for continuous and systematic study. Webb was pastor of several churches in North and South Carolina before being called to the chair of theology in the Southwestern Presbyterian University. Here he followed Joseph Ruggles Wilson, who had filled this position since the opening of the divinity school at Southwestern University in 1885. Webb agreed to teach at Louisville only after being assured that the seminary stood for co-operation between the Northern and Southern Presbyterian churches but not for organic union.

The subject of Dr. Webb's inaugural address at Louisville was 'The Old Theology and the New.' 'The hour has not come for the abandonment of the faith of the fathers,' Webb said. He continued:

[11] Sally Girardeau died soon after her marriage to Robert Webb. He married Roberta Chauncey Beck in 1888.

> For centuries the Church has been laboring to develop . . . a system of Christian doctrine. Through controversies within and without, by criticisms friendly and hostile, by study and prayer, by altering and amending, by readjusting and restating, progress has been made in clarifying and defining and articulating the tenets of the Christian faith. In this way an historical outline of the faith has been created, the general trend of doctrine has been established, a traditional orthodoxy has been defined, the *communis consensus* of Christendom has been registered. These generic findings of the past, verified by the studies and experiences of the fathers, baptized by the blood of the martyrs, have come to be denominated the 'Old' or the 'Traditional' theology, and define the lines within which the conservative student prosecutes his investigations and seeks to make more accurate adjustments. He declines to nullify historical results achieved by a Church which has been under the tuition of the Spirit—to abandon that highway which is crowded with the foot-prints of the flock of Christ.[12]

One of his associates at Louisville said of Webb that 'he was a master of definition, and his depth and clarity of thought were a marvel of all who knew him.'[13] Webb was an exacting teacher. He did not allow the students to take notes, but required them to write out summaries of his lectures after leaving the classroom. 'In his questions he was very skillful,' wrote Charles Hemphill, 'and while he would sometimes play the student as a fisherman plays the fish, it was always in kindest spirit. He threw his whole soul into his teaching and often the professor's chair became the preacher's pulpit

[12] John R. Richardson, Introduction, in Robert Alexander Webb, *The Reformed Doctrine of Adoption* (Grand Rapids: Wm. B. Eerdmans Publishing Company, 1947), pp. 9-10.

[13] Sanders, *Louisville Seminary*, p. 55.

and he bore down on the heart and conscience of the student with powerful appeal.'[14] Students loved his tender prayers in the morning chapel at the seminary, and they appreciated his preaching on the great fundamental doctrines of the Bible.

R. A. Webb was a strict Calvinist, as can be seen in his book *The Theology of Infant Salvation*.[15] This book was published during the time that the Northern Presbyterian Church was debating whether to add a statement to the Westminster Confession affirming the salvation of all those who die in infancy. Webb surveyed the different views of salvation—Pelagian, Semi-pelagian, Catholic, and Mystic—and concluded that Calvinism, 'instead of implicating the damnation' of any child dying in infancy, gives 'a biblical, rational, and theological basis for the doctrine' of the salvation of all infants dying in infancy and of those people who are 'incapable of being outwardly called by the ministry of the Word.' Certainly not all infants are elect, but all who die in infancy are elect, he believed.

In 1914 Webb returned to Columbia Seminary to give the Smyth Lectures. His subject was 'The Christian's Hope,' and he used as his key text the words of Zechariah 9:12, 'Ye prisoners of hope.' Webb said that Christians are 'prisoners' in that they are 'chained to the order of things which now prevails,' but they are not prisoners of despair, but prisoners of hope. 'The people of God have an outlook and a future . . . the hope of a happier life and a better world.' The Christian's hope 'circles around four great objects.' First, the Christian

[14] Charles R. Hemphill, 'A Sketch,' in Robert Alexander Webb, *Christian Salvation: Its Doctrine and Experience* (Harrisonburg, Va.: Sprinkle Publications, 1985), [pp. 7-8].

[15] Robert A. Webb, *The Theology of Infant Salvation* (Richmond: Presbyterian Committee of Publication, 1907).

hopes for 'personal triumph over death and a blessed immortality beyond the grave.' Second, the Christian hopes for the complete triumph of the gospel and the conversion of all people. Third, the Christian hopes for Christ's triumphant return to the earth 'and an endless reign of bliss and glory on this globe which has been the theater of [the] human story.' Fourth, the Christian hopes for the triumphant restitution of all things and the establishment of the 'new heavens and the new earth.' Webb said:

> These are the four sublimest objects which loom on the horizon of Christian hope . . . Every man wonders what is to become of him after death. Every Christian must wonder what is to be the outcome of the cause to which he has committed himself and every precious interest which he has. Every disciple of Jesus must wonder what has become of his Lord and Savior who has gone from the world and left a train of splendid promises behind Him. Every dweller on this earth must wonder what is to be the final fate of the old homestead where he was born and lived and died.

Webb's published lectures were dedicated to the memory of his teacher at Columbia Seminary and the father of his first wife, John L. Girardeau—'Illustrious Teacher, Golden Mouthed Preacher, Erudite Philosopher, Saintly Christian.' Webb captured something of the eloquence of Girardeau in these lectures when he said:

> The Christian Scriptures represent God as having taken three looks at this earth of ours. First, in the morning of its creation, when it swam, a new-made thing in the amplitudes of space; and then He stood on the steps of His throne and admired it as good, very good, superlatively good. Second, in the day of its fall, when it lay before Him, a sin-blighted

> and perverted globe; and then He rose in His judicial wrath and cursed the very 'ground,' because of the moral infamy of the race for which He had made it and to whom He had graciously given it. Third, in the consummation of the redeeming work of Christ, when it floated before His vision as 'the new heavens and the new earth, wherein dwells righteousness'; and then He stood upon the steps of His great white throne and admired its beauty, and crowned His Son for His glorious success in 'the restitution of all things.'[16]

Dr. Webb's classic features and snow-white hair formed a striking figure in any company. According to John R. Richardson, Webb was 'a born gentleman, to use a phrase common in the old days in the South.'[17] After he died in 1919, five presbyteries asked the 1920 General Assembly to collect Webb's theological lectures and writings in a published volume of his work. The editors decided to limit the work to Webb's teaching on soteriology, so *Christian Salvation: Its Doctrine and Experience* was published.[18] The preface stated that the book was being 'sent forth to the Church in recognition of an able and loyal son and a gifted teacher of many of her most useful ministers, and in the conviction that by it her faith in the doctrines of Grace will be confirmed.'[19]

Henry E. Dosker, pastor in the Dutch Reformed Church and professor at Western Theological Seminary in Holland, Michigan, came to Louisville Seminary in 1903 and for twenty-three years taught church history, pastoral theology, and missions. He believed that R. A. Webb was 'the greatest

[16] Robert Alexander Webb, *The Christian's Hope* (Jackson, Miss.: Presbyterian School for Christian Workers, 1914), pp. [3-4], 19-20, 94.

[17] Richardson, 'Introduction,' p. 6.

[18] Robert Alexander Webb, *Christian Salvation: Its Doctrine and Experience* (Richmond, Va.: Presbyterian Committee of Publication, 1921).

[19] Webb, *Christian Salvation,* [p. 9].

theologian of the Southern Church' and after B. B. Warfield of Princeton, the greatest theologian 'in all the Presbyterian Church.'[20]

[20] Richardson, 'Introduction,' p. 10.

25

'A PASSING BREATH'

IN the fall of 1897 Robert Lewis Dabney gave lectures at Columbia Seminary on 'Christ our Substitute and Sacrifice for Imputed Guilt.'[1] Old and blind, Dabney nonetheless spoke with precision and power. The Columbia Seminary faculty praised Dabney's 'well-known clearness of statement, force of reasoning, energy of expression and aptness of illustration' and recognized 'gratefully the goodness of the Lord in sending his servant among us.'[2]

One Sunday Dabney preached at First Presbyterian. *The State* newspaper reported, 'As Dr. Dabney sat in the pulpit of the First Presbyterian Church, the other day, and preached a sermon long to be remembered by those who heard it, his appearance was both venerable and patriarchal.'[3]

Dabney visited his old friend, John Girardeau, now stricken with partial paralysis. George Blackburn, Girardeau's son-in-law, had succeeded Girardeau as pastor at Second Presbyterian Church (now Arsenal Hill Associate Reformed Presbyterian Church). One Sunday during Dabney's visit in

[1] The lectures delivered at Davidson College and Columbia Seminary were published under the title of *Christ Our Penal Substitute*. Thomas Cary Johnson states that 'this little book contains a masterly presentation of the Old School Presbyterian view of the atonement.' Johnson, *Dabney*, p. 522.

[2] Johnson, *Dabney*, p. 521.

[3] *The State*, January 9, 1898.

Columbia, Girardeau led the service at Second Presbyterian and Dabney preached the sermon. Blackburn described the scene:

> When the service was over the two men came down the aisle together; they were men of imposing presence, each like the son of a king . . . Dr. Girardeau said: 'Doctor, that was a glorious sermon this morning.' Dr. Dabney replied, 'This has been a sweet service to me, and this singing carries me back to old Tinkling Spring.' Dr. Girardeau said: 'But what will it be in heaven?' The answer of Dr. Dabney was lost in the tramping of the congregation. And so, blind and lame, these princes in Israel walked on, talking of the past and future worship of God. A few months after this meeting they both joined the general assembly of the church of the first born in the majestic worship of their God and Saviour.[4]

Robert Lewis Dabney died on January 3, 1898. Six months later, John Lafayette Girardeau died. Years earlier, Girardeau had written a poem called 'Life.'

> Life! 'Tis a passing breath,
> A vapor of today,
> Appearing for a little while,
> And vanishing away.
>
> Life! 'Tis a courier swift
> With tidings from the fray;
> With bending form and foaming steed
> He posteth on his way.
>
> Life! 'Tis the eagle's flight
> Across the trackless way;

[4] Blackburn, *Girardeau,* p. 368. Girardeau left among his papers a small sheet with the title 'Points Upon Which I Disagree with Dr. Dabney.' There are not too many. See Blackburn, *Girardeau,* p. 367.

His rapid pinion beats the air—
He hasteth to the prey.

Life! 'Tis the gallant ship
With pennon floating free;
The favoring gale swells all her sails,
Look now! She's far at sea.

Life! 'Tis a fleeting dream
That ends a troubled night;
But start not—Lo! the morning beam
Of everlasting light.

Life! 'Tis the setting sun
That sinks in storms away;
But see! The morrow is begun
Of Heaven's eternal day.[5]

Girardeau's funeral service was conducted in the Arsenal Hill church, and he was buried in Elmwood Cemetery near the grave of his beloved teacher, James Henley Thornwell. His pulpit-shaped tombstone features an open Bible and bears the inscription 'After he had patiently endured, he obtained the promise. Heb. 6:15.'

* * * * *

In 1899 John Adger died. After teaching at Columbia for seventeen years, Adger had resigned from the seminary in 1874. Henry Alexander White wrote, 'The transparent honesty of Dr. Adger, combined with the simplicity of his religious faith, left deep impressions upon the hearts of all

[5] Blackburn, *Girardeau,* p. 353. Blackburn gives nineteen pages of poems and paraphrases of Psalms by Dr. Girardeau.

who sat at his feet.'[6] Adger returned to Pendleton in the Upcountry, where he served the Presbyterian church until 1896. For two years he worked on his massive *My Life and Times*, which includes almost a hundred pages of commentary on Calvin's Book Four of the *Institutes*, and two hundred and fifty pages of the Southern Presbyterian controversy about evolution. As Adger was dying, his friends often heard him say, 'Master, Master, come quickly, come today.' When he died, one of those friends wrote: 'We who stood there with uplifted eyes saw him ascending to heaven, with a kind of joyful feeling. His "spirit is with Christ"; and our hope is in God.'[7] Forty-five years earlier, in 1854, Thornwell had written to Robert J. Breckinridge, 'I have a very high opinion of Adger . . . He is indeed a noble Roman, or rather an Israelite in whom there is no guile.'[8]

* * * * *

Richard Clark Reed became professor of ecclesiastical history and church polity at Columbia Seminary in 1898. Born in Tennessee in 1851, Reed studied at King College and Union Seminary in Virginia and served churches in Tennessee, Virginia, and North Carolina, before coming to Columbia.

Reed delivered his inaugural address at the seminary on the topic 'How to Make Our Brief Course in Church History Most Profitable.'[9] He said that the fact that he had been chosen to teach church history at the seminary must indicate

[6] White, *Southern Presbyterian Leaders*, p. 300.

[7] Adger, *My Life and Times*, p. 665.

[8] Palmer, *Thornwell*, p. 383.

[9] R. C. Reed, 'How to Make Our Brief Course in Church History Most Profitable,' *Presbyterian Quarterly* (July 1899), pp. 453-69.

'a woeful lack in our ministry of men properly furnished for this work.' Even so, Reed promised to do his best 'to take the study of church history out of the category of the dull and irksome, and place it where it properly belongs in the category of the pleasing and inspiring.' He stressed that the only reliable standard in teaching church history is God's infallible Word. 'As we look upon the ever-shifting panorama of history, with its mingling of light and shade,' he said, 'we have the key to its interpretation in the book which Christ placed in our hands, and by the use of this we can assure ourselves of his presence.'

History studied in the light of the Bible and with God's presence in the person of the Holy Spirit will become 'the sustainer and nourisher of both our faith and our hope.' 'The golden age of the church is not behind us,' Reed said. With the Bible's promise of God's ultimate and complete victory, 'we dare not become pessimistic . . . Amid the shadows, hope rejoices and abides his time.'

Studying church history in the light of Scripture, Reed continued, enables us to test the claims of churches, both ancient and modern. He illustrated his point:

> Human nature has not waited till the nineteenth century to devise new expedients for hastening on the triumphs of the Gospel. It has been equally busy in all other centuries. The history of the church is largely a history of expedients devised by those who were impatient of God's slow methods.

No age of the church has improved on 'the simple devices of the Gospel,' he insisted. 'Preaching and praying and holy living are the regenerating forces still as in apostolic times.'

Reed believed that 'Reformation theology represented a progress backward. The Presbyterian Church believes that all true progress in theology lies in [going back] in the direction of the Divine Teacher and his apostles. The goal is behind us.'[10]

Reed was a strong Calvinist with a charitable spirit toward Christians of other convictions. He wrote in the introductory chapter to his little book *The Gospel as Taught by Calvin:*

> For many years Calvinism and Arminianism were at deadly strife. They could not speak peaceably to one another. Experience has proven conclusively that Christ can live at peace with both. He can use both for his glory and for the saving of men. He has at length 'broken down the middle wall of partition,' and abolished the enmity between them. They exchange civilities, stand in each other's pulpits, and join hands in concerted warfare against the common enemy. This is as it should be, and it is far from our purpose to stir the embers of the old strife. We delight to sing
>
> Blest be the tie that binds,
> Our hearts in Christian love.
>
> But there is no shutting our eyes to the fact that the standards of the Presbyterian Church are constructed, from foundation to turret, out of Calvinism pure and simple, the Calvinism of the Reformation period. If these standards are to mean anything to the rank and file of the church, they must be held up to view. The graciousness of their doctrines, which is somewhat obscured by the ruggedness of statement, must be exhibited. Our design in what follows is to set forth the 'five points,' against which a considerable part of modern Christendom has revolted, in such a logical, lucid and scriptural manner as to win for them a heartier assent from Presbyterians. We firmly believe that Calvinism was true in those dark

[10] R. C. Reed, *The Gospel as Taught by Calvin* (Richmond, Va.: Presbyterian Committee of Publications, 1896; repr. Banner of Truth, 2009), p. 2.

> days when at the cost of much precious blood it won its great victories for God and humanity. If true then, it is true today. If true it should be believed and loved.[11]

In *The Gospel as Taught by Calvin* Reed presented the famous 'five points' in a fresh and appealing way: (1) 'the fatal image' (total depravity); (2) 'an opened heart' (unconditional election); (3) 'first choice' (limited atonement); (4) 'boundary lines' (irresistible grace); and (5) 'grace linked to glory' (perseverance of the saints).

In his little book Reed championed the free offer of the gospel. He wrote:

> 'Whosoever will, let him take the water of life freely.' Any so-called Calvinism that does not chime with this sweet gospel bell deserves to 'be cast out, and to be trodden under foot of men.' We ask for no leniency of judgment on any argument or inference that would tend to make the strait gate straiter, or the narrow way more narrow. Above all things, let us believe that 'Jesus Christ came into the world to save sinners,' and that 'him that cometh to him he will in no wise cast out.'[12]

Reed's book *A History of the Presbyterian Churches of the World* met the need for a comprehensive view of worldwide Presbyterianism.

Reed was quite critical of his own church's ministry—or lack of it—among African Americans. Since emancipation, he wrote, 'the Southern Presbyterian Church has done very little for the religious instruction of the negro . . . is now doing very little, and without a change of method is not likely to do any better.' He noted that the Southern Presbyterian

[11] Reed, *The Gospel as Taught by Calvin,* pp. 12-13.
[12] Reed, *The Gospel as Taught by Calvin,* pp. 81-82.

Church seemed to be content with supporting its school in Alabama for the training of black Presbyterian pastors, and deplored the inadequate education that they received there. He listed the mere handful of black Presbyterian churches that had been planted. Furthermore, he argued, the Southern Presbyterian Church had not incorporated its black churches into its own organic structure, but has merely tacked them on to 'its skirts as a loose fringe.' Reed described the 'peculiar relations existing between the emancipated negroes and the Southern white population,' which dampened the church's enthusiasm for greater commitment to evangelizing 'the African in the midst of us.' Social equality of the Negroes, he wrote, was something the South did not accept. 'We have one hand on their head holding them down socially; how much can we lift them up religiously with the other?' The refusal to accept political equality with the Negroes was another reason for the church's failure to promote fully its mission to them. Reed wrote: 'The negro is a citizen, dignified with all the honors, privileges, and responsibilties which belong to that character. The way is open to places of the highest official preferment.' Reed was not optimistic that the Southern Presbyterian Church would overcome its 'timid and inefficient policy, where interests so momentous are involved.' He suggested that the Southern Church 'turn the management of the whole work over to the Northern [Presbyterian] Church, and that we cooperate with that Church in the way of sending young men to their schools to be educated, and contributing of our money to their support.'[13]

Reed was moderator of the General Assembly of 1922. This kind and gentle man, because of his strong conviction

[13] R. C. Reed, 'The Southern Presbyterian Church and the Freedmen,' *Southern Presbyterian Review* (January 1885), pp. 83-108.

that truth was being sacrificed to avoid offence, preached the retiring moderator's sermon to the 1923 General Assembly on the subject of 'Hell.'

* * * * *

On May 25, 1902, Dr. Benjamin Morgan Palmer died from injuries he had suffered when he was struck by a streetcar. People in New Orleans and all over the South mourned his death. The city had not seen such a large gathering for a funeral since the death of the Confederate president, Jefferson Davis. Streetcars stopped running, businesses closed, and the flag on City Hall floated at half-mast, as thousands of people of all classes and denominations filled the First Presbyterian Church and overflowed into Lafayette Square. A Jewish rabbi said at the funeral that when Dr. Palmer 'went home to his Father's house, we all became poverty stricken. New Orleans . . . lost her foremost citizen [and] her public conscience.'[14] The people of the city loved him—Roman Catholic cardinals, Jewish rabbis, Episcopal bishops, and people of all faiths or none—and yet they knew that he 'was a Presbyterian of the Presbyterians, a Calvinist of the Calvinists, a Christian of the Christians.'[15]

In South Carolina, Governor M. B. McSweeny paid tribute to the state's most famous preacher:

> The news of the death of the venerable Dr. Palmer has been received in his native State with expressions of sincerest sorrow . . . [He] was one of the many bright stars of the firmament of learning produced by the Palmetto State. His name will go into our history with those of Calhoun, McDuffie,

[14] Wells, *Southern Presbyterian Worthies*, p. 140.
[15] Wells, *Southern Presbyterian Worthies*, p. 170.

> Hayne and Rutledge. In Columbia, where Dr. Palmer served for fourteen years at the opening of his brilliant career, he was most dearly loved, and to the members of his congregation he served so faithfully here the news of his death brought the deepest sorrow. Dr. Palmer undoubtedly ranked as one of the greatest preachers of the Gospel and exponents of theology that the United States has ever produced.[16]

* * * * *

Joseph Ruggles Wilson died in January 1903, one month before his eightieth birthday, in Princeton, New Jersey. After leaving Columbia, Dr. Wilson had served First Presbyterian Church in Wilmington, North Carolina, until 1885. When a teaching position opened at the struggling theological school of the Southwestern Presbyterian University, Wilson moved to Clarksville, Tennessee, where he taught until 1893. He was stated clerk of the Presbyterian Church in the United States, the Southern Presbyterian Church—a position he had held since 1865—until 1898. The office did not carry much power in the decentralized Southern Church, but it was often said that Wilson 'could kill an unwise overture by the way he would read it and then glare at the Assembly as if lost in wonder that any such thing had ever been thought of'![17] Wilson's increasingly poor health necessitated his moving to Princeton in the spring of 1901 to live with his son Woodrow, who was then president of Princeton University. As Wilson's body rested in a coffin in the bay window of Woodrow Wilson's Princeton study, Ellen Axson Wilson told her daughters to look at their grandfather's now serene and 'beautiful old

[16] Johnson, *Palmer,* p. 636.
[17] Mulder, *Woodrow Wilson,* p. 26.

face,' so that they could remember him with dignity rather than as a helpless, sick old man.[18] After a brief service in Princeton, Woodrow Wilson accompanied his father's body to Columbia for the funeral and burial next to his wife, who had died in 1888, in the graveyard of First Presbyterian Church. The son provided the epitaph:

> Pastor, teacher, ecclesiastical leader. For thirty-four years Stated Clerk of the General Assembly of the Presbyterian Church of the United States. Steadfast, brilliant, devoted, loving and beloved. A master of serious eloquence, a thinker of singular power and penetration, a thoughtful student of life and God's purpose, a lover and servant of his fellow men, a man of God.

* * * * *

On January 17, 1907, James Woodrow died. He was seventy-nine years old. Despite the controversy over his views of evolution, Woodrow was honoured in Columbia and throughout the Southern Presbyterian Church. Although he was removed from his chair at Columbia Seminary, he continued to serve, without bitterness, the denomination he loved. On one occasion, he mortgaged his Columbia house to raise $4,000 needed to pay the salaries of Southern Presbyterian missionaries. Before James Woodrow died, the board of directors of Columbia Seminary passed a resolution 'removing any and all aspersions or implications upon his character, standing, or theological orthodoxy' that might be drawn from actions of the board.[19]

[18] Frances Wright Saunders, *Ellen Axson Wilson: First Lady Between Two Worlds* (Chapel Hill: University of North Carolina Press, 1985), p. 146.

[19] Gustafson, *Woodrow*, p. 262.

S. L. Morris, one of Woodrow's seminary students, said of him: 'He was a universal genius; one of the greatest scholars the South ever produced. He taught me more than all the other professors combined, and so grounded me in the truth of the Bible that no power on earth can successfully assail my faith. Many a time have I heard him say, "I fear God, and in fearing him I have nothing else to fear."'[20]

William Childs Robinson writes that 'in his final illness James Woodrow was visited by a close friend and former student. All the tangled threads of this life had been pushed aside and the dying Christian was resting in these words of faith which his mother had taught him as a child in the old country:

> For Jesus hath loved me,
> I cannot tell why.
> Only this I do find—
> We two are so joined,
> He'll not be in Heaven
> And leave me behind.'[21]

Referring to the way in which he was wheeled from one room in the home to another, Woodrow said that 'dying meant just passing to another room in the Father's house.'[22]

Thomas Woodrow Wilson, president of Princeton University and soon to be the twenty-eighth president of the United States, wrote that his uncle's death took away

> one of the noblest men I ever knew. A man of many small failings, I am glad, for my own comfort, to remember, but a man to love (in the quiet, self-contained Scottish fashion,

[20] LaMotte, *Colored Light*, pp. 212-13.

[21] William Childs Robinson, *Our Lord: An Affirmation of the Deity of Christ* (Grand Rapids: Wm. B. Eerdmans Publishing Company, 1949), p. 59.

[22] Robinson, *Our Lord*, p. 59.

> but very, very deeply, none the less) and to be loved, and gifted in an extraordinary degree with the powers that make a great thinker and a great man of science. He followed duty to obscure places and kept himself in mere faithfulness from the eye of fame; but his friends and intimates knew him for a man who might have placed his name among the great names of our men of learning. It pleases me to think of the gracious and helpful influences he has brought into the lives of many generations of students, and not least into the life of a nephew who never told him how much he owed to him.[23]

On May 10, 1908, the Woodrow Memorial Presbyterian Church in Columbia was dedicated. The Reverend Melton Clark, pastor of First Presbyterian Church of Greensboro, North Carolina, and son-in-law of Dr. Woodrow, preached from 1 Chronicles 22:16, 'Arise and be doing; and the Lord be with thee.' Several members of First Presbyterian Church had conducted a mission in the Waverly suburb since 1899; Mr. David W. Robinson, deacon at First Presbyterian, and Dr. R. C. Reed of Columbia Seminary were leaders in this work. In 1906 the mission was turned over to the session of First Presbyterian Church. The Men's Auxiliary raised money and purchased a lot for a church building in 1907. Mrs. Woodrow became interested in the project and gave $15,000 as a memorial to her husband. At the dedication of the new church building, Mr. Robinson ended his historical sketch with a tribute to Mrs. Woodrow, who had provided the church 'its furniture and furnishings complete, from the foundation stone to tower cap' as a 'worthy memorial of the distinguished scholar and minister whose name it honors and

[23] Ray Stannard Baker, *Woodrow Wilson, Life and Letters; Youth; 1856-1890* (New York: Doubleday, Page, and Co., 1927), p. 20. Quoted by Gustafson, *Woodrow,* p. xi.

bears.' Dr. Reed and seminary student G. M. Wilcox ministered together in the new church. Within a year, there were twenty-four communicants and over two hundred enrolled in the Sunday school.

* * * * *

Samuel Macon Smith died suddenly on Monday morning, January 10, 1910. On Sunday, January 2, he had preached on the words of the Apostle Paul—'None of these things move me' (*Acts* 20:24). The next morning he met seminary professor Henry Alexander White on the street. White described their conversation:

> We stood together at the edge of the sidewalk and the conversation turned at once to his sermon. He spoke of a certain part of the sermon and told me about the source from which he drew the material for it. This source he had found in some books, a loan to him from my private library, containing accounts of the advances made by Federal soldiers against the Confederate position at Fredericksburg, and the advance by the division of Pickett and Pettigrew against the Federal works on Cemetery Ridge at Gettysburg. These bold advances were described by Dr. Smith in his sermon and then applied to his theme as illustrating the steadfastness and aggressiveness of the Apostle Paul in his campaign of evangelistic work.
>
> Even thus, while we were speaking still of Paul and Stonewall Jackson and other heroes of the faith, we parted, even as pilgrims part on the highway, and now I shall see him no more until we meet again face to face in the Father's house. And verily we shall meet. Heaven seems now not very far away. Our dear friend has been translated in a moment of

time, and has already found his place in the presence of Him to whom he gave the service of his life.

In the evening of January 9, Smith's text was 'He that soweth abundantly shall reap also abundantly' (2 *Cor.* 9:6). The next morning he died. He had sown abundantly at First Presbyterian Church for over twenty years and was held in high esteem by all Columbians. The day after his death a full page of letters appeared in *The State* with the title 'Samuel Macon Smith, D.D.—Men of Many Creeds and Callings Pay Tribute to the Memory of This Great Presbyter Who Died Yesterday.' Governor Ansel wrote that 'a prince and a great man' had fallen 'in Israel.' Dr. William McPheeters of Columbia Seminary wrote that in Dr. Smith 'were mingled insight, understanding, the salt of wit, the grace of humor, sympathy and genuine humility.'[24] Presidents of Columbia's colleges, professors at the seminary, elders of the church, and his fellow townsmen expressed their love for Dr. Smith.

[24] White, *Southern Presbyterian Leaders*, p. 460.

26

'THE LINE OF DESCENT'

ERNEST Trice Thompson wrote: 'At the close of the 19th century the Southern Presbyterian Church seemed solidly conservative, strongly Calvinistic, distinctly sectional, and remarkably homogenous in outlook and belief.'[1] Already, however, there were signs that changes were coming in the new century. Douglas Kelly explains how many 'churches lapsed into a broadly evangelical, man-centered type of soteriology, a lack of serious church discipline, and an all-too-frequent separation . . . between personal piety and business, educational and social/cultural life. Much of this decline from sound Calvinism in the Southern denominations occurred between approximately 1870 and 1930.'[2]

William McPheeters, who joined the Columbia Seminary faculty in 1888, noted that the views of the 'higher critics' were 'being rapidly popularized and propagated among all the more intelligent people of our churches.'[3]

McPheeters and the other professors at the seminary defended the Bible as the Word of God. He wrote, 'It is upon this foundation—the integrity, authenticity, genuineness,

[1] Thompson, *Presbyterians in the South*, 3:215.

[2] Kelly, *Preachers with Power*, p. xxv.

[3] Thompson, *Presbyterians in the South*, 3:212.

supernatural origin and divine authority of the Bible—that the church needs to center her most serious attention.'[4]

As they faced the challenges to come, McPheeters and his colleagues held fast to the infallibility of the Scripture and championed the Thornwellian doctrine of the spirituality of the church. Christ gave the church a definite mission, they argued—to bring people to the cross and train them in the teachings of the Bible. The church is not at liberty to substitute for this any other end, they insisted. The Christian church will be the source of great benefits, moral as well as economic, to the world, but these things are to be accomplished by Christians trained by the church, and not directly by the church in its corporate capacity.

During his long ministry, Benjamin Morgan Palmer struggled to correctly apply the doctrine of the spirituality of the church. 'He stood so uncompromisingly for civic righteousness and so unyieldingly for the spirituality of the church that his position was a difficult one,' wrote John Wells. Palmer fought to preserve Sabbath observance in New Orleans and to defeat the lottery, while maintaining the position that the church as church must restrict its work to instructions it receives from the Bible. Christians as Christians can, and must, be active in many movements to safeguard and advance human life on earth, but the church as church must follow its mandate—to preach the gospel throughout the world and to train Christians in the Scriptures.

The Westminster Confession asserts the right of church bodies to make appeals to the state 'by way of humble petition in cases extraordinary.' The Southern Presbyterian Church on rare occasions availed itself of this constitutional

[4] Thompson, *Presbyterians in the South*, 3:214.

privilege: a memorial addressed to Christian nations around the world concerning the arbitration of international disputes (1890), the adoption of more effective child labour laws (1908), and support for the prohibition amendment to the Constitution (1914). The General Assembly's first two declarations attracted little attention; approval of the prohibition amendment, however, brought a storm of protest by many Southern Presbyterians who believed that in doing so the church had moved away from its doctrine of the spirituality of the church. In 1919 the General Assembly sent a telegram to President Wilson, the son of a Columbia Seminary professor, declaring that the Southern Presbyterian Church was confidently relying upon him to carry out his 'gigantic task to a righteous consummation.' Because he believed that this petition violated the doctrine of the spirituality of the church, McPheeters voted against it. This time, however, he stood almost alone.

In 1913 James R. Howerton, Columbia Seminary graduate of 1885 and professor of philosophy at Washington and Lee University, published a book, *The Church and Social Reforms,* in which he attempted to clarify the doctrine of the spirituality of the church. 'The church . . . as an organization,' he wrote,

> cannot and ought not to engage in secular reforms, political or economic. She always makes mischief when she does so . . . The only real good the Church has ever done in promoting such reforms is by her influence in forming the character, the principles, and the motives of men and women whose real business in life is to engage in such service to business, to society, and the state . . . Let [the church] preach the Gospel as a rule of justification; but she must preach the law as a rule of life, and insist that obedience to it in all the relations of life

> is the only valid evidence of a saving faith . . . The separation of church and state does not mean that morals and religion must be kept out of politics. That the church herself must not engage in secular reforms is not to be interpreted to mean that her preachers and her members shall have nothing to do with such reforms. That the ecclesiastical organization itself cannot be used to promote such reforms must not mean that preachers and church members may not form voluntary and interdenominational organizations in order to unify and systematize their work for social reforms.[5]

* * * * *

William Thomas Hall was professor of theology at Columbia from 1895 to 1911. A North Carolinian, Hall studied at Davidson College and Columbia Seminary. He served pastorates in South Carolina, Mississippi, and Virginia before coming to the seminary. He was, according to Morton Smith, 'a thoroughgoing Calvinist in the historic sense of that term.'[6]

* * * * *

Henry Alexander White taught New Testament literature and exegesis from 1903 until 1926. Descended from sturdy Scotch-Irish stock, White was born in 1861 in Greenbrier County in Virginia. He graduated from Washington and Lee in 1885 and from Princeton Seminary in 1889. He married Fanny Beverley Wellford and taught history at his alma mater, Washington and Lee, from 1889 to 1902. White was engaged in special study at the University of Glasgow when called to Columbia Seminary in 1902. Through the years, hundreds

[5] LaMotte, *Colored Light*, pp. 252-53.
[6] Smith, *Studies in Southern Presbyterian Theology*, p. 256.

of students, colleagues, and other friends enjoyed the 'old Southern hospitality' of Dr. and Mrs. White, whose home in Gibbes Court was 'an art gallery,' as the Whites brought back from Europe hundreds of copies or photographs of famous masterpieces.

White wrote books on the history of South Carolina and the Scotch-Irish in America, biographies of Robert E. Lee and Stonewall Jackson, and a work about *Southern Presbyterian Leaders 1683-1911*. He dedicated this book to his wife's father and uncle, one a ruling elder and the other a deacon in the First Presbyterian Church of Richmond, Virginia—'worthy types of that efficiency in service, that nobility of character and that purity in thought and purpose that from the beginning have marked the office-bearers in our Southern Presbyterian Church.'

Dr. White gave the principal address at the Tercentenary of the King James Bible in 1911 and delivered the Stone Lectures at Princeton in 1920 on 'The Gospel of Comfort.' He died early on Sunday morning, October 10, 1926. The preceding week he had given a series of sermons on the Holy Spirit for the faculty and student body in the seminary chapel.

'The old Covenanter fighting blood was strong in this sweet and gentle soul on questions of principle,' First Presbyterian Church elder George A. Wauchope said at the memorial service for White in the seminary chapel. The Memorial Bulletin of Columbia Seminary stated that in an age of growing attacks on the Christian faith, White 'remained sweet and calm and confident of the truth for which his Church stood.'[7]

* * * * *

[7] LaMotte, *Colored Light*, p. 181.

In 1911 Thornton C. Whaling succeeded William Thomas Hall as professor of theology. Whaling was born in Virginia in 1858. He studied at Davidson College, Roanoke College, and Union Theological Seminary in New York. He returned to the South and received his bachelor of divinity degree from Columbia Seminary in 1883 and that same year married Lucy Muller of Columbia. Whaling served churches in South Carolina, Alabama, Virginia, and Texas, including First Church, Lexington, Virginia, and First Church, Dallas, Texas, which for many years was the largest Presbyterian church in the South. He taught theology at Southwestern Presbyterian University.

On the occasion of his becoming professor of theology and the first president[8] at Columbia Seminary, Whaling said:

> It is essential to preserve uncorrupted and to extend more widely the influence of that type of Calvinistic theology of which Columbia is the representative. Calvinism has never received more convincing and reasonable exposition than at the hands of Thornwell and Girardeau, and our day and our Church cannot be more effectively served than by the unchanged and consistent presentation of this scriptural and rational theology, as was so faithfully done by my distinguished predecessor, Dr. W. T. Hall. The greatest asset of our seminary is this Columbia type [of theology] which inherits the best results of the past and further expands and develops the system to meet the new issues of the present time. The line of descent is Paul, Augustine, Anselm, Calvin, Owen, Edwards, Hodge, Howe, Thornwell, Girardeau.[9]

Thornton Whaling was an ardent supporter of Dr. Woodrow in the evolution controversy. Whaling dedicated his book

[8] Before Dr. Whaling became the seminary's first president, the faculty chose one of its members to serve as chairman of the faculty.

[9] Smith, *Studies in Southern Presbyterian Theology*, pp. 257-58.

Science and Religion Today in memory of 'that peerless scholar and saint James Woodrow, a scientist and a "man of God" who was above all a masterly expounder of the right relations between science and religion.'[10]

Whaling's praise of Woodrow did not lessen his admiration for Woodrow's greatest opponent, Dr. Girardeau. For *The Life Work of John L. Girardeau,* compiled and edited by Girardeau's son-in-law George A. Blackburn, Whaling contributed two chapters: 'The Philosopher' and 'The Theologian.' Whaling admitted that on some issues he had disagreed with Girardeau but praised him wholeheartedly, almost extravagantly, as a man 'who filled a large place in the eye of the Church as preacher, theologian, teacher, writer and ecclesiastic.'[11]

Students appreciated Whaling's devotion to Calvinistic theology as expounded by Charles Hodge, his standard assignments of twenty pages for the next lesson, his explanatory diagrams used to interpret the mysteries of theology, and his dramatic 'interviews' with various historical heretics, who were abruptly kicked out of the classroom after their heresies had been properly demolished![12]

In reviewing Sherwood Eddy's *New Challenges to Faith,* in which Eddy undertook to show how the church could accept the truth of scientific methods and discoveries and reformulate Christian belief in ways that would appeal to modern people, Whaling said that *New Challenges to Faith,* a good example of modernist thought, was quite wrong in its

[10] Gustafson, *Woodrow,* p. 232.

[11] Blackburn, *Girardeau,* p. 283. The substance of these two chapters had appeared in the *Union Seminary Magazine.*

[12] Sanders, *Louisville Seminary,* p. 59. Morton Smith stated that Whaling 'accepted the Scriptures as infallible, and followed his predecessors in the acceptance of the historic Calvinism of the Westminster Standards.'

approach and conclusions. Whaling rejoiced at the reprinting of Dabney's *Systematic and Polemic Theology* and hoped it would prompt a reissue of the writings of James Henley Thornwell, Breckinridge, Beattie, and others. That would, he stated, provide an answer to the views of popular liberals, such as Eddy and Harry Emerson Fosdick, who were 'theological pygmies' by contrast.[13]

In 1921 Whaling became professor of theology and apologetics at Louisville Theological Seminary, succeeding Robert A. Webb in that position. When the *Presbyterian Standard* asserted that 'progressive' theology was making inroads into the Southern Presbyterian Church, Whaling answered with 'The Crises of the Presbyterian and Reformed Churches.' He urged people to remember 2 Timothy 2:24, 25, which exhorts believers to patience and meekness in answering those who oppose them. He suggested that those who could not accept historic Reformed theology should withdraw to another denomination. He argued that the so-called progressive theology was, in fact, antiquated, bearing the marks, he stated, of Neoplatonism, Gnosticism, and pantheism. He urged the church to exercise better oversight of its colleges and seminaries to ensure that the Westminster Standards were taught. Churches, he declared, should be ready to try for heresy those who refused to accept the teaching of the Standards.[14]

In 1929 Whaling retired and spent his last years in Columbia. An associate at Louisville Seminary characterized him as 'a man of fine appearance and address, scholarly, fluent, quick in repartee, delightful in conversation.'[15]

[13] Nutt, *Many Lamps, One Light*, pp. 86, 87.

[14] Nutt, *Many Lamps, One Light*, pp. 92, 93.

[15] Sanders, *Louisville Seminary*, p. 56.

* * * * *

Robert Gamaliel Pearson taught English Bible at the seminary from 1911 to 1913. He grew up in a Quaker family that moved from North Carolina to Mississippi, where Robert was born in 1847. He made a confession of faith as a child and wanted to become a preacher. He served first as pastor of a Cumberland Presbyterian Church in Mississippi and then in several Cumberland churches in Tennessee. Pearson became an evangelist, preaching from New York to Missouri, in Texas, and throughout the South. He did not emphasize the number of conversions, as was commonly done by evangelists, often saying that 'there was a snare in the counting business and that David had sinned that way.' He did not emphasize denominations, maintaining that he had not been 'sent forth as a denominational recruiting officer but as a worker for the kingdom of God.'[16] During the World's Fair in Chicago, Robert Pearson was preaching at the Empire Theater when D. L. Moody came in and said, 'Pearson, you go over to the Haymarket Theater and preach to my congregation and I will preach to yours here.'[17] Pearson taught Bible at the Montreat Conference of the Southern Presbyterian Church for three summers. Whaling was so impressed that he invited Pearson to teach at Columbia Seminary. But after just two years at the seminary, Pearson died in Columbia on March 19, 1913.

* * * * *

[16] LaMotte, *Colored Light,* p. 184.
[17] LaMotte, *Colored Light,* p. 186.

On October 23 and 24, 1912, the Synod of South Carolina celebrated the centennial of the birth of James Henley Thornwell. It was held at First Presbyterian Church in Columbia—the church, Synod noted, 'which Dr. Thornwell had twice served as pastor, and in the city where nearly all his eminent services to the Church had been rendered.'[18] Large congregations, including the president, faculty, and students of the university, the members of the theological seminary, the congregation of First Church, and the people of the city, gathered to hear three special addresses. Dr. Thornton Whaling, president of Columbia Seminary, spoke on 'Dr. Thornwell as a Theologian,' and Dr. A. M. Fraser of Staunton, Virginia, on 'Dr. Thornwell as an Ecclesiologist.' Dr. Thomas H. Law, pastor in Spartanburg, South Carolina, who had studied under Thornwell at the seminary and had listened to his sermons at First Church, addressed the synod on 'Dr. Thornwell as Teacher and Preacher.' Law concluded with the words, 'Let us cherish tenderly and sacredly his memory, as we learn the many lessons of his illustrious career; and let us fondly and devotedly conserve the grand and noble work which he performed for our State and for our Church.'[19]

* * * * *

In 1912 Columbians celebrated the election of Woodrow Wilson as the twenty-eighth president of the United States. William Plumer Jacobs noted in his diary for December 20 that 'this is the 52nd anniversary of the ordinance of

[18] *Centennial Addresses, Delivered before the Synod of South Carolina in the First Presbyterian Church, Columbia, October 23, 24, 1912* (Spartanburg, S.C.: Band & White Printers, 1913), p. 3.

[19] *Centennial Addresses*, p. 21.

Secession,' and then optimistically added 'The [Civil] War is over. There is no longer North or South. A Virginian will enter the Presidential chair.'[20] Wilson's ties with South Carolina and Columbia were strong. His father, Joseph Ruggles Wilson, was a professor at Columbia Seminary, and Woodrow's boyhood years were spent in Columbia. The Wilson home was just a block from the seminary, and it was in the seminary chapel that Woodrow professed personal faith in Christ. He joined First Presbyterian Church. Both his mother and father were buried in the church's cemetery. His sister, Annie, lived in Columbia; she was married to George Howe, the son of the long-time seminary professor. When President Woodrow Wilson came to Columbia on September 18, 1916, for the funeral of his sister, he stopped at the chapel of the seminary, where he had accepted Christ as a boy back in 1873. 'I feel I ought to take off my shoes,' he commented. 'This is holy ground.'[21]

[20] Jacobs, *Diary of William Plumer Jacobs,* p. 440.
[21] Mulder, *Woodrow Wilson,* p. 38.

27

'THE PROPHET'S CALL AND THE SHEPHERD'S HEART'

IN May 1914, Dr. James Reavis resigned from his pastorate at First Presbyterian Church, where he had served since 1911, to become professor of pastoral theology, sacred rhetoric, and English Bible at Columbia Seminary. Born in Missouri, Reavis studied at Westminster College in Fulton, Missouri, Louisville Presbyterian Seminary, New York University, and Princeton Seminary. He married Eva Fullton Witherspoon. He was pastor of First Presbyterian Church in Louisville, Kentucky, and First Presbyterian Church in Dallas, Texas, before becoming Secretary of Foreign Missions for the Southern Presbyterian Church in 1905. As pastor in Columbia, Reavis brought the cause of world missions before the church and the city. He preached on missions, lectured at the seminary on missions, and brought missionaries to the church. A church member, in a farewell poem dedicated to Reavis, wrote, 'Thou hast stirred us in that work! Our song: the Gospel give to every needy one!' One of those challenged by his missionary appeals was Aurie Lancaster, daughter of Robert Alexander Lancaster, beloved doctor and faithful elder at First Presbyterian. She married Columbia Seminary student James Montgomery, and they went as missionaries to China late in 1917. Reavis taught at the seminary until 1920, when he once again became secretary of foreign missions for the Southern Church.

* * * * *

From 1885 to 1927, when the seminary moved to Decatur, Georgia, at least thirty-three Columbia Seminary graduates went out as foreign missionaries to Mexico, Japan, China, Brazil, Siam, Central America, Persia, Korea, and to the Belgian Congo and Cameroon in Africa. C. Darby Fulton, a graduate of 1915, served in Japan until 1925, when he was brought home to become Secretary of the Southern Presbyterian Committee of Foreign Missions.

Other students found areas of useful service at home. Davison McDowell Douglas graduated in 1899. He became a pastor in North Carolina and then Maryland. He came back to his native South Carolina in 1911 to become president of Presbyterian College, where, according to Daniel Hollis, he had 'outstanding success.' In 1927 Douglas was elected president of the University of South Carolina, becoming the third man with a Columbia Seminary connection to become president of the state university. Thornwell had been president from 1852 to 1855, and Woodrow from 1891 to 1897. Douglas's sudden death on August 1, 1931, ended his brief presidency at the university. His 'greatest contribution,' Hollis wrote, 'was his firm insistence that expansion should not come at the expense of academic standards.'[1]

* * * * *

[1] Hollis, *University of South Carolina*, 2:328, 331.

Edgar D. Kerr, a graduate of Davidson College and Columbia Seminary, with graduate studies at the University of Chicago and Princeton Seminary, was pastor of several churches before being called to Columbia Seminary as professor of Greek and Hebrew in 1915. He also served as pastor of the Presbyterian church in Newberry, South Carolina. A superb teacher of the biblical languages, Kerr's strong faith made a deep impression on his students. One day in class a student asked, 'Dr. Kerr, do you think God could possibly be just and send any man to hell?' Kerr paused for a little and then answered, 'Yes, God could be just and send me to hell.'[2]

From time to time the practice of teaching Greek and Hebrew in the seminary came up for discussion in church courts and papers. There was a growing sentiment to reduce the study of the languages or replace them with something more 'practical.' The professors of Columbia Seminary, however, were united in insisting that a good knowledge of both biblical languages was essential for effective preaching and teaching.

* * * * *

In September 1914 First Presbyterian Church extended a call to Andrew Watterson Blackwood, pastor of the Sixth United Presbyterian Church of Pittsburgh, Pennsylvania.

Andrew Blackwood was born on August 5, 1882, in Clay Center, Kansas. His father's parents were Reformed Presbyterians (Covenanters) from Northern Ireland. His mother was of Associate Presbyterian (Seceder) stock from Scotland. Isabella and Thomas Blackwood dedicated Andrew to the

[2] Richards, *As I Remember It,* p. 42.

Christian ministry the day he was born, but, not wanting to impose their plans on him, they did not tell him until after he was ordained.[3]

Andrew grew up in Kansas, Ohio, and Pennsylvania. He attended Franklin College, a nondenominational school with Presbyterian roots in New Athens, Ohio. His studies centered largely around mathematics, languages, writing, and debate. He went to Harvard University in 1903, when Harvard, especially the English department, was at the height of its 'golden age.' In 1905 he received his second BA degree, awarded, as the first had been, *magna cum laude*.

Andrew considered law as a career, but when he 'learned more about the law,' he decided that he would prefer to teach English. The possibility of a ministerial career was always in the back of his mind, but he believed that he would fail at this because he was not 'a good mixer.' While he was a student at Harvard working on a debate about education in France, Blackwood suddenly felt 'an inner call to the ministry.' From that time on he never had any questions concerning his future.

In the fall of 1905 Andrew Blackwood began his ministerial studies at Princeton Seminary—known for its outstanding faculty and conservative theology. At Harvard, he had moved far from his Covenanter-Seceder upbringing toward liberal theological beliefs. He decided to study at Princeton to see 'the other side.' There he came under the influence of Princeton's president, Francis Landey Patton, and the seminary's teachers, especially Benjamin Breckinridge Warfield, Geerhardus Vos, and John Davis. At Princeton, Blackwood's personal theological convictions

[3] Biographical material on Andrew Blackwood is from Jay E. Adams, *Studies in Preaching*, vol. 3, *The Homiletical Innovations of Andrew W. Blackwood* (Presbyterian and Reformed Publishing Company, 1976).

returned to the historic Christian orthodoxy of his childhood. Blackwood studied only one year at Princeton; he transferred in 1906 to Xenia Seminary, nearer his home in Ohio—forced to make the change because of what he called a nervous breakdown.

Andrew Blackwood was ordained in the United Presbyterian Church on May 18, 1908.[4] He worked as a home missionary in Oklahoma and served several small congregations in Kansas. On April 10, 1910, he married Carolyn Phillips. In their rural community, where the farmers went to bed at dark, there were few evening meetings; and 'all that first winter,' Carolyn wrote, 'I could hem napkins or embroider linen' while Andrew read aloud from Lamb's *Essays* or Thackeray's *Vanity Fair*. 'Often I said to myself,' Carolyn continued, 'This is the life! How grand to have married a minister!' But Andrew was called to the Sixth Presbyterian Church in Pittsburgh in 1912, and in that busy city, the idyllic life of the country pastorate came to an end. Blackwood faithfully served his city congregation and, for three months in 1913, during the absence of a professor, taught Old Testament at Xenia Seminary—'very successfully,' declared the faculty minutes.

Dr. Blackwood described his Columbia congregation: 'The president and a third of the faculty of the State University were active in our church. Also the Columbia Theological Seminary was there. All the professors but one, and all the students came to our church. The Presbyterian College for Women was there. The president, the professors, and the students attended with us. In addition we had a good congregation of people from the city.'

[4] This denomination was formed in 1858 as a result of the merger of Covenanter and Seceder churches.

First Presbyterian maintained a bulletin board at the Southern Railroad passenger station on Lady Street, to announce its services and activities to visitors. The Sunday morning crowd was 'taxing the capacity of the building.' Sunday evening open-air services were held in the churchyard during the summer. 'Cottage prayer meetings' met in twelve locations throughout the city.

Before long there was another opportunity for outreach in Columbia. War with Germany was declared on April 6, 1917. Fort Jackson, named in honour of Andrew Jackson, who was born on the North Carolina-South Carolina border, soon garrisoned over 40,000 soldiers. Downtown Columbia was filled with khaki-clad men, many of whom joined the American Expeditionary Forces under General John J. Pershing and played a key role in the final campaign that resulted in the Armistice on November 11, 1918. First Presbyterian Church adopted a 'War Time Membership Affiliate Plan' and reached out to the troops.

Andrew Blackwood's first book, *The Prophets: Elijah to Christ,* was published in 1917. He later described an experience that led to this book. Writing in the third person, he explained:

> One day the parson was preaching about heavenly recognition. He insisted that in the other world we shall not only recognize those whom we have known and loved on earth; we shall likewise know and love the men of the Bible, such as Hosea and Amos. The next day one of the deacons said to the minister: 'Don't you think it will be embarrassing for me to meet the Minor Prophets and have to confess that I have never read one of their books? I wish you would tell me how to read Amos and Hosea.'

'The parson,' Dr. Blackwood, prepared a series of evening sermons on the prophets, from Elijah to Christ, for his Columbia congregation, which he delivered again at the Montreat Bible Conference and then published in a book for lay people.

Andrew Blackwood was a popular preacher, although he had what he called 'one unfortunate tendency' from his debating days in college. A teacher at the University of South Carolina who regularly heard Blackwood preach told him that he was 'arguing' with his people. 'So I was,' Blackwood said, 'until I learned better.'

Blackwood studied the great preachers of the past and their sermons, seeking, he said, 'the source of their power.' He wrote, 'In Columbia we often ask the secret of the power of the three mighties, Thornwell, Palmer, and Girardeau.' One of their secrets, he discovered, was that 'each of them was a doctrinal preacher.' Benjamin Palmer, especially, impressed his successor. 'If we study the sermons of Palmer,' he wrote, 'we quickly agree that this man adorned his doctor's degree.'

Despite his early fears that he was not a good mixer, First Presbyterian's pastor took seriously the work of visitation and counselling.[5] Every weekday, from nine in the morning until two o'clock, he gave himself to his study and books. The afternoons he spent in calling—but not until after the late-midday South Carolina dinner, which was the main meal of the day. He observed what he called 'the pastor's hour,' when he would be present in his study at the church to which people could come with their problems and needs. Blackwood took an interest in the life of the city—visiting principals of schools, city librarians, and those responsible for the maintenance of playgrounds, as well as newspaper editors and city officials. He called on new pastors in town or sent a friendly

[5] For Dr. Blackwood's ministerial practice, see his *Pastoral Work: A Source Book for Ministers* (Philadelphia: Westminster Press, 1945), and his many other books.

letter of welcome. Carolyn Blackwood formed Bible study groups for girls and businesswomen, which also sponsored socials, and became involved in community service.

Blackwood taught at Columbia Seminary as 'special lecturer on selected portions of the English Bible.' Often the seminary students would confer with him about their sermons or ask him questions about his preaching and ministry. Blackwood taught Bible at the University of South Carolina, which awarded him the honorary doctor of divinity degree in 1918.

In January 1921, Blackwood was called to the Indianola Presbyterian Church of Columbus, Ohio. He wrote to the Columbia congregation:

> I rejoice that I have been counted worthy to labor in such a field as this, and my loftiest hope for the new field of labor is that in time it may command such an influence in the State of Ohio as this beloved First Church has long had in the State of South Carolina. I am glad that I came to be your pastor and I am finding it increasingly hard to go away . . . I trust that you may ere long be guided to choose a man of God who has the prophet's call and the shepherd's heart and that under his leadership you shall as never before begin really to 'possess your possessions.'

In 1925 Blackwood became professor of English Bible at the Presbyterian seminary in Louisville, Kentucky—another link in the Columbia-Louisville connection. In his inaugural address, entitled 'Your Mother's Bible,' he said: 'For me the greatest work in the world is to aid in preparing consecrated young men to preach the Gospel of our divine Lord and Redeemer, as it is written in the Book. But if I am to teach the English Bible to others, I must first believe it for myself.' In 1930 Blackwood became professor of homiletics at Princeton

Theological Seminary. From 1950 to 1958 he was professor of preaching at Temple University. He published twenty-two books, including *The Fine Art of Preaching* (1937), *Preaching from the Bible* (1941), and *The Preparation of Sermons* (1948). 'It is a serious question,' Jay Adams has written, 'whether any other man in the history of American homiletics' has been more influential than Blackwood.[6]

[6] Adams, *Studies in Preaching*, p. 1. The January 1953 issue of the *Pulpit Digest* was dedicated to Dr. Blackwood, 'whose influence,' it said, 'will be discernible in a large proportion of the sermons preached in the United States next Sunday, or any Sunday.' The *Pulpit Digest*, 33 (1953), p. 16.

28

THE LAST COMMENCEMENT

IN the summer of 1920, Columbia native Melton Clark, after pastorates in the Carolinas, came to Columbia Seminary as professor of English Bible and pastoral theology. He was welcomed by the First Presbyterian Church session back to the church of his boyhood. Melton was married to Mary Charlotte Woodrow, daughter of Dr. and Mrs. James Woodrow. Graduate of the University of South Carolina and Columbia Seminary, Clark was a polished gentleman, at home in any circle. Because of his kindness and gentleness, the seminary students called him 'Sweet Thing'! Before joining the seminary faculty Clark served several churches in the Carolinas, including Second Presbyterian Church in Charleston where Thomas Smyth was pastor for so many years. In 1932 Clark resigned from the seminary to go back into the pastorate at the First Presbyterian Church of Anniston, Alabama.

Hugh R. Murchison graduated from Columbia Seminary in 1897, served a number of churches in South Carolina, and returned to the seminary in 1920 as teacher of missions, secretary to the board of directors, and business manager.

John Miller Wells, pastor of the First Presbyterian Church of Wilmington, North Carolina, came to Columbia Seminary in 1921 as president and professor of pastoral theology. Dr. Wells was convinced that the best solution for Columbia

Seminary's financial problems was to merge with Union Seminary in Virginia. When it became apparent that the merger would not happen, Wells resigned in 1924 and became pastor of the Presbyterian church in Sumter, South Carolina. In 1936 he gave the James Sprunt Lectures at Union Seminary. He was asked to discuss some phase of practical theology. He wrote in the preface to his published lectures, *Southern Presbyterian Worthies,* that he felt 'the best way to discuss practical theology is by discussing practical theologians.' Wells gave lectures on seven Southern Presbyterian 'worthies': 'James Henley Thornwell—The Scholar'; 'John Leighton Wilson—The Foreign Missionary'; 'Daniel Baker—The Evangelist'; 'Moses Drury—The Preacher'; 'Benjamin Morgan Palmer—The Christian Statesman'; 'Givens Brown Strickler—The Pastor'; and 'Walter William Moore—The Educator.' Three of these 'practical theologians'—Thornwell, Wilson, and Palmer—had a close association with Columbia Seminary.[1]

James Benjamin Green came as professor of theology in 1921. Born in Alabama, Green studied at Peabody Normal College in Nashville and Union Seminary in Virginia. He served as pastor in two churches in Tennessee and then, for thirteen years, in Greenwood, South Carolina. Dr. Green had a keen, insightful mind and was a master of Reformed theology. As a teacher he had few equals. He used Hodge's *Systematic Theology* as his text until, in his latter years, he replaced Hodge's three volumes with Louis Berkhof's one volume. Green's *Harmony of the Westminster Presbyterian Standards* remains a valuable guide for students of the Confession and Catechisms.

Green also taught English Bible, continuing a long tradition at Columbia Seminary, and homiletics. He could be quite

[1] Wells, *Southern Presbyterian Worthies,* preface.

blunt in his critiques of sermons, as many students found out the hard way. On one occasion after a student sermon, he commented: 'There were three problems with this sermon: first, it was read; second, it was read poorly; third, it wasn't worth reading.' On another occasion a student chose to preach a sermon with the sensational title 'The Double-Barreled Gospel.' Green responded at the end of the sermon, 'What a subject! "The double-barreled gospel". Unfortunately, neither barrel was loaded.'[2]

* * * * *

When Columbia Seminary was founded, South Carolina and Georgia formed one synod of five presbyteries. There were now five synods—Alabama, Florida, Georgia, Mississippi, and South Carolina—that owned and operated the school. Many Southern Presbyterians believed that to survive the seminary had to move to a larger city nearer the centre of the five synods. As early as 1887, there were proposals to move the seminary to Atlanta. William Plumer Jacobs attended the meeting of the Synod of South Carolina in October 1904. He wrote in his diary:

> Synod has come and gone. It was a great body—genial, splendid, but alas, it voted to give away the Seminary to Georgia. I voted, prayed, and talked against it—all in vain. The vote was 96 to 52. I was with the 52. I here record my protest. It was a wrong, a silly thing, to do. And Synod will regret it but once and that is always.[3]

The seminary did not move to Georgia then, but in the early 1920s the Synod of South Carolina discussed the possibility

[2] Richards, *As I Remember It*, p. 62.
[3] Jacobs, *Diary of William Plumer Jacobs*, p. 368.

of relocating the seminary or merging it with Union Theological Seminary in Richmond, Virginia. Columbia's First Presbyterian Church did all it could to prevent such a move. A resolution from the session to the seminary directors on October 21, 1923, stated:

> It is with profound regret that we, the Session of the First Presbyterian Church of Columbia, learn of the movement to remove from our bounds that time-honored and beloved institution, the Columbia Seminary. The Seminary is virtually a child of this congregation, and is strongly rooted in the memories and affections of all our people. To remove it from its present location would be a disastrous blow to Presbyterians in our church and capital city.

In 1924, however, the Synod of South Carolina, facing the financial pressures of keeping the school open, approved the move of the seminary to Atlanta. Presbyterians in the Atlanta area donated a site of forty acres and provided $250,000 for buildings; the Synod of Georgia promised an additional $250,000. During the school year 1926-1927—its last year in Columbia—the seminary enrolled sixty-two students.

* * * * *

Richard Thomas Gillespie, pastor of the First Presbyterian Church of Louisville, Kentucky, was elected president of Columbia Seminary in 1924. Gillespie was born in South Carolina to godly parents and reared in a home deeply loyal to the Southern Presbyterian Church. He graduated from Davidson College and Columbia Seminary. A strong biblical preacher and a faithful and beloved pastor, Gillespie served the First Presbyterian Church in Florence, South Carolina, for eight years, the Maxwell Street Presbyterian Church of Lexington, Kentucky, for four years, and First Presbyterian of Louisville for four years. When Gillespie became president, the decision already had been made to relocate Columbia Seminary to Atlanta. He moved to Atlanta to raise funds and plan for the seminary's move, but travelled frequently to Columbia. Gillespie died unexpectedly while attending the General Assembly in Charlottesville, Virginia, in 1930. At this assembly George L. Petrie, Columbia Seminary graduate of 1862, was honoured as the oldest living alumnus of the seminary and the only living commissioner to the first General Assembly in 1861. He had served the Presbyterian church in Charlottesville, Virginia, for fifty years, from 1878 to 1928.

After Dr. Gillespie's death, Melton Clark, professor of English Bible, became acting president and served for two years, while teaching Bible, homiletics, pastoral theology, and Christian education.

R. C. Reed taught church history at Columbia Seminary until his death in 1925. In his will he provided Columbia Seminary with money to create the Cantey Venable Reed Memorial Scholarship in honour of his wife.

Dr. Reed was followed by William Childs Robinson, who became professor of ecclesiastical history, church polity, and missions in 1926. A native of Columbia, with degrees from the University of South Carolina, Columbia and Princeton seminaries, and Harvard University, Robinson was a loyal and determined champion of the Old Columbia theology.

* * * * *

The funds for the Thomas Smyth Lectures at Columbia Seminary became available in 1911, and a succession of distinguished scholars was invited. Francis Landey Patton lectured on 'The Theistic View of the World' and 'Christianity and the Modern Man' (1911 and 1919); Robert E. Speer, on 'Some Missionary Problems Illustrated in the Lives of Great Missionary Leaders' (1913); Columbia Seminary graduate R. A. Webb, on 'The Christian's Hope' (1914); and W. S. Plumer Bryan, 1878 graduate of Columbia Seminary and pastor of the Church of the Covenant in Chicago, on 'The Grace of God' (1917). The next year the lecturer was Benjamin B. Warfield of Princeton Theological Seminary, who spoke on 'Counterfeit Miracles.' In 1927 J. Gresham Machen, also of Princeton, gave the last of the Smyth Lectures in Columbia. He preached at the Sunday morning service at First Presbyterian Church on March 27 and, beginning on Monday night, delivered lectures on 'The Virgin Birth of Christ.' Machen spoke in a 'largely extemporaneous' manner, the newspaper reported, and his lectures were enthusiastically received by large audiences.

Gresham Machen's beloved grandfather, John Jones Gresham, had served as a member of the board of Columbia Seminary and endowed the LeRoy Gresham Chair in memory of his deceased son. A prominent judge and businessman in Macon, Georgia, Mr. Gresham served twice as Macon's mayor. For forty-four years he was a member of the session of First Presbyterian Church in Macon, for forty-one of which he was clerk of session.

In the fall of 1926 Dr. Gillespie, acting for the Columbia Seminary board, visited Dr. Machen in Princeton to urge him to come to Columbia as professor of New Testament. Ned B. Stonehouse, in his biography of Machen, writes: 'Southerner that he was in tradition and in various aspects of his outlook and spirit, and anxious as he had become for the future of the [Southern Presbyterian] Church in which he was brought up, Machen could not but be moved by this approach. But . . . the urgency of the Princeton situation, and his sense of responsibility in the crisis of its life, did not allow of a favorable response.'[4]

* * * * *

A full history of a Presbyterian seminary would include an account of the role of the presbyteries and synods involved, as well as the General Assembly. It would describe the work of the board of directors. It would, of course, feature the lives and activities of the faculty and students. It would include the seminary's setting and some notice of the history of the times. It would also tell of the supporters of the seminary, the men and women who prayed for it and contributed to it. And it would include some account of the seminary's staff, those men and women who worked behind the scenes to keep the institution going. In this study of the Old Columbia Seminary there is very little about these people, because very little is known about them. Many, no doubt, were African Americans, most probably slaves before emancipation.

Worthy of highest praise was a Methodist preacher, Joseph Dixon, a black man who served the seminary as custodian. Dixon had lost one arm in a railway accident but wonderfully overcame his handicap. He cared for the seminary's buildings and kept the school's two large boilers stoked with coal, coming early in the morning to see that the buildings were

[4] Ned B. Stonehouse, *J Gresham Machen: A Biographical Memoir* (Edinburgh: Banner of Truth, 1987), p. 424.

comfortably heated before the students rose. Dixon prepared a device that he fixed to one handle of a wheelbarrow and then slipped over the shoulder of his missing arm, enabling him to handle the wheelbarrow with ease. He could remove light fixtures and replace them more skillfully with one hand than most persons could with two. Dr. McPheeters said that Mr. Dixon was the best sermon he had ever seen or heard on using what God gives you in his service. When Mrs. Dixon had triplets after they already had three children, a student greeted the father the next day, 'Well, I hear you had an addition to your family yesterday.' 'Yes,' Dixon replied, 'it may have been an addition, but it seemed more like a multiplication.' Dixon was asked from time to time to preach in the morning chapel service at the seminary. His sermons were always edifying and well received, although it was difficult for him to terminate them!

Plato Henderson began work in the seminary kitchen in Columbia when he was less than twenty years old. He proved to be a master chef. Henderson said that he could tell when a man was going to be a really good preacher by the size of his appetite. When asked on one occasion whether there were any promising preachers in the student body, Henderson replied, 'Yes sir, we got some great preachers coming on at Columbia Seminary now!'[5]

* * * * *

The last commencement of the Theological Seminary in Columbia took place in 1927. The seminary was ending its ninety-ninth year of existence, ninety-seven of which were

[5] Richards, *As I Remember It*, pp. 48-49.

spent in Columbia. Twenty-three students graduated, the largest class since 1875. The First Presbyterian Church bulletin for April 24, 1927, announced, 'with heartfelt and mingled feelings . . . the last commencement service of Columbia Theological Seminary that will be held in this church.' The next Sunday, May 1, Dr. W. M. McPheeters presided at the baccalaureate. That evening the annual missionary address was given under the auspices of the Society of Missionary Inquiry. On Tuesday evening, Dr. Richard T. Gillespie—who had been serving as president since January 1925, succeeding Dr. John M. Wells—was inaugurated.

On Wednesday, May 4, commencement exercises were held in First Presbyterian Church. The benediction was given, the choir sang the 'Amen,' and the Columbia years of the seminary's history came to an end. Margaret Babcock Merriwether wrote, in her history of Columbia, that when the seminary 'moved to Georgia . . . an irreplaceable quality was lost from Columbia's civic personality.'[6]

First Presbyterian Church felt most keenly the departure of the seminary—'Our Southern Zion.' For many years, the church had given a reception each fall for the seminary faculty and students and was the site of the seminary's commencement exercises in the spring. The church had supported the seminary with its prayers and money. It had drawn on the seminary for supply preachers and Sunday school teachers. Lectures and special services of the seminary were held in the church's buildings, enriching the congregation and the

[6] The old seminary property in Columbia was sold to Columbia Bible College for $75,000. After 1959, when Columbia Bible College moved to a 300-acre campus on the edge of the city, the old Ainsley Hall building, which had housed both Columbia Seminary and Columbia Bible College, was beautifully restored by the Historic Columbia Foundation. It is now known as the Robert Mills House.

city with solid Bible teaching and historic Reformed theology. Pastors of First Church had taught at the seminary, and some had become faculty professors there.

Columbia Seminary opened its first session in its new home in Decatur, an attractive suburb of the city of Atlanta, on September 14, 1927. The 1928 General Assembly, meeting in Atlanta, celebrated the centennial of Columbia Seminary. The *Presbyterian Standard* for May 23, 1928, commented, 'No Assembly is complete unless a gavel of some famous wood is presented. Dr. J. B. Green, of Columbia Seminary, was on hand with a gavel made, one-half of wood from the old seminary, and one-half of wood from the new. He presented it in a happy speech of excellent taste.'[7]

[7] The *Presbyterian Standard* (May 23, 1928), p. 2.

CONCLUSION: 'THIS PURE LIGHT'

THE reorganization of the board of Princeton Theological Seminary by the General Assembly of the Presbyterian Church (USA) in 1929 forced the departure of J. Gresham Machen and began a slow but steady decline in historic Reformed orthodoxy in that school. The move of Columbia Theological Seminary to Decatur, Georgia, in 1927 saw in time the departure from the theological convictions of its founders. The professors who went with the seminary to Decatur, notably William McPheeters, J. B. Green, and William Childs Robinson, kept alive the old teachings of Howe, Palmer, Thornwell, and Girardeau for another fifty years, but gradually the seminary's interests and emphasis shifted to more modern views.

In his *Studies in Southern Presbyterian Theology*, Morton Smith wrote: 'In this Columbia Theology we find a line of thought that is fully as orthodox and sound as that of Princeton . . . Coupled with the theology of Union Seminary, the two give a statement of the Christian faith of which the Southern Presbyterian Church need never be ashamed.'[1]

In his insightful book *Crisis in the Church: The Plight of Theological Education*, John H. Leith, Pemberton Professor

[1] Smith, *Studies in Southern Presbyterian Theology*, p. 267.

of Theology Emeritus at Union Theological Seminary in Virginia, chronicled the changes taking place in the Presbyterian seminaries during the last half of the twentieth century.[2] Leith wrote:

> The seminaries have lost their depth in time and history . . . The three seminaries I know best, Columbia, Union Theological Seminary in Virginia, and Princeton demonstrate little pride in or memory of their past . . . It is significant that the writings of nineteenth-century Presbyterian theologians are continually being reprinted, though they are seldom to be found on mainline seminary bibliographies or in Presbyterian seminary bookstores . . . Yet it was the theology that was contained in these volumes that built Princeton, Union, and Columbia seminaries as well as the church community of which they are a part.[3]

In a letter to Columbia Seminary on the occasion of its semi-centennial in 1881, Princeton's Alexander T. McGill, who taught at Columbia for a year, wrote:

> [Columbia Seminary's] traditions of the past should be treasured up for an earnest of the future. Its men of God, before and after that sojourn of mine—Goulding, Jones, Leland, Thornwell, and Plumer—who have gone to the 'church of the first born, which are written in heaven'—shed a luster on your institution which the Church on earth should be glad to perpetuate on the same spot and with the same surrounding of good and faithful men . . . who cherished it with so much

[2] John H. Leith writes in the preface of his *Crisis in the Church* that Westminster John Knox Press, the denominational publishing house of the Presbyterian Church (USA), requested Leith to write the book. He comments: 'My only qualification is that my whole life has been given to preaching and teaching theology. I was born in a Presbyterian home and in the fellowship of a Presbyterian church. I can no more leave the Presbyterian Church than I can change my name or leave my family' p. ix.

[3] Leith, *Crisis in the Church*, pp. 14-15.

> zeal in the past generation of that beautiful locality. The conservative character of Columbia Seminary cannot be spared from the visible Church at this day. The true inspiration of God's word, the cardinal doctrine of atonement by substitution, the full development of scriptural polity in the structure, government, and discipline of the Church, indispensably need this pure light, where it was kindled at the first.[4]

Led by a line of stalwart theologians and faithful pastors, the Old Columbia Seminary stood firmly for a hundred years for the Bible as God's inspired Word, for the Calvinism of the Westminster Confession of Faith as a true theological expression of the Bible's teaching, for a true Presbyterian church, and for the spread of the gospel throughout the Southern United States and the whole world.

[4] *Memorial Volume,* p. xxii.

INDEX

SOME OTHER BOOKS
BY
THE BANNER OF TRUTH TRUST

Preachers with Power,
Douglas F. Kelly

224 pp. clothbound,
ISBN: 978 0 85151 628 8

Douglas Kelly here reintroduces one of the richest periods of evangelical history, spanning the years 1791-1902, and captures its ethos in the lives of four of its most influential men: Daniel Baker, who spent his life as a missionary and itinerant evangelist though sought by a church and two U.S. Presidents for Washington; James Henley Thornwell, equally able as a pastor and professor but best remembered as a preacher 'wrapt in wonder at the love, humiliation and condescension of the Trinity'; Benjamin M. Palmer, who, in the words of a Jewish rabbi, 'got the heart as well as the ear of New Orleans'; and John L. Girardeau, 'the Spurgeon of America', who was so remarkably used among the black people of South Carolina. In addition to these moving lives, Dr. Kelly gives us many illuminating side-lights on Christians of the South. The author is not only well-qualified to write on 'the old South' but, more important, he inspires a fresh vision of the great lessons embodied in his subjects. He convinces us of the truth of the words of R. L. Dabney: 'The real *desideratum* is not new methods, but fidelity to the old, a real revival in the hearts of ministers and Christians themselves, a faith that "feels the power of the world to come", a solemn and deep love for souls. What we need most is repentance, and not innovation.'

Southern Presbyterian Leaders,
Henry White

512 pp. clothbound,
ISBN: 978 0 85151 795 7

White's fascinating biographical sketches of leaders in the Southern Presbyterian Church, from the establishment of Presbyterianism in the American Colonies in the 1680s to the beginning of the twentieth century, has never been superseded. The better known names read like a roll-call of many of the finest representatives of evangelical piety and experiential Calvinism in America: Samuel Davies, Archibald Alexander, Daniel Baker, William S. Plumer, James Henley Thornwell, John L. Girardeau, Benjamin M. Palmer, Robert L. Dabney, Thomas J. ('Stonewall') Jackson and Thomas E. Peck. But many lesser-known names are also brought before the reader, from Francis Makemie in the 1680s to leaders still living when White wrote his account in 1911. The pages of this book teem with fervent evangelists, faithful pastors, learned professors, accomplished statesmen, and soldiers likely to inspire fear in the heart of any tyrant, all owing the inspiration of their lives to the saving truths they learned from the Scriptures and the Westminster Standards.

Making Many Glad: The Life and Labours of Daniel Baker, **William M. Baker**

560 pp. paperback,
ISBN: 978 0 85151 781 0

This stirring biography tells the story of Daniel Baker, the great evangelist of the American South, largely in his own words. Baker was one of those preachers who could not resist the call to 'preach Christ where he was not named', and wherever he went it was 'in the fulness of the blessing of the gospel of Christ'. His longest stay in one pastorate amounted to just nine years, whereas he was involved in gospel ministry for almost forty years, itinerating from Pennsylvania and Ohio, through Virginia, the Carolinas, his native Georgia and around the southern states to Texas. Citing Isaiah 52:7, Professor Douglas Kelly writes of Baker: 'There could not be a better way of characterizing the effects of the life and preaching of this great Southern evangelist . . . than this verse about beautiful feet hastening with glad tidings across waste places.'

The Life and Letters of Benjamin Morgan Palmer, **T. C. Johnson**
704 pp. clothbound
ISBN: 978 0 85151 522 9

This biography of Benjamin Morgan Palmer (1818-1902), takes us behind the public figure to the humble, prayerful Christian whose life was marked by affliction. His only son was lost in childhood and four daughters were to die, one after another, followed by his wife. As Palmer saw it, 'The earthly lights are put out that no earthly love may come in between Him and us.' This is not only a great biography; it is an outstandingly relevant record in an age when the church needs a recovery of spiritual strength and vision. It would be hard to read it sympathetically without being led to pray.

The Writings of Thomas E. Peck, 3 vol. set

ISBN: 978 0 85151 770 4
Cloth-bound

As a teacher, Peck was in the front rank. 'As an expositor of truth, as an exegete of Scripture,' his successor C. R. Vaughan believed, 'he was probably without a rival in his day.' It was not mere teachers that he laboured to prepare for the gospel ministry but rather men 'with a tongue set on fire'. In this his own life was a constant example, possessed as he was with a moral conviction and a resolute fidelity to Scripture which 'sometimes puzzled the lovers of expediency'. Yet this was ever combined with a generous enthusiasm and warm affections. Devotion to principle is the only biblical remedy for our age of religious uncertainty and compromise. In these volumes, Peck's life work will be continued in another generation.

THE BANNER OF TRUTH TRUST

The Banner of Truth Trust originated in 1957 in London. The founders believed that much of the best literature of historic Christianity had been allowed to fall into oblivion and that, under God, its recovery could well lead not only to a strengthening of the church today but to true revival.

Inter-denominational in vision, this publishing work is now international, and our lists include a number of contemporary authors along with classics from the past. The translation of these books into many languages is encouraged.

A monthly magazine, *The Banner of Truth*, is also published and further information will be gladly supplied by either of the offices below.

3 Murrayfield Road,
Edinburgh, EH12 6EL,
UK

P O Box 621, Carlisle,
Pennsylvania 17013,
USA

www.banneroftruth.co.uk

COLUMBIA, S. C. Columbia The